TOWARDS ILLIBERAL DEMOCRACY
IN PACIFIC ASIA

Towards Illiberal Democracy in Pacific Asia

Daniel A. Bell
*Carnegie Council on Ethics
and International Affairs*

David Brown
*Lecturer in Politics
Murdoch University, Western Australia*

Kanishka Jayasuriya
*Lecturer in Politics
University of Sydney, Australia*

and

David Martin Jones
*Lecturer in Politics
National University of Singapore*

St. Martin's Press

in association with
ST ANTONY'S COLLEGE
OXFORD

First published in Great Britain 1995 by
MACMILLAN PRESS LTD
Houndmills, Basingstoke, Hampshire RG21 6XS
and London
Companies and representatives
throughout the world

FTW
AJL5532

This book is published in the St Antony's / Macmillan Series
General Editor: Alex Pravda

A catalogue record for this book is available
from the British Library.

ISBN 0–333–61399–6

10	9	8	7	6	5	4	3	2	1
04	03	02	01	00	99	98	97	96	95

Printed and bound in Great Britain by
Antony Rowe Ltd
Chippenham, Wiltshire

First published in the United States of America 1995 by
Scholarly and Reference Division,
ST. MARTIN'S PRESS, INC.,
175 Fifth Avenue,
New York, N.Y. 10010

ISBN 0–312–12686–7

Library of Congress Cataloging-in-Publication Data
Towards illiberal democracy in Pacific Asia / Daniel A. Bell . . . [et
al.]
p. cm.
"In association with St. Antony's College, Oxford."
Includes bibliographical references and index.
ISBN 0–312–12686–7
1. Democracy—East Asia. 2. East Asia—Politics and government.
3. East Asia—Economic policy. I. Bell, Daniel A.
JQ1499.A91T68 1995
320.95'09182'3—dc20
                                        95–4169
                                        CIP

Contents

Preface

During 1992, when we were all members of the Political Science Department of the National University of Singapore, we each contributed departmental seminar papers on different aspects of political change in East and Southeast Asia. The book grew out of the realization that these papers, while differing markedly in focus, shared two characteristics. They each constituted attempts to rethink, in the light of the Asian experience, the conceptualizations of democracy and democratization which comprised the conventional armory of western-trained political scientists. Moreover, they each reflected a suspicion of the growing sentiment that Asia offered a new model which combined economic growth, cultural self-confidence, and political stability in a new 'Asian democracy' – a new utopia which the West would do well to emulate.

The recognition that Asian democratization was intrinsically problematical came not just from the examination of the particular issues which each of us explored in our papers, but also from the experience of living and working in Singapore. Singapore is unique in East and Southeast Asia in the extent to which its managerial state is able effectively to engineer the economic, cultural and political behaviour of its society. But it is this very characteristic which makes it the paradigmatic Asian polity. It exhibits in an exaggerated form both the managerialism, and the tensions arising from that managerialism, which constitute the problematical politics of Asian democratization. Certainly, these problems manifest themselves differently in each state; in the parliamentary confrontations of Taiwan and the aggressive money politics of Malaysia, as well as in the anxiety of Singaporean politics.

The common themes and interests of our seminar papers were explored in a series of discussions in bars and coffee shops, as well as in repeated oral and written critiques of each others successive drafts. Each individual approached the discussions from the perspective of his particular interests in the politics of democratization, democratic theory, traditional culture, the role of the middle classes, the political economy of industrialization, and the role of ethnic and state nationalisms. The book is thus organized as a series of chapters which explore contemporary political change in Pacific Asia from these different angles, and which are tied together by an overall argument as to the illiberal character of Asian democratization.

DANIEL A. BELL
DAVID BROWN
KANISHKA JAYASURIYA
DAVID MARTIN JONES

1 Understanding Illiberal Democracy: A Framework

Daniel A. Bell and Kanishka Jayasuriya

Liberal democratic ideals and institutions command almost universal allegiance in Western societies, a phenomenon to be understood in the light of the West's shared history and culture. In what seems like an all too obvious theoretical mistake, however, it is often assumed without argument that liberal democracy also meets the deeper aspirations of the rest of the world, most notably by Francis Fukuyama with his now infamous claim that we are witnessing an 'end of history' in which liberal democracy has finally triumphed over all its rivals. More concretely, this blind faith in the universal potential of liberal democracy takes the form of a US governmental policy to promote liberal democracy abroad, regardless of local needs, habits, and traditions, and not unexpectedly moral exhortation has proven far less effective than in the days when General MacArthur could forcibly impose democratic forms of government on recalcitrant countries. In short, democracy activists have encountered much resistance in non-Western contexts, and the task of exporting liberal democracy appears to be a great deal more complicated than optimists had supposed in the heady days after the collapse of communism in the Soviet bloc.

The problem, modernization theorists may respond, lies with the expectation that stable and legitimate democratic arrangements could be successfully established and maintained in other than modern, dynamic, pluralistic societies; only economic development, the argument goes, produces the social forces that seek the democratic transformation of the political system. As the authors of a concluding chapter to a recent book on political change in the Asia–Pacific region put it, at higher levels of growth

> we should expect the economy then to have become too complex for the state to manage alone. We should also expect that at least some of the new social classes would have become too large and politically conscious to be willing any longer to defer to the judgements of the bureaucracy or to be excluded from the political process. An important threshold should be crossed, the internal balance of power should tip, and authoritarian rule should give way to a democratic transformation. (Crouch and Morley, 1993: 288)

Where this model clearly does not fit, as in Singapore, theorists invoke special factors explaining why, with respect to such 'deviant cases' (ibid.: 306), liberal democracy is not the inevitable outgrowth of economic development.

Nowhere has economic growth been so sudden and spectacular in the last two decades as in the Asia–Pacific region, and one may be led to expect a liberal democratic transformation toward the 'end of history' in the newly industrialized and industrializing states of Taiwan, South Korea, Singapore, Indonesia, Thailand, and Malaysia, as well as the full blossoming of liberal democracy in Japan and the beginnings of a transformation in China. The co-authors of this book, however, do not now or in the foreseeable future expect a 'triumph' of liberal democracy in the modernized polities of East and Southeast Asia. This is not to deny that Taiwan, South Korea, and Thailand have been democratizing, if by 'democracy' we mean nothing more (or less) than a political procedure for 'the filling of offices through contested elections, held at suitably frequent intervals, decided by the majority, on the basis of universal adult suffrage' (Kateb, 1992: 59), or that once secure democratic rights to participate in elections and offices have been dealt serious blows of late in Malaysia and Singapore. Rather, our claim is that democratization in East and Southeast Asia can be interpreted as a grafting of democratic practices and institutions on to societies with an alternative cultural baggage, with different ways of organizing their economic life, and with distinctive answers to the question of who counts as 'we the people'. That is, whereas democratic practices were adapted in part to serve the liberal ends of freedom and equality in the West, a different set of values and needs underlies and justifies democracy in Asia (see Miller, 1993: 74). This leads us to the following questions – what, then, explains the process of democratization in Asia, if not the growing presence of liberal social groups clamoring for more freedom and equality, and what is the likely shape of the illiberal democracy that may emerge in Asia? But the first step is to say more about what Bhikhu Parekh aptly terms 'the cultural particularity of liberal democracy' (Parekh, 1993: 156).

I THE CULTURAL PARTICULARITY OF LIBERAL DEMOCRACY

While Athenian democracy preceded liberalism by nearly two millenia, in the modern age liberalism preceded democracy 'and created a world to which the latter had to adjust' (ibid.: 157). The entrenchment of liberalism prior to democratization gave Western liberal democracy its historically specific form, namely, a democracy shaped and structured within the limits set by liberal values and assumptions. More precisely, the practices and institutions of Western representative constitutional democracies have been informed and justified by the liberal ideals of equality and freedom, along with a pragmatic recognition of 'the fact of pluralism' (Rawls, 1988: 275). Let us clarify by highlighting the culturally distinctive features of Western liberal democracy, contrasting these briefly with the regulative ideals shaping the political systems and the processes of political change in East and Southeast Asia.

1   The Value of Equality

Western political thinkers generally share a belief that 'all persons are by nature equal', a principle of equal respect for the moral status and intrinsic worth of each person (Kymlicka, 1990: 4). Needless to say, this principled commitment to equality has been imperfectly applied in practice – Western social and political systems have systematically excluded large numbers of persons from access to political power and a fair share of the benefits of social cooperation – but at least at the level of theory most Western thinkers since the birth of liberalism in seventeenth century England begin with an assumption that the interests of each member of the community matters, and matters equally. And as Robert Dahl notes, even earlier and deeper religious sources – the common doctrine of Judaism and Christianity that we are equally God's children (Dahl, 1989: 86) – help to explain the taken-for-granted, uncontroversial status of an egalitarian premise.

As one might expect, things have worked themselves out differently elsewhere and consequently the ideal of equality may not resonate to the same extent with the habits and traditions of people living in different times and places. Most obviously, the assumption in traditional Hinduism that people come into the world unequal as a result of differences in karma inherited from previous incarnations conflicts with an egalitarian premise, but more relevant for our purposes is the fact that dominant understandings in East and Southeast Asia also tend to prioritize a hierarchical world view – in East Asia, for example, the moral and political status of each person has traditionally varied both in theory and practice in accordance with a person's unchosen position within a hierarchical family unit, and a Chou period theory that society consists of four classes, with warrior-administrators on the top, merchants and traders on the bottom, and peasants and artisans in between, 'remained East Asian dogma for the next two millenniums' (Fairbank and Reischauer, 1989: 34). This is not to deny the presence of egalitarian ideals in Asian social and political theory, such as the Confucian stress on meritocratic education or the legalist idea that all persons (with the exception of the emperor) are equal before the law; all things taken into account, however, egalitarian norms are not as deeply entrenched in Asian culture as they may be in the West, at least in the sense that Western political and moral argumentation rules out explicit appeal to a hierarchical world view (it is difficult to imagine a sane Western version of a Lee Kuan Yew publicly expressing regrets that his government had given women equal rights, thus limiting their marriage prospects to Asian men who prefer women learning the skills that would make them 'marvellous helpers of their husband's career' (*Straits Times*, 26 April 1994)). Most interesting (and disturbing) of all, hierarchical shared meanings grounded in Asian culture and history fit in well with the needs of modern, technocratic managerial regimes in East and Southeast Asia, an argument developed in Jones's contribution to this volume.

2 The Value of Freedom

The value of equality standing alone, it is important to emphasize, cannot by itself justify a democratic procedure in the form of majority rule with universal suffrage – if Lee Kuan Yew is correct that a middle aged family man is 'more likely to vote in a serious way than a capricious young man under 30' (*Straits Times*, 11 March 1994), then his idea for a political system that gives two votes for family men between the ages of 40 and 60 may well yield a government more likely to ensure the equal consideration of people's interests than a government elected by a one person one vote procedure. A second premise, to be called freedom or autonomy, is necessary to justify a political practice of equal rights to self-government – the idea that ordinary persons ought to make the decisions that affect them most closely and importantly, as opposed to being led by external and impersonal forces. Free or autonomous individuals have an overriding interest in shaping a particular life plan or moral outlook, consistent with the equal right of others to do likewise, and since important matters of public policy affect the way that we lead our lives, everyone should have an equal right to choose a government.

But note that a premise of equal rights to autonomy leads to much more than 'minimal democracy', the mere act of putting a cross on a ballot every four or five years. Given the impact of political decisions on our everyday lives, free citizens ought to participate in the making of those decisions, and if continual and direct involvement in politics requires too much time and effort, free and equal citizens ought to be encouraged to deliberate and to make judgements about public issues. In a liberal communicatory regime of this sort, Stephen Macedo notes, 'criticism of the government is accepted and even encouraged, and liberal citizens expect to be answered with reasons rather than mere force or silence' (Macedo, 1990: 41), requiring a free press that supplies argumentative citizens with the material essential for making judgements about public policies and more generally the institutions and social practices that maintain the conditions for free and open public speech (Habermas, 1987; Minogue, 1987). Anything less, liberals believe, and the state fails to respect our capacity freely to choose our own conception of the good.

Arguments to liberalize the political process in the name of equal rights to freedom (defined as a capacity to choose, enact, and revise a life plan, not merely as the absence of constraints), moreover, also apply to the workplace, schools, families, in short, all those social institutions where decisions are taken that govern the course of our lives. And since most social institutions provide few opportunities for the exercise of democratic autonomy, Western theorists worried about the large gap between 'actually existing liberal democracies' and the ideal of autonomy argue for radical changes regarding the way that we organize our social lives. Economic enterprises, for example, ought to be radically restructured since 'these organizations are not only immensely important in the everyday lives of most citizens, but they stand out starkly because . . . their internal governments are in fact systems of guardianship at best and despotic at worst' (Dahl, 1989: 327; but see Arneson, 1993: 138–43).

But once again we notice the 'cultural particularity' of the liberal project. Whereas many in the West tend to assume that the demand for freedom or individual autonomy is a universal phenomenon, the sociologist Orlando Patterson points out that freedom developed into a core value in Western civilization as a result of a specific configuration of historical factors, emerging initially in response to the experience of slavery in ancient Greece and spreading to the rest of the Western world along with the expansion of the Roman empire and the Christian religion (Patterson, 1991). In the non-Western world, however,

> freedom was, and for many still remains, anything but an obvious or desirable goal. Other values and ideals were, or are, of far greater importance to them – values such as the pursuit of glory, honor, and power for oneself or one's family and clan, nationalism and imperial grandeur, militarism and valor in warfare, filial piety, the harmony of heaven and earth, the spreading of the 'true faith', nirvana, hedonism, altruism, justice, equality, material progress – the list is endless. But

almost never, outside the context of Western culture and its influence, has it included freedom. (ibid.: x)

More specifically with reference to East Asia, the traditional focus in Confucian ethics on duties and obligations owed to elderly parents, departed ancestors, and future generations continues to exert a powerful influence over the general population. Greater exposure to Western contact, moreover, may not have the desired liberal effect – attending to the unpredictable and time-consuming needs of family members often conflicts with the desire to 'live one's life in one's own way', and East Asians may feel that the former ought to have priority, particularly in view of such apparent phenomena as family breakdown and social disintegration in liberal Western societies. Politically, a cultural preference for familism over freedom will manifest itself as a preference for a Singapore-style regime that provides individuals with special incentives to attend to the needs of family members (e.g. tax and housing breaks for those who care for elderly parents) over a liberal system operating on the premise that individuals ought to have a fair opportunity to freely pursue their own conception of the good, regardless of the consequences. Thus, Western liberals will likely experience serious difficulties persuading East Asians of the superiority of a political system informed and justified first and foremost by the ideal of freedom, although East Asians may be more receptive to the idea that the practice of democratic competitive elections is an essential bulwark against attempts by the government to subvert and destroy traditional family arrangements – this argument is developed in Bell's chapter.

Recall, however, that the Western conception of freedom as the capacity to shape one's own world requires more than mere voting in periodic elections – free and equal citizens are treated with respect only when provided with the social conditions allowing for open deliberation and public criticism of the government's policies. Yet again, significant and perhaps irreconcilable cultural differences lead one to question the universalizability of the liberal project: far from taking the view that 'shying away from open and candid public justification entails high costs' (Macedo, 1990: 67), the Javanese resort to highly ritualised pretense in interpersonal behavior as a socially acceptable way of avoiding contention and conflict (Geertz, 1960); Chinese political culture has been shaped by the role models of wise and virtuous mandarin bureaucrats and out of sight, semi-divine superhuman emperors, helping to explain 'the total failure of the Chinese to develop the arts of oral persuasion, rhetoric and oratory as nurtured and admired first in Athens and Rome and then in parliaments and congresses'

(Pye, 1993: 416); and in the more modernized polities of East and Southeast Asia, major political and economic decisions are made not by elected politicians following open debate in parliaments and public deliberation among informed citizens, but rather by highly esteemed bureaucrats chosen on the basis of high educational qualifications and professional competence, working in the context of a public opinion that 'is more trusting of behind-the-scenes, political maneuvering and paternalistic decision-making by a small group of officials' (Rozman, 1991: 37). Even with the adoption of democratic elections, in short, Asian political systems are not adopting the rest of the liberal-democratic baggage shaped and justified by the value of freedom (in Taiwan, for example, non-elected KMT officials continue to play the dominant role in policy decision making (Leng and Lin, 1993: 833) and vote buying and intimidation seem to have increased in the latest local elections (Bellows, 1994: 120)); and it goes without saying that most Asians do not feel a burning need to free individuals from the 'despots', 'guardians', and impersonal forces governing the internal workings of economic enterprises, schools, families, religions and the other 'unfree' social institutions that Western liberal democrats worry about.

3   The Fact of Pluralism

Whatever the importance of equal rights to moral freedom, modern constitutional democracies cannot operate on that principle alone – after all, Jean Jacques Rousseau constructed a model of a small homogenous community that makes no provision for the protection of individual rights and yet respects every person's freedom of will (Rousseau, 1968). Rousseau's model, however, cannot fit a modern world that must recognize and accomodate 'the fact of pluralism – the fact that a plurality of conflicting comprehensive religious, philosophical and moral doctrines are affirmed by citizens in a modern democratic society' (Rawls, 1988: 275). Whereas citizens in the West may once have been committed to a harmonious vision of the common good, people today disagree about socio-economic interests as well as moral outlooks, and liberals are increasingly drawing attention to the fact that, contrary to previous assumptions of culturally homogeneous nation-states, political systems must also accommodate the competing claims of diverse cultural and linguistic groupings inhabiting the same territory (Weinstock, 1993: 19).

The Western world came to recognize the permanent fact of social pluralism by institutionalizing the principle that citizens were to live within a common legal and constitutional system that secures individual rights held as 'trumps' against 'the tyranny of the majority'. Thus, decisions taken by governments elected by majority rule with universal suffrage are circumscribed by various anti-majoritarian devices such as a constitutional bill of rights enforced by non-elected judges holding final powers of review. More generally, liberals argue that democratically elected majorities can never legitimately justify policies on the grounds that some ways of life are better than others, as the state has an overriding obligation to protect peoples' equal right to freely form and realize their own conception of the good life in a world of ineliminable pluralism. The principle of keeping the government out of the business of judging the good life is known as state neutrality, a principle that explains the uneasiness liberals feel when, for example, democratic majorities enact policies favouring a certain conception of family life as against the preferences of an unpopular minority.

Turning to the historical roots of the Western response to the 'fact of pluralism', one is struck yet again by the uniqueness of the Western experience. A commitment to liberal neutrality developed out of a response to civil strife and religious warfare in the sixteenth century, when both Catholics and Protestants sought to impose their own conception of true faith on the other. Both sides learned the futility of their endeavour, eventually drawing 'the obvious lesson of our political history since the Reformation and the Wars of Religion' (Rawls, 1987: 13; but see Kymlicka, 1992: 33–56) – that 'a practicable political conception for a constitutional regime cannot rest on a shared devotion to the Catholic or Prostestant faith' (ibid: 5), a principle of religious tolerance that liberals subsequently extended to other controversial questions about the good life.

Not having undergone the same history, East and Southeast Asian states never did draw the 'lesson' that political systems must by founded on general principles acceptable to widely different moral outlooks and interest groupings, much less the idea that the state ought to be neutral between all conceptions of the good life. Instead, East and Southeast Asian political understandings place great value on substantive moral consensus that denies or suppresses moral pluralism and social diversity (*see* Jones' contribution), whether in the traditional Confucian appeal to a past golden age of virtue and universal harmony to be memorialized and used as a basis to criticize the 'chaotic' present, or in the form of contemporary bureaucratic-managerial elites mobilizing society via mass organizations, moral exhortation, and the dissemination of national 'core values' underpinning social and economic goals (e.g. in January 1989 the Singapore government identified four official core values – communitarianism, familism, decision making by consensus, and social and religious harmony – 'which Singaporeans must espouse to ensure national unity' (Quah, 1990: 92)).

Even the democratically elected governments of South Korea, Taiwan, and Thailand remain a long way from strict adherence to a principle of liberal neutrality – the Korean government, for example, recently banned a Michael Jackson musical performance said to be expressing the wrong sort of values (note that this occurred prior to allegations of child molestation) and proposes to establish a commission to define the 'Korean national identity' said to underpin governmental policies.

To summarize this section of the introduction: a liberal democratic political system, informed and justified by the ideals of equality and freedom as well as by a recognition and accomodation of 'the fact of pluralism', is a culturally distinct, historically contingent artifact, not readily transferable to East and Southeast Asian societies with different traditions, needs, and conceptions of human flourishing. Consequently, 'Western' political practices such as competitive elections may be adopted selectively, without the whole gamut of liberal democratic practices and institutions, and if adopted, may be put to use for a unique set of illiberal purposes. What then explains 'democratization' in Asia?

II INTERPRETATIONS OF POLITICAL CHANGE

Whereas chapters two and three focus primarily on the dominant, nonliberal social and political understandings informing East and Southeast Asian societies – Bell contrasts the liberal idea of autonomy with Confucian familism while Jones traces the Asian preference for hierarchy and harmony as against liberal notions of equality and pluralism and the manner in which the former have been redeployed by contemporary Asian technocrats – the next three chapters attempt to explain the problematic nature of political change and democratic transition in Asia.

Consistent with the methodological core of our research project, chapters 4 to 6 are informed by a recognition of the essentially contingent nature of democratic transition and of the need for a historically grounded and sensitive interpretation of democratization and political change in Asia. In contrast to the universalist claim that economic modernization – read as liberal capitalism – inevitably flowers into a vibrant civil society and an open political system, it will be argued that the overwhelming dominance of state power in the economic and social life of economically modernized East and Southeast countries diminishes the possibility of a liberal route to democracy. But first let us review the dominant explanations of transitions to liberal democracy, explanations grounded in the historical experience of liberal capitalism in Western Europe.

1 The Unique Process of Democratization in Western Societies

The literature on democratic transition in Western societies is based on a model of state–society relationships that is especially problematic in the East and Southeast Asian context. As a rule, in these studies democratic political forms are represented in terms of a weakening of state power and the consequent empowering of civil society. In other words, the state–society relationship is a zero sum game. From this perspective, democracy can only be sustained by a vibrant and active civil society; it is a relationship of mutual dependence. The studies in this section all challenge – albeit from different perspectives – this model of state–society relations. Instead, it will be argued that strategies of democratization in East Asia may contribute to a strengthening of state power. Before discussing these findings it is useful to outline the manner in which these models of state–society relationships have influenced studies of democratic transition.

The empowerment model of civil society is implicit in both 'strategic' and 'structural' theories of democratic transition. The strategic view of transition, exemplified by O'Donnell *et al.* (1986), places emphasis on the negotiated nature of democratic transition between authoritarian and oppositional leaders. This negotiation in turn requires an initial period of liberalization. In order that oppositional activity can take place there must be space for oppositional politics. This space can only be sustained through the development and consolidation of civil society. For example, Arato (1990) argues that limited liberalization in central Europe, ushered in by reformist regimes, created political space for the birth and consequent nurturing of oppositional political movements. However, in the East Asian context – with the possible exception of South Korea – there is little evidence for the importance of formally or informally negotiated pacts. In fact, in the Singaporean case, Brown and Jones argue that the brief period of liberalization under Goh Chok Tong provided a means of pre-empting, rather than responding to, political opposition. This policy of pre-emption was also apparent in Taiwan where the KMT, through a series of gradual reforms, attempted to coopt possible political opponents. In both cases, political reform was driven by a desire to pre-emptively manage potential opposition, rather than as a response to an emerging autonomous civil society 'from below'.

Structural explanations of democratic transitions for their part focus on the importance of social structural factors rather than the strategic choices of key elites. In these accounts the drama of democratization is governed by a script that authorizes well defined social classes to be the central subjects of the performance. The logic of this explanation, as Rueschemeyer *et al.* (1992) argue, is simple: democracy has a differential effect on the position and interests of various classes; therefore those groups or classes that benefit from democracy are likely to promote these forms of political representation. Conversely, those classes or groups likely to lose out are prone to be hostile to democratic political forms.

Intrinsically connected with this explanatory logic of class is the development of capitalism. Capitalism as an economic system brings in its wake new and dramatically transformed class structures. The perspective of modernization theory places great weight on the important effects of economic development on the pattern, level, and cultural basis of social mobilization, leading to the emergence of a pluralistic and differentiated social structure which enables autonomous social groups – particularly the middle class – to play a decisive role in the transition to democracy. This perspective can be traced to de Tocqueville's analysis of democracy in America, which stressed the importance of civil society in sustaining democratic life. But these ideas do not lie entirely within the province of modernization theory; they are also widely shared by Marxist theorists. As Rueschemeyer *et al.* (1992) point out, these 'Tocquevellian ideas are closely paralleled in the Marxist literature by Gramsci's contention that rule through consensus is made possible by the development of "dense civil society". A deeper and stronger civil society is a by-product of capitalist development' (1992: 49).

In other words, it is the changing constellation of class power that provides the dynamic of democratization. Pre-eminent among these theories is the comparative historical work of Barrington Moore, whose basic concern was to explore the complex social roots of modern authoritarianism; more specifically, he argued that while there was but one path to democracy there were multiple paths to authoritarianism. His focus on the English route to democracy identified the role of the bourgeoisie, the outgrowth of the commercialization of agriculture, as the central components of an explanation of the transition to parliamentary democracy in England. Moore concluded that 'we may simply register strong agreement with the Marxist thesis that a vigorous and independent class of town dwellers has been an indispensable element in the growth of parliamentary democracy' (1966: 418), an argument that has been particularly influential in establishing a research tradition concerned with probing and examining the relationship between the strength of the middle class or bourgeoisie and the presence/absence of democratic regimes. But this argument, as we will see, cannot readily be transposed to an East Asian context.

2 Political Change in an Asian Context

One study that represents the clearest exploration of East Asian political change within the Barrington Moore tradition is *Democracy and Authoritarianism in Southeast Asia* by Hewison *et al.* (1993). Hewison *et al.* propose that the growth of capitalism in East Asia has led to the emergence of a powerful capitalist class – a class that is politically asserting itself against neo-mercantilist regimes. They argue that:

> in so-called late industrializing societies, capitalist classes are nurtured within the protective framework of authoritarian, neo-mercantilist regimes and thereby constitute its political allies as long as they remain dependent upon the resources – protection of the state. The critical point in the political histories of such societies comes when the development of industrial capitalism and the interests of the bourgeoisie become contradictory to the continued existence of authoritarian forms of state power; when the regime constrains the social order. (1993: 27)

Regime change and transition is therefore to be understood in terms of the requirements and needs of capitalist development. The pact between state and capital that underpinned statist growth strategies is no longer necessary for the needs of the emerging domestic and international capitalist order. The emerging capitalist class seeks a new political relationship with the state – a process that eventually leads to the collapse of authoritarian regimes.

A surprisingly similar conclusion is reached by a group of scholars working within the research tradition of modernization theory (Morley, 1992). In the conclusion to this study, Crouch and Morley argue that with economic growth,

> the society has evolved too far for economic reforms alone to work. The modern classes – the working, middle, business, and, sometimes, farming (as opposed to peasant) classes – have become too large, too highly educated, too politically conscious, and too well mobilized under their own leadership to accept any longer the authority of a state that excludes them from real political participation, and when the balance of power between state and society has shifted decisively, the new social forces demand and secure, whether by negotiation or violence, movement toward the democratic transformation of the political system. (Crouch and Morley, 1992: 282)

This conclusion substitutes the language of modernization for the language of class used by Hewison *et al.* (1993) – social mobilization rather than class power, middle class rather than the bourgeoisie, economic development rather than capitalism – but there is an affinity in the logic of both arguments.

This explanation is contested by Brown and Jones, and Jayasuriya in this volume. Brown and Jones argue that there is no basis to the claim that the middle classes are the historical bearers of political liberalization in East Asia. Indeed, they contend that the middle classes in fact may be the prime beneficiaries and supporters of authoritarianism. The strategy of state economic paternalism has given the middle class a strong stake in the perpetuation of the mercantilist regimes of East Asia. Whereas the experience of liberal capitalism helped to nurture an entrepreneurial middle class grounded in a culture of competitive individualism in Western Europe, in East Asia the experience of statist economic paternalism has produced a middle class grounded in a culture of dependence and anxiety. These cultural traits in turn produce a middle class constantly anxious about instability and insecurity – strikingly illustrated by middle class demonstrators in South Korea, who chanted for order in the midst of demands for democratic reform.

Political elites have been adept at utilizing these middle class concerns to demand political acquiescence. The 'iron cage' in East Asia, far from being a prison, provides a source of security and stability. Indeed, there are two interpretations of the iron cage metaphor: in the 'iron cage as prison' model, more typical of the West, politics is about the limitation and regulation of bureaucratic and state power; whereas in the 'iron cage as security' metaphor, predominant in East Asia, politics is about the management and effective organization of state power. The latter interpretation suggests that 'democratization' in an Asian context is primarily about problem solving rather than the accommodation of a plurality of interests. Therefore, in East and Southeast Asia, a technocratic and managerial approach to politics appears in the guise of political liberalization.

Jayasuriya's contribution, from a somewhat different standpoint, also maintains that there is no basis to the claim that the middle classes are the historical bearers of political liberalization. Jayasuriya argues that in the East Asian economies of Japan, South Korea, and Taiwan the state fostered the creation of a market economy. Unlike in other 'standard' late industrializers, capital in this new group of industrializers is heavily dependent on the mode of development. The blurring of the boundaries between the market, state and civil society markedly distinguishes contemporary East Asian economies from liberal capitalism. The state remains the single most important factor in the social and economic development of East Asia; consequently, it follows that under these conditions there can be no independent and autonomous group of capitalists able to challenge state power. The impetus for political reform arises not from the autonomous assertion of independent interests by social classes but from conflict within the state; political reform is about the management of intra-elite conflict rather than about the fundamental restructuring of state–society relationships. Therefore, political liberalization in these states is manifested in the changing architecture of the state with civil society remaining both limited and circumscribed. Indeed, the term 'liberalization' is employed guardedly in this context to refer to the management of differences within the state rather than the enlargement of civil society, suggesting a managerial model of democracy at odds with the liberal democratic account that implicitly or explicity underpins the interpretation of political development proposed by Hewison *et al.* (1993) and Morley (1992).

More generally, our study raises concerns over the value of conventional understandings of class and class interest in the study of political change in East Asia where the mercantilist or state dependent nature of the industrialization process reduces the opportunities for the autonomous development of classes and groups. In contrast to the assumption that economic development 'stimulates a growing awareness of group identity and interests, and it encourages the organization of the new groups and strata into politically active bodies' (Crouch and Morley, 1992: 280), the dependence of groups on state patronage and benefits in East Asia attenuates rather than accentuates differences between classes, leading one to the conclusion that conventional understandings of class – be it modernization theory or Marxist oriented – are limited because they are implicitly premised on a model of liberal capitalist economic development.

Brown's chapter critically evaluates yet another problematic assumption of the modernization school – the idea that the formation of a cultural and political nation constitutes a necessary precondition for the development of a democratic polity. In contrast to the European experience, Brown argues that in the East and Southeast Asian states the lack of national consciousness and identity and the lack of congruity between ethnic and state borders might not act as breaks on the democratization process, but might indeed be facilitating it. Regimes which hitherto were sufficiently cohesive and ideologically determined to keep the lid on debates about problems of national identity, are now suffering from self-doubt and dissensus. They are beginning therefore to change their strategies in order to coopt and accomodate the competing visions of nationhood.

But there is again nothing liberal about this politics; it is an emerging debate which is being managed primarily on the state's terms. It is conducted not in the language of the 'rights' of the various identity groups, so much as in terms of the pragmatic utility of accommodationist politics in facilitating the maintenance of regime support, national unity, and further economic development. Moreover, the emergent debates as to national identity do not offer any kind of model or formula, other than a particularly problematical form of contemporary politics in which the tensions both within society and within the state are beginning to be articulated, and to be reflected in overt politics and government. The articulation of such tensions does not imply – unless one were an optimist or an apologist – the likelihood of their resolution.

In sum, recent political change in East and Southeast Asia does not represent the growth of liberal democracy. Whereas the Western experience of 'democratization' emerged as a response to a growing demand for autonomy on the part of groups and classes in civil society, the dominant and intrusive role of state power in most aspects of East and Southeast Asian social life channels political change to serve the managerial and technocratic ends of the state. Where 'democratization' occurs – in the sense of fair democratic procedures that may allow for an alteration of ruling parties – a political language deeply rooted in traditional non-liberal concepts of hierarchy, familism, and the possibility and desirability of the harmonization of potentially conflicting interests renders unlikely the emergence of a 'liberal' alternative.

III AN ASIAN DEMOCRACY

Let us conclude this introduction with a brief summary of the features that distinguish the political systems of economically modern Asian states from liberal democratic systems in the West, keeping in mind the possibility (if not likelihood) that things may change in radically unforeseen ways.

The contemporary East Asian understanding of politics continues to hold the view that the state had both a tutelary and a disciplinary function. In contrast to the neutral state of liberal theory founded on the assumption that rulers must respect an individual's equal right freely to choose his or her own conception of the good life in a world of incommensurable values, East Asian political actors conventionally maintain that governments can justifiably intervene in most if not all aspects of social life in order to maintain or to create a harmonious and balanced polity. Given the interventionary character of the East Asian state, law functions more as a technique for adjusting citizens to the current requirements of a national plan formulated by a wise and virtuous bureaucratic elite than as a mechanism for the protection of individual rights.

The dominant and intrusive role of the state in most aspects of social and economic life and the concomitant absence of a free public space allowing for the articulation of differentiated and potentially conflicting interests carries certain implications for political change. Instead of 'democratization' resulting from a demand for autonomy on the part of civil society and its individual members, political reform ought to be viewed primarily as a state strategy to maintain or increase commitment to national goals.

This is not to deny that the adoption of democratic practices such as free and fair competitive elections may entail certain benefits such as the minimization of fear. But a 'reversion' to more crude methods of social control remains a distinct possibility, and, whatever the extent of 'democratization', illiberal Asian political systems will most likely not extend individual rights and liberties when these conflict with the collective aims articulated by state and economic managers.

2 Democracy in Confucian Societies: The Challenge of Justification[1]

Daniel A. Bell

Westerners rarely question the importance and desirability of democracy, but the story is rather different in East Asia. Many Hong Kong business-men would gladly put Mr Patten on the next flight back home, democratic ideals have little allure among Chinese peasants preoccupied with pressing family and economic matters (Schue, 1992: 161–2), and Singaporean officials will unabashedly assert that relatively benign authoritarian systems do better at providing such benefits as safe streets, good jobs, and political stability (Roy, 1994). In short, there is widespread indifference if not hostility to the idea of democracy in East Asia, a phenomenon which poses a problem for democracy activists seeking to promote their preferred system of government. Some may plunge into despair, others may campaign for a General MacArthur-style forced imposition of democracy, but my concern here is with those thinking about the issue of how democracy can be *justified* to East Asians.

The central argument of this paper is that justifications for democracy derived from the Western experience cannot readily be exported to East Asia. Part I of the chapter examines what is perhaps the most common justification for democracy, namely, the idea that democracy is the best form of government for autonomous individuals who freely choose their own individual and collective destinies, and Part II evaluates the arguments of those who justify democracy on the instrumental grounds that it leads to socially desirable consequences. Neither autonomy-based nor instrumental justifications for democracy, I argue, will capture the 'hearts and minds' of East Asians still impregnated with Confucian values and habits. But rather than end on a pessimistic note, I conclude with the suggestion in Part III that an as yet undeveloped (instrumental) defence of democracy, the idea that democratic governments protect and facilitate communitarian ways of life, may hold some promise for pro-democracy forces relying ultimately on moral persuasion.

I DEMOCRACY JUSTIFIED BY AUTONOMY

Democracy in Western countries is most often justified on the grounds that citizens in human political communities ought to live as they choose for themselves, as opposed to being led by external and impersonal forces outside of their control. As John Dunn puts it,

> The power and appeal of the idea [of democracy] come from its promise to render the life of a community something willed and chosen – to turn the social and political existence that human beings share into a texture of consciously intended common action. In a democracy, the people (the *demos*), its human members decide what is to be done, and in so deciding they take their destiny firmly into their own hands. The power and appeal of democracy comes from the idea of autonomy – of choosing freely for oneself. (Dunn, 1992: vi)

Thus, the normative appeal of democracy rests on the supreme importance of exercising for oneself the human capacity to decide for oneself the things worth being, achieving, and doing. Ordinary human beings have an essential interest in making the decisions that affect them most closely and importantly (Arblaster, 1987: 103; Held, 1989: 273), and a democratic political regime is a system of self-rule that expresses the fact that we are creatures capable of genuine autonomy. Democracy, in short, is the best form of government because only it embodies our capacity to choose our own individual and collective life plans; it is crucial for human well being, to be valued regardless of its consequences for society (see Kateb, 1992, especially chapter 2).

But how universal is the belief that the key to human flourishing lies in consciously choosing and enacting one's own life-plan? While the idea that people ought to lead autonomous lives undoubtedly has great appeal in Western societies,[2] members of other societies may not have such a deeply felt need to exercise their powers of choice. Such is the case, as we will see, in East Asian countries which share a Confucian heritage that downplays the significance of self-mastery, control, and personal autonomy. Before I go on, however, it is important to defend the claim that Confucian values in fact matter in East Asia, more specifically, what does it mean to say that a society is predominantly 'Confucian' in outlook?

What is a Confucian Society

A society can be labeled 'Confucian', it seems to me, if it displays the following characteristics:

1. Values originating from the Confucian tradition's sacred texts continue to have widespread impact on people's behaviour. Just as 'Judaeo-Christian' societies must display significant commitment to values expounded in the Bible and other religious texts, so people in 'Confucian' societies will manifest attachment to values embedded in the Confucian tradition.

2. Confucianism is more than an official ideology manipulated by elites for their own purposes[3] (similarly, when we say that Western countries share a Judaeo-Christian heritage, we mean that Judaeo-Christian values have filtered down to affect the lives of ordinary people regardless of the behaviour of political elites). The claim that Confucianism is nothing but an official ideology can be tested in the following manner – if Confucianism were merely a set of values and practices promoted through deliberate government policies, one would expect most traces of Confucianism to vanish once the government adopts a different ideology (consider the fate of Marxism in the ex-Soviet Union). But elites in China have occasionally forsaken conscious allegiance to Confucianism, and yet Confucian values were maintained by ordinary people: from the early third to the late sixth century, and later in the Tang dynasty (618–907), Taoism and Buddhism dominated the intellectual and spiritual scene in China, but this 'did not mean that the Confucian tradition had disappeared [because] Confucian ethics was by then virtually inseparable from the moral fabric of Chinese society' (Tu, 1989: 16). More recently, the Chinese Communist Party attempted to stamp out the 'feudal legacy' of Confucianism, but several scholars have argued that some Chinese Communist Party ideas and practices during Mao's era were essentially Confucian in inspiration, notwithstanding the CCP's own self-understanding of what it was doing (Metzger, 1977: chapter 5; Dawson, 1981: 86–7; Munro, 1977: chapter 4; Li, 1991: 244–5; Whyte, in Dernberger, *et al.*, 1991: 714–5), and more than one observer has noted that post-Mao China has experienced a revival of traditional Confucian values and practices (Goldstein, in Dernberger, *et al.*, 1991: 718; De Bary, 1988: 34). In short, whatever the latest 'belief system' fashion at elite levels, Confucianism has continued to persist in significant forms among ordinary people.

3. Given that Confucianism originated from an elite class of intellectuals and/or scholar bureaucrats, it is crucial that one be able to demonstrate (at least in principle) by means of an historical investigation precisely *how* it is that the values espoused in 'high culture' Confucian texts came to exert an influence on the culture of the people. One can defer to the findings of sociologists and historians for this task – a recent book edited by Gilbert

Rozman traces the spread of Confucian values and behaviour in East Asian countries, concluding that China was the first country to be 'Confucianized' in the sense that the teachings closely identified with Confucius's teachings became widely disseminated among the Chinese people, followed by Korea and Japan: 'In Korea the Confucian legacy was introduced later and did not spread widely until the fifteenth century. In Japan mass acceptance of Confucian principles was accelerated in the eighteenth and nineteenth centuries' (Rozman, 1991: ix). With regard to the means employed to disseminate and maintain Confucian values, suffice it to say at this point that the state did play an important role at times, but that Confucian ethical instruction was carried on primarily in the family and within local schools, i.e., in ways not directly dependent on the decisions of state elites (Rozman, 1991: part I; De Bary, 1988: 23–4), thus helping to explain the persistence of Confucianism 'among the masses' even when the winds had shifted at higher levels.

To conclude this section: evidence available from the historical record suggests that Confucianism has become widely disseminated in China, Japan and Korea, and one may also include (at the risk of oversimplification) Hong Kong, Taiwan and the Chinese majority in multi-ethnic Singapore, societies whose ancestors left China when Confucianism had established itself as the dominant worldview.[4] It will be noticed, however, that nothing yet has been said about the *content* of Confucian ethics, a topic that presents us with a host of problems – the Confucian tradition is a complex and changing centuries long argument dating back to the legendary sage-kings Yao and Shun, interpreted differently in different times and places and complemented in sometimes conflicting ways with Legalism and Taoism, not to mention the problem of the gap between the Confucianism of books and the 'vulgar' Confucianism of peasants and workers. In this essay I abstract from these considerations to focus on two Confucian values that are (1) central to *The Analects*, 'our most reliable source for the early Confucian school, if not for the vision of the Master himself' (Schwartz, 1985: 61) and (2) still resonate with what many East Asians feel and think to be the truth, or so one can deduce given the presence of certain distinctive and empirically verifiable social phenomena.

The Importance of the Family in Confucian Societies

A basic assumption of Confucian ethics is that the moral life is possible only in the context of particularist personal ties (Moody, 1988: 3). A necessary condition for leading a moral life is behaving in accordance with the duties and obligations embedded in socially sanctioned roles: 'Let the prince be a prince, the minister a minister, the father a father, and the son a son' (*The Analects of Confucius*: book XII.11). For the general population, the most important relationship by far in Confucian ethics is the family,[5] the sphere within which one concentrates on such virtues as 'gratitude toward parents for their nurturing love, responsibility of adult children for aged and feeble parents, and a prolonged sense of loss when they depart' (Schwartz, 1985: 99; see also Ebrey, 1991: 45; Ivanhoe, 1991: 247; De Bary, 1986: 10; Harland, 1993: 10). At this point, the Western reader may object: 'I love my parents just as much as persons from "Confucian" societies care for their parents, and there doesn't seem anything novel or interesting about family-based Confucian ethics.' A legitimate sentiment, but nevertheless a claim can be made that the family carries more ethical weight in Confucian societies, for the following reasons:

1.   Confucian social and political theorists place greater value on the family than their Western counterparts. A brief comparison of Confucian and Western views on the family will demonstrate this point:
   (i)   *Confucians say that the family is the first and most important school of virtue*: 'Surely proper behaviour towards parents and elder brothers is the trunk of Goodness?' (*The Analects*: Book I.2). And: 'Filial piety is . . . the root of virtue and the source of all teaching' (*The Book of Filial Piety*, quoted in Dawson, 1981: 47).
   The natural love and obligations obtaining between members of the family, then, is made the basis of a general morality applicable in everyday life. Benjamin Schwartz helpfully contrasts this outlook with Plato's conception of the family:

> Plato . . . provides us with all the reasons why the family is not the source of virtue. It is a particularistic 'private' group within the polis bent primarily on the promotion of its own economic interests. Instead of focusing men's minds on large public matters, it locks men into an overwhelming concern with the petty joys and sorrows of other family members. The company of wives and children provides little room for intellectual enlargement. (Schwartz, 1985: 100)

Few Western theorists paid much attention to the family as an actual or potential source of virtue until liberal feminist thinkers such as Mary Wollstonecraft and John Stuart Mill critically discussed the subordination of women within the family context and speculated about the educative function of a radically restructured egalitarian family (Wollstonecraft, 1975; Mill, 1975). Such feminists, however, differ from Confucians in two important respects. First, they argue that there is an immense gap between the actually existing family, the 'school of despotism', and the family as it ought to be, the 'school of the virtues of freedom and equality'. Susan Moller Okin, a prominent contemporary feminist theorist inspired by liberalism, argues that reform of the family requires nothing less than a situation where 'one's sex would have no more relevance than one's eye colour or the length of one's toes' (ibid.: 181), i.e., members of the family would have no sense of being either male or female. While many contemporary Confucian thinkers seem to be somewhat embarrassed by Confucians of the past who endorsed or at least tolerated the subordination of women within the family, and some have explicitly tried to meet the challenge of including women as fully human subjects,[6] they still find more of value in actually existing families than feminists of the Okin mode, similar, perhaps, to feminist 'care theorists' who celebrate women's traditional roles while criticizing the devaluation of those roles by a male-dominated culture (*see* note 12).

Secondly, whereas feminists tend to think of the family as an educative institution for *children* (Okin, 1989: 17–23), Confucians focus primarily on the family as an educative institution for *adults* (Schwartz, 1985: 101). That is, human beings learn such virtues as responsibility and self-sacrificing love not just *qua* children learning from adults, but also (especially) *qua* adults caring for elderly parents. It is the focus on filial piety, 'the essential way of learning to be human' (Tu, 1989: 13), that explains in large part the Confucian stress on the family as an educative institution, an emphasis that goes beyond even recent feminist work on the family's (potential) role in transmitting (desirable) morality.

(ii)   *Confucians say that proper behaviour in the family context has important implications not just for ethics and everyday social life, but also with respect to politics*:

> Those in private life behave well towards their parents and elder brothers, in public life seldom show a disposition to resist the authority of their superiors. And as for such men starting a revolution, no instance of it has occurred. (*The Analects*: Book I.2)

> When gentlemen deal generously with their own kin, the common people are incited to Goodness. When old dependents are not discarded, the common people will not be fickle. (*The Analects*: Book VIII.2)

> Someone, when talking to Master K'ung, said, How is it that you are not in the public service? The Master said, The Book says: 'Be filial,

only be filial and friendly towards your brothers, and you will be contributing to government'. There are other sorts of service quite different from what you mean by 'service'. (*The Analects*: Book II.21)

That is, persons displaying the right sorts of virtues in the family context, such as loyalty and respect for legitimate authority, will also, as a by-product, be good citizens, and they may affect others by means of their positive example in a way that contributes to good political community (see Schwartz, 1985: 102). Moreover, rulers learn the dispositions and habits that underpin the benign exercise of power from the family,

precisely the domain within which the authority comes to be accepted and exercised not through reliance on physical coercion but through the binding power of religious and moral sentiments based on kinship ties. . . . The choice is not between 'a government of freemen and equals' and a government of hierarchy and authority, but between a government which is suffused with the spirit that maintains the harmony of an ideal family life and a government in which hierarchy and authority are based on brute force or mere interest without any sense of spiritual-moral constraint. (ibid.: 70; see also De Bary, 1989: 17)

With the exception of 'liberal communitarians' such as William Galston, who argue from empirical evidence that stable families contribute to the formation of 'secure, self-reliant young people' valued by politically liberal societies (Galston, 1991: 222), most social and political theorists in the West persist in drawing a sharp separation between the virtues appropriate for the 'private' realm of the family and those appropriate for the public sphere.

(iii) *Confucians say that family obligations should outweigh all other obligations, including one's obligation to obey the law*:

The 'Duke' of She addressed Master K'ung [Confucius] saying, In my country there was a man called Upright Kung. His father appropriated a sheep, and Kung bore witness against him. Master K'ung said, In my country the upright men are of quite another sort. A father will screen his son, and a son his father – which incidentally does involve a sort of uprightness. (*The Analects*: Book XIII.18)

This passage can be interpreted to mean that the requirements of filial piety justify breaking the law, no matter how just the law. While much of the Confucian tradition is a long argument about how obligations to the family are to be complemented by the responsibility of subjects to be loyal to rulers and of friends to be loyal to friends, and legalist opponents of Confucianism explicitly argued for the priority of obligations to the state in cases of conflict,[7] few if any Western political theorists have even pondered the hypothesis that the care owed to elderly parents ought to be a pre-eminent aim in one's life.

It would seem, then, that Confucian social and political theorists think of the family as the key to a good life as well as the sphere where virtues are learned and applied to social and political life, with the ethical implication that individuals have a supreme duty to nurture their family bonds. But Confucian 'familism' is more than an official ideology espoused by an elite group of Confucian scholars, for it informs, justifies, and at least in part helps to explain distinctive and empirically verifiable social phenomena, the second reason justifying the claim that the family carries special ethical weight in Confucian societies (on the matter of specifying a historical connection between Confucian conceptions of the family in *The Analects* and the fabric of East Asian societies past and present, see Rozman, 1991: especially part I; Dutton, 1992: section I).

2.   East Asians have supported and strengthened the family even at great cost. That is, the ultimate test of one's commitment to family members is the willingness. to set aside personal happiness in the interests of the family unit, and on this score Confucians have manifested a remarkable capacity to endure hardship:

(i)   *Divorce rates in Confucian societies remain well below Western levels.* While this may be due in part to the fact that legal marriage dissolution is relatively difficult to obtain in East Asia,[8] there is little evidence that variations in the strictness of divorce laws influence the degree of marital breakdown (Phillip: 1988), and one can surmise that a willingness to de-emphasize personal happiness, romantic love, and sexual fulfillment in the interests of the family bond plays an important role in ensuring family stability.

(ii)   *East Asian parents regard their children's education as a long-term undertaking in which great effort must be invested up to and including university entrance exams.* Not atypical is the Japanese 'education mama [who] helps with homework and test preparation at successive rungs on the ladder of schooling' (Rozman, 1991: 193; see also Fallows, 1994: 414). The children, in turn, face immense pressure to perform well at school, forsaking the opportunity to engage in playful activities most Westerners would consider to be a normal part of childhood.

(iii)   *Willingness to work hard, endure short-term economic sacrifices,*

and defer rewards can be explained (at least in part) by reference to
concern for the family's future:

> The importance of the future generations can be seen by the anxiety
> of the parents to see their sons married, and to accumulate property
> for the prospective children. With this in mind they work hard and
> live thriftily so that they can pass some capital for the prospective
> children. They feel guilty when unusually good food or extra-money
> is spent, not because they cannot afford these things, but because they
> want to have something to leave to their descendants. (Yang, 1945:
> 45, quoted in Ebrey, 1991: 46)

As one might expect, East Asian countries have significantly higher savings rates than Western countries (Vogel, 1992: 88). While the difference
can also be explained by governmental policies such as the forced savings
scheme in Singapore, certain cultural preferences undoubtedly make it
easier for East Asian governments to enact such policies.

(iv) *Most important, and most distinctive, is the East Asian emphasis on*
filial piety, the virtue of virtues. For some insights on the behavioral implications of this virtue, one can turn to Confucius himself: in response to a
question about the meaning of filial piety, Confucius said 'While they
[one's parents] are alive, serve them according to ritual. When they die,
bury them according to ritual and sacrifice to them according to ritual'
(*The Analects*: Book II.5). The details of Confucian rituals have of course
changed over the years, but relatively constant have been care for elderly
parents (once again, governmental policies such as housing benefits in
Singapore to those who care for elderly parents and marriage laws in
China requiring that young people provide support for their elderly parents
(Whyte, in Dernberger *et al.*, 1991: 307) may help to explain such practices, but laws promoting filial piety are generally accepted at least in the
sense that they are not thought to be among the more oppressive aspects
of authoritarian governments, and it is difficult to imagine Western governments even contemplating legislating filial piety into law), elaborate
funerals and burial rituals,[9] and respect toward one's departed elders in the
form of ancestor worship rituals at home, at graves, and at lineage halls.[10]

In comparison with Westerners, then, East Asians typically fulfill more
duties and obligations for the sake of family members[11] – in a manner
consistent with dominant Confucian values, they expend much effort in
the interests of elderly parents, children, spouses, future generations and
departed ancestors, often forsaking their own personal well-being in the
process of attending to family responsibilities (but see *The Economist*, 28
May 1994: 23–4).

Having established the relative importance of the family in Confucian ethical theory and practice, it is appropriate to return to the earlier discussion about the value of autonomy, the prevailing 'Western' justification for democracy. Does autonomy conflict with the Confucian requirement to fulfill family obligations? Autonomous or self-determining selves, modern day liberals say, must conceive of their selves to be prior to their ends, not in the sense that one can ever perceive a self totally unencumbered by any attachments, but rather 'in the sense that no end or goal is exempt from possible re-examination' (Kymlicka, 1989: 52; see also Caney, 1992: 277; Dworkin, 1989: 289; Macedo, 1990: 247), including (presumably) responsibilities to family members. But the very idea of putting into question family obligations is morally perverse from the Confucian point of view, and if the Confucian has to choose between personal autonomy and family duties, the latter more often than not will have priority. Nor is this a purely theoretical point – at the individual level, it means individuals will often side with obligations to the family when these compete for time and energy (as they commonly do) with one's own freely chosen projects,[12] and at the political level it means that East Asians will prefer, say, a Singapore-style paternalistic regime that provides individuals with special incentives to attend to the needs of family members and officially discriminates against those who relinquish their duties to care for elderly parents and children over a liberal system whose principal virtue is that it provides individuals with the opportunity to exercise their moral powers of choice.

The Importance of Public Service in Confucian Societies

A second basic assumption of Confucian ethics of special relevance to 'gentlemen' successful in a meritocratic educational system is that man's ultimate mission is public service:

> Tzu-lu asked about the qualities of a true gentleman. The Master said, He cultivates in himself the capacity to be diligent in his tasks. Tzu-lu said, Can he not go further than that? The Master said, He cultivates in himself the capacity to ease the lot of other people. Tzu-lu said, can he not go further than that? The Master said, He cultivates in himself the capacity to ease the lot of the whole populace. If he can do that, could even Yao or Shun find cause to criticize him? (*The Analects*: Book XIV.45)

In contrast to Plato's philosopher king burdened with the task of public duty among unenlightened 'cave-dwellers', and to Aristotle's idea that intellectual contemplation is the highest pleasure, and to 'the prophets of Israel and the West, who appear to be more free standing and less professionally committed to such secular functions' (De Bary, 1989: 16), Confucius's superior men achieve complete self-realization in their public vocation (Tu, 1989: 8–9, 12; Schwartz, 1960).

Only ethical and intellectual elites have a vocation to lead society, it is important to note, as the bulk of persons ('those who toil painfully without ever managing to learn' – *The Analects*: Book XVI.9; and see Book VIII.9 and Book XII.19) are not thought capable of exercising such initiative. Confucius does speak of 'teaching' the people (see, e.g., *The Analects*: Book XIII.9) but Schwartz notes that what they are taught 'is presumably no more than the rudiments of family relationships. They are hardly in a position to achieve the extensive cultivation required for the achievement of full self-realization, and it is obvious that only those in public service can do anything substantial to order human society.' (Schwartz, 1960: 53; see also Schwartz, 1985: 96–108)

In short, only those who acquire knowledge and virtue ought to participate in government, and the common people are not presumed to possess the capacities necessary for even the most indirect form of political participation. This brand of political elitism does not differentiate Confucianism from, say, Plato's views in *The Republic*, but most distinctive is that Confucian societies *institutionalized* a stable mechanism capable of producing at least on occasion what was widely seen as a 'government of the best men' – China's famous two-thousand year old meritocratic civil service examination system.[13] Entry to the civil service through competitive examination was open to all males with a few exceptions (Dawson, 1981: 19), and those who eventually succeeded in passing (often having to undertake half a lifetime of study to do so – see ibid.: 9) were thought to be in sole possession of the moral and intellectual qualities necessary for public service.[14] Put differently, scholar–bureaucrats proved their ability by succeeding in a fair and open examination system, as opposed to merely arguing in favour of their superior virtue in political theory texts, universities, churches, and so on, and consequently they were granted uncommon (by Western standards) amounts of legitimacy, prestige, and respect.

What does all this mean for those who would promote democracy founded on the value of autonomy? Autonomy requires that individuals be 'free and equal in determining the conditions of their own association' (Cohen and Rogers, 1983: 149; see also Held, 1992: 35), but it is far from obvious that most East Asians want to be free and equal with respect to political decisions even in principle – on the bottom, the traditional political culture of the East Asian commoner continues to be one of passivity and dependence on one's betters (Pye, 1985: 1988), and on the top, unelected but highly esteemed bureaucrats continue to wield power and authority that would make even their colleagues in *Yes Minister* envious,[15] a combination that does not augur well for 'pro-autonomy democrats' in East Asia. But rather than pursue this controversial point, let us turn to problems posed by the issue of feasibility.

The (Un)Feasibility of Democratic Autonomy

Critics of contemporary democratic systems have drawn attention to the gap which exists between democratic ideals and 'actually existing democracy' (see Zolo, 1992: 102) in the form of national political representative institutions. In comparison with the citizens of ancient Athens who literally ruled themselves (Dunn, 1992: 240–3, 255, and Hansen, 1991), the sovereignty of the modern democratic citizen, says a particularly pessimistic critic, 'can now hardly amount to more than empty verbiage' (Zolo, 1992: 170). Citizens have the formal right to participate in the shaping of their individual and collective destinies, but most are in fact at the mercy of apparently uncontrollable external and impersonal forces governing their lives. Just to name a handful of the more serious problems facing would-be-modern-day autonomous citizens:

1. Citizens of political communities are (or will soon be) involuntarily subjected to the effects of world-wide phenomena such as:

> the current demographic explosion, coupled with the growing disparity between the small number of democratic (and rich) countries and the large number of non-democratic countries, which, far from experiencing economic growth, are actually seeing the living standards of millions of their people progressively worsen; the mass movements of population which these conditions are likely to cause, and the racist reactions and violent conflicts over the apportionment of citizenship which the objective pressure for equality behind these movements seems certain to provoke; the ever-present military threat, now further increased by the widespread diffusion of nuclear, chemical and biological weapons in the countries experiencing growth and, in the poorer countries, by an uncontainable spread of terrorism, which has now been taken to international levels . . . ; the escalation of the trend towards ecological disequilibrium with incalculable consequences not only for the quality of life on the planet but also for the political structures themselves of industrialized countries. (Zolo, 1992: 178–9; see also Kennedy, 1993)

2. At the national level, the promise of popular sovereignty 'has been completely drained of effect by the growth of public bureaucracies. The functional logic of large-scale organizational bureaucracies is, as a result of their unrestrainable hierarchical and oligarchal tendencies, quite opposite to the logic of democracy' (Zolo, 1992: 102).

3. Moreover, even if citizens wanted to counterbalance the growth of public bureaucracies by taking a more active part in politics, it may be impossible for them to do so. That is, relevant issues and policies in the political systems of modern societies have become so complex that 'no one can ever hope to master more than a few' (Dahl, 1992: 50). The sheer complexity of public affairs, and the implications this has for citizens trying to comprehend a wide sense of public issues, renders all but meaningless the 'underlying assumption behind the notion of representative democracy – i.e., the sovereignty, rationality, and moral autonomy of the individual' (Zolo, 1992: ix. and chapter 4 more generally).

4. In the workplace, a minority presiding over companies and factories direct and control the working lives of producers. The economy is perhaps 'the decisive area of society's life' (Arblaster, 1987: 103), yet most firms are run by unelected and unaccountable owners and managers, and even governments feel relatively powerless in relation to great agglomerations of private economic power.

5. Families are not run along democratic lines – women in particular are vulnerable to dependency, exploitation, and abuse within the context of gender-structured marriage and family life (Okin, 1989: especially chapter 7). Moreover, inequality of family circumstances – women being assigned 'the functional role of actual or potential wife and mother and, as primary parent, to basic or at least periodic dependence upon a man' (ibid.: 173) – raises psychological and practical barriers against women's participation in democratic life outside the family (ibid.: chapter 6).

In short, citizens of 'actually-existing democracies' are dominated and controlled by a bewildering array of external and impersonal forces, and the idea that autonomous individuals should set their own life plans and participate in the collective life of the community amounts to little more than a pleasant mirage. In response to this phenomenon, some 'pro-autonomy democrats' reluctant to revise their normative premise have proposed various ways of narrowing the gap between the ideal of democratic autonomy and the reality: (1) to deal with the problem of global issues currently beyond the reach of national democratic mechanisms, David Held proposes a 'cosmopolitan model of democracy' that includes a global Parliament and an interconnected global legal system (Held, 1992: 31–9); (2) to counter large-scale bureaucratic power and the perception that national politics appears too distant from our ordinary concerns, 'strong democracy' theorists favour political decentralization in the form of 'a national system of neighbourhood *assemblies* in every rural, suburban and urban district' (Barber, 1984: 269; see also Macpherson, 1977 and Pateman, 1970); (3) to overcome the tendency towards greater complexity of public affairs and the attendant implications for citizen competence, Robert Dahl advances the idea of randomly selected citizen assemblies that 'could provide what opinion surveys cannot – judgements arrived by a body of well-informed citizens after deliberation assisted by experts' (Dahl, 1992: 55; see also Fishkin, 1991); (4) several democratic theorists, both socialist and non-socialist, have argued that workplace democracy is required as a realization of more general democratic principles (see, e.g., Gould, 1988: especially chapters 4–9; Arblaster, 1987: 103–4; Cohen and Rogers, 1983: 162–5; Dahl, 1985; Walzer, 1983: 117–19, 161–2, 301–3); and (5) feminist thinkers argue that gender relations can be equalized by such means as payment for homemakers, subsidized day care, and flexible time for working parents, hence making democracy more of a reality for the female half of our species (see, e.g., Okin, 1989: especially chapter 8; Gutmann, 1987: 290).

Whatever the desirability of these proposals, it must be recognized by even the most optimistic among us that implementing meaningful democratic autonomy entails an intimidatingly radical programme for political change, and that very few of the above proposals are anywhere near the top of the agenda in democratic countries more preoccupied by such issues as economic decline, urban crime, threats to national security, family breakdown, and so on. And the news is even worse when one turns to the East Asian context – since East Asians are not likely to be moved by proposals for democratization justified by appeals to the idea of autonomy, they will be even less favourably disposed to the ideal of democratic autonomy once it becomes clear that meaningful autonomy requires not just (as commonly thought) the democratization of national political institutions, but also a radical re-structuring of interstate, bureaucratic, work, and family practices and institutions. In brief, democratic autonomy is neither very desirable nor very feasible from the East Asian perspective, with the implication that pro-democracy activists need to consider justifications for democracy decoupled from notions of autonomy and substantial self-determination in our everyday lives. At this point, let us turn to an evaluation of the suitability of various *instrumental* justifications of democracy in an East Asian context.

II INSTRUMENTAL JUSTIFICATIONS FOR DEMOCRACY

Those who think democracy can be justified on instrumental grounds, by the fact that it usually if not always leads to desirable outcomes, normally adopt a *procedural* definition of democracy. On this view, democracy is nothing more (nor less) than a means of constituting authority in which the ruled choose the rulers. As Samuel Huntington puts it,

> In other types of political systems, people may become rulers by virtue of birth, appointment, lot, examination, wealth, or coercion. In democracies, in contrast, either the rulers and ruled are identical, as in direct democracy, or rulers are selected by vote of the ruled. A modern nation-state has a democratic political system to the extent that its most powerful decision-makers are selected through fair, honest, periodic elections in which candidates freely compete for votes and in which virtually all the adult population is eligible to vote. (Huntington, 1993: 28)

Elections, in short, are the essence of democracy in the contemporary world, but Huntington adds that 'free, fair, and competitive elections are only possible if there is some measure of freedom of speech, assembly, and press, and if opposition candidates and parties are able to criticize incumbents without fear of retaliation' (ibid.). Democracy thus includes a competitive struggle for the people's vote *and* the freedoms required to make the elections a meaningful exercise, but democracy understood in procedural terms (see also Schumpeter, 1943; Dahl, 1956; Lipset, 1960; and Barry, 1991: 25–7; but see Kateb, 1992: chapter 2) cannot be *defined* by the content of outcomes often associated with it, such as political stability or economic growth.

Still, if certain benefits or socially desirable goals often flow from democratic procedures, they can *justify* those procedures. While consequentialist justifications are necessarily contingent, meaning that 'where democratic procedures fail to produce desired outcomes, there appears to be little reason to follow such procedures' (Mostov, 1992: 103),[16] sufficiently overwhelming empirical evidence about probable (desired) outcomes can persuade reasonable individuals to support democracy. Hence, claims about outcomes commonly thought to result from democracy, if true, may hold the key to promoting democracy in East Asia. What outcomes are said to flow from democracy, and is there sound empirical evidence linking democratic procedures and desired outcomes? The next section will consider these questions, with special focus on significant counter-examples from East Asian countries close in historical and cultural terms that are more likely to pose difficulties for pro-democracy forces in East Asia.

1. Democracy Leads to Social Peace (within the State)

Democracy leads to social peace, one can argue, because it correspond to people's shared understandings about how political systems ought to be structured. As Rawls justifies his principles of justice (the first principle of justice includes democratic procedures and attendant freedoms):

> What justifies a conception of justice is not its being true to an order antecedent and given to us, but its congruence with our deeper understanding of ourselves and our aspirations, and our realization that, given our history and the traditions embedded in our public life, it is the most reasonable doctrine for us. (Rawls, 1980: 519)

But of course this justification will not appeal to those who have little or no history of democracy, and one would be hard pressed to argue that democracy meets, say, the deeper aspirations of Chinese peasants.

A more promising claim is that democracy leads to social peace in *pluralistic* modern societies. That is, members of contemporary societies have different socio-economic interests and sometimes conflicting beliefs, faiths, and cultural outlooks, and democracy can be defended on the grounds that it provides a mechanism for the peaceful resolution of conflicts. Without democracy, individuals and groups with competing interests and conceptions of the good life will resort to force to resolve their differences.

Focusing strictly on the issue of diverse cultural and linguistic groupings inhabiting the same territory as a potential source of conflict, it is noteworthy that some East Asian countries (e.g., Japan and Korea) are relatively homogeneous in comparison to Western multi-national states, and an argument which assumes irreconcilable differences between individuals and groups may not appeal as much in this context (not to mention the fact that East Asians are socialized in such a manner as to suppress their differences, or at least not to express them openly). Moreover, there is not an invariable link between democracy and social peace even in those countries that cannot fail to recognize the fact of ethnic pluralism, as democracy's majoritarian principle can sometimes exacerbate conflict by causing minorities to feel systematically excluded from the political system (think of Northern Ireland, Sri Lanka, and Croatia). In the Southeast Asian context, multi-ethnic Singapore (76 per cent Chinese, 15 per cent Malay, 6 per cent Indian) assures social peace not by democratic mechanisms[17] but by means of authoritarian measures designed to prevent the

outbreak of violence between ethnic and religious groups, including restrictions on intercommunal proselytizing,[18] on public gatherings of more
than a few people, and on certain 'sensitive' racial and religious issues
from being raised in the press.

Another argument is that democracy leads to social peace by facilitating
smooth transitions of political power. As Friedrich Hayek said, the democratic procedure is the 'only method of peaceful change of government yet
discovered' (Hayek, 1979: 5). Without a democratic systems, competing
political elites have no peaceful way of sorting out their differences.

But non-democratic hereditary monarchies have often experienced peaceful transitions of political power, and the Chinese dynastic system, notwithstanding some uncertainty about dynastic succession, enjoyed long
periods of stability for most of this millennium. Japan experienced remarkable political stability during the Tokugawa Shogunate (1603–1868), as
did Korea during the Yi Dynasty (1392–1910). More recently, Taiwan
experienced a smooth non-democratic transition of power after the death
of Chiang Kai-Shek in 1975 and later after the death of his eldest son,
Chiang Chingkuo in 1988. In terms of the future, Samuel Huntington
suggests that in the absence of a Western-style democratic system allowing for the ouster and replacement of incumbents an economic downturn
may produce 'revolutionary change' (Huntington, 1993: 42), but an equally
plausible claim can be made that authoritarian governments are easier to
justify in crisis situations (e.g., the economy nosedives and foreign capital
must be attracted by a 'healthy investment climate', which may require
authoritarian measures to temporarily restrict worker's rights and benefits
– this tactic was successfully employed by the Singaporean government
to emerge from a serious economic downturn in 1985), particularly if the
political leadership in generally trusted and viewed as being seriously
committed to economic development and cannot plausibly be blamed
for the economic downturn (e.g., in the event of a world-wide war or
depression).

2 Democracy Co-exists with Economic Prosperity

This justification is the most compelling, according to John Dunn:

> The practical power of modern democratic institutions today comes
> from their very ordinariness, and especially from their peculiar apt-
> ness to the economic world in which we now live. . . . The principal
> contribution of modern constitutional democracy has been to make
> both the modern state and the standard of democratic legitimacy

compatible with the operating requirements of an international and domestic economic order founded an private ownership and market exchange – to reconcile the needs of capitalist production with the practical and ideological requirements of effective rule in the modern world. (Dunn, 1992: 251)

But the experience of Meiji Restoration Japan, Nazi Germany in the 1930s and the four 'mini-dragons' (South Korea, Taiwan, Singapore and Hong Kong) in the post-World-War-II era proves that authoritarian rule can co-exist with capitalist mechanisms and high growth rates. Moreover, the experience of rapid development in authoritarian China since the early 1980s as compared with the disastrous economic performance of post-socialist Russia dramatically illustrates the risks of a sudden *volte face* to democracy in countries moving from a state-socialist system of directive planning into some form of a market economy (White, 1994: 80; but see McCormick: 1994).

Empirical evidence does support the claim that democracy is closely related to the socioeconomic systems of *developed* countries, but not that democracy *always* co-exists with economically developed status (Diamond, 1992: 487), and the continued existence of authoritarian rule in economically prosperous Singapore is a clear enough lesson for East Asian countries (the Chinese government sent over 200 delegations in 1992 to learn from the Singapore experience, and Lee Kuan Yew has been asked to advise governments ranging from the Vietnamese communist leadership to the ANC). Moreover, in view of the economic difficulties in developed welfare states such as Sweden, Holland, and Canada, a good argument can be made that democratic majorities in prosperous states have a tendency to sacrifice the interests of future generations by voting themselves extensive benefits in the present (compare the welfare-induced deficit figures in Western liberal democratic states with the huge national reserves accumulated by relatively benign authoritarian states in East Asia and what this means in terms of the capacity of governments to uphold the living standards of future generations as well as to help them in the event of 'rainy days') and to vote out of office a government that threatens to rein in entitlements (in a 'graying Holland', for example, the elderly are organizing themselves to fight against a government that may freeze pensions and divert funds to create jobs for young people, notwithstanding the fact that the number of people receiving benefits will soon outstrip the number of those who work – see the *International Herald Tribune*, 3 May 1994). If people have an essential interest in prosperity, in other words, democracy may not increase the probability of either becoming or staying wealthy.

3. Democracies Safeguard Civil Liberties

All human beings, it is commonly believed, need basic civil freedoms, such as the rights to physical integrity, to travel, marry, have children, speak freely, and so on. Even persons not prone to the critical reflection required of the autonomous ideal (Larmore, 1987: 74; Kymlicka, 1993: 218–9) have an interest in being left alone by their government, and if democracy minimizes or eliminates fear and oppression, this is a good reason to support democracy.

The recent adoption of fair democratic procedures in Taiwan and Korea, including the right to run for the opposition without fear of retaliation, along with what appears to be a reduction in fear (compared with the same countries ten years ago, or Singapore today) does lend some support to the hypothesis that free and fair elections can minimize fear, but still many relevant counter-examples lead one to think otherwise. Authoritarian rule during the 4000-year cycle of dynasties in China, for example, interfered very little with the ordinary lives of the vast majority of people in China (Simon Leys argues that this 'hands-off' approach to ruling helps to explain the stability of the dynastic system, in contrast to the communists who 'betrayed a strange incapacity to understand their own people' (Leys, 1990: 10) by organizing recurrent waves of terror invasive of the lives of common people), and the non-democratic colonial government of Hong Kong extends to its citizens perhaps the most extensive set of civil liberties anywhere in Asia. Moreover, democratic regimes have more than once suspended fundamental civil liberties (e.g., the internment of Americans and Canadians of Japanese descent during World War II). Last but not least, a good case can be made that on occasion civil liberties *should* be curtailed, which may be more difficult if the vote is granted to a short-term minded electorate – nearly all intellectuals in China accept the necessity of the one child per family policy meant to curb China's staggering post-1949 population explosion (Link, 1992), but this policy is highly unpopular in the countryside (where most Chinese live), and it is not implausible to imagine that a democratic China would revoke this measure even if it had disastrous effects at the collective level (interestingly, Fang Lizhi and other democracy movement leaders in China 'have expressed only horror at a democratic formula that would give equal voting rights to peasants' – Shue, 1992: 163).

4. Democracy Leads to International Peace

More precisely, the claim is that democracies don't fight each other – citizens' interest in staying out of bloodshed and war, and the establishment of democratic norms of peaceful resolution of conflict and of other people's right to self determination, among other factors introduce an element of restraint in the way democracies deal with each other (see, e.g., Sorensen, 1992).

But the US has more than once subverted democratic regimes in Latin America that threatened the interests of US based multi-nationals (e.g., Guatemala in 1954). More recently, Croatia, Serbia and Bosnia have moved towards democracy, and this has not prevented inter-state wars of unimaginable cruelty (one can argue that bloodshed occurs only in the early stages of democratic states in the process of determining who counts as 'we the people', but this thought will bring little comfort to countries in Southeast Asia where it is unclear whether people's primary allegiance lies with the national community or their ethnic group).[19] In the East Asian context, a plausible case can be made that mutual hostility runs deeper among the people (e.g., between Koreans and Japanese, Chinese and Japanese, Malaysians and Singaporeans) than among their political leaders, and that more democracy may actually increase the probability of war.

In short, commonly advanced instrumental arguments that democracy facilitates the functions of modern states cannot readily be confirmed by empirical hypotheses linking such arguments.

III DEMOCRACY AND COMMUNITY

I will explore in greater depth an uncommon (instrumental) justification for democracy most likely (I believe) to capture the 'hearts and minds' of East Asians, namely, the idea that democracy protects and promotes communitarian ways of life, with special emphasis on the family.

The argument begins with the observation that excessively interventionist political regimes, by seeking to control and dominate people's lives, actually undermine communitarian ties. As Allen Buchanan explains,

> At least in our century, the greatest single threat to communities probably has been totalitarianism. As the name implies, the totalitarian state recognizes no limits on its authority, seeking to control every aspect of its citizens' lives. It cannot tolerate genuine communities within its boundaries because they would limit the individual's dependence upon and allegiance to the state. And it is a matter of historical record that totalitarian regimes have employed the most ruthless measures to undermine traditional communities – the

family and the church in particular – in the name of achieving an all-inclusive political community.[20] (Buchanan, 1989: 858)

There is no better illustration of this point than China's experience under the Communist Party. Communist leaders 'were convinced that one of the weaknesses of the old system was precisely its lack of control over the populace and the failure to utilize their energies by engaging them in the political system' (Goldstein, in Dernberger *et al.*, 1991: 171–2). Family ties and obligations, which far outweighed other bonds, were undoubtedly the most threatening from the point of view of communist leaders out to establish primary allegiance to the state, and consequently the Party set out 'to transform families so that they will mobilize their members to serve state interests' (Whyte, in Dernberger *et al.*, 1991: 306–7; see also Dutton, 1992: 260–1). The claim that the CCP tried to destroy the family so that individual members would be released to give loyalty to the Party and to Mao may be an exaggeration (Whyte, in Dernberger *et al.*, 1991: 306), but the new 'state-first' policy did mean (at minimum) that obligations to the state overrode obligations to the family in cases of conflict, as confirmed by the sorry history of family members betraying each other for political reasons during the Cultural Revolution, and to a lesser extent after 4 June 1989 (it will be recalled that some individuals were publicly rewarded for informing against family members).[21] Gone were the days when 'A father will screen his son, and a son his father' (*The Analects*: Book XIII.18).

What all this means for democratization needs to be made explicit – modern day democratic governments ultimately dependent on support from citizens at election time will not risk incurring displeasure by employing ruthless measures to undermine traditional communities, and for family-oriented East Asians this is not an insignificant point. One can argue in reply that families are doing worse in the democratic West than in 'soft authoritarian' states such as Singapore that view the family as a social institution whose flourishing is essential to the interests of the state, but things may change (if, say, Lee Kuan Yew becomes convinced that rearing children in communal barracks will increase the growth rate by 5 per cent), and 'the people' may still want the 'insurance' of free and fair competitive elections. Moreover, the democratic method cannot plausibly be blamed for the breakdown of family structures in Western countries (excessive emphasis on individual autonomy without social responsibility is undoubtedly a more important cause). Democracy, in short, is a strong bulwark against attempts to deploy the coercive apparatus of the state to destroy or radically transform family and other community structures, and it need not lead to the erosion of family life (in fact, the democratic system is perfectly compatible with active 'pro-family' governmental policies, so long as it's not a liberal government operating according to a political principle of state neutrality that rules out measures justified on the grounds that family life is an especially worthy form of life – see Bell, 1993: 230–1).

Contrary to what some Confucians seem to imply, however, stable families cannot secure sufficient attachment to the overall political community. While the family may well inculcate certain virtues appropriate to good citizenship such as loyalty, discipline, and respect for legitimate authority, strong arguments can be made that human beings have an interest in establishing a relatively strong (direct) sense of attachment to the political community: a deep human need for community beyond the family can be met by participating in or identifying with the collective achievements of one's community, e.g., the pride of a Frenchman partaking of an esteemed culinary tradition or of an American for her country's triumph over the Nazis (Tamir, 1993); a particularist sense of identification with fellow citizens provides the motivational force for an effective scheme of distributive justice favouring the weak and the helpless (Rorty: 1989, 191); people who care for their community will be more likely to overthrow a corrupt and oppressive government (Chee, 1994: 14–5); and so on.

But rather than rehearse these arguments, I will focus more narrowly on the issue of patriotism required for common defense. Some countries can get by with professional, quasi-mercenary armies, but others require much more with respect to provisions for common defense and preparations for warfare – Singapore and Taiwan, for example, are small countries surrounded by large, potentially hostile neighbours, and consequently both have a policy of military conscription for all adult males, a need recognized by even the most radical opponents of these regimes (though some argue for a shorter period of national service and/or the inclusion of women). Moreover, it is (or should be) of prime concern to instill a strong sense of patriotism, as measured by the degree to which one is prepared to take risks and face harm and danger on the nation's behalf (see MacIntyre, 1988: 40), a requirement of any community that relies on its own citizens to provide for common defense (consider, for example, the crucial role that patriotism played for the Vietnamese in their victory over a technologically superior US military machine).

At this point, however, we encounter a problem with (at least some) authoritarian regimes. In Singapore, for example, the government relies on official propaganda (e.g., 'communitarianism', defined as 'community over self', has been declared one of the four national core values by an official act of Parliament in January 1989) and extensive legal regulations (e.g., stiff fines for littering and not flushing toilets) to foster a sense of loyalty, public responsibility and concern for the fate of others in the community,[22] but perhaps not surprisingly one sees much selfish behavior[23] in contexts where individuals feel free from legal regulations (e.g., inconsiderate behaviour of people boarding a bus, not giving up seats for elderly persons and pregnant women, and so on). Even the government voiced its concern about Singaporeans feeling little attachment to the country and its people (e.g., Minister for Information and the Arts, Brig. Gen. (res) George Yeo compared Singapore to a 'five star hotel' where residents might like to spend a vacation because the economic benefits are good but not a lifetime (*Straits Times*: 21 June 1991), and Dr Chee Soon Juan, acting Secretary General of the opposition Singapore Democratic Party, opens his political manifesto with a chapter on the gap between the rhetoric of communitarianism and the more individualistic reality in Singapore, arguing for measures that would lead to greater national cohesion (Chee, 1994: chapter 1).

So how does this bear on the question of democracy? For one thing, the vindictive way the Singaporean regime deals with political opponents sends an 'unpatriotic' message to the community at large – 'stick to your own (family, religious, and business) affairs, because it's dangerous for those who haven't been specially anointed by the top leadership of the ruling party to become involved in public affairs'.[24] One can predict that if there really were free, fair, and competitive elections for political power, including the right to run for the opposition without fear of retaliation, this would do more to promote a sense of attachment to the community at large than ineffectual 'courtesy campaigns' (consistent with this view, patriotism appears to be on the increase in Taiwan following the adoption of democratic practices).

Secondly, and equally important, 'there is abundant historical evidence to support the hypothesized linkage between a vigorous associational life and a stable democracy' (Diamond, 1992: 483), in contrast to authoritarian regimes like Singapore where independent forces in civil society have by and large either been coopted into official organizations or expunged from the political scene (one exception is the relatively autonomous women's group 'AWARE'). This is relevant for those concerned with patriotism because as Hegel explained, participation in intermediary groups leads to a broader notion of public spiritedness:

Unless he is a member of an authorized corporation . . . , an individual is without mark and dignity[25] [and] his isolation reduces his activity to mere self-seeking. . . . The single individual attains his actual and living destiny for the whole only when he becomes a member of

a corporation. . . . [Hence] the secret of patriotism [lies in recognizing
that] the proper strength of the state lies in its associations. (Quoted
in Buchwalter, 1992: 572)

More famously, de Tocqueville depicted intermediary associations as 'large
free schools' (quoted in Diamond, 1992: 483)[26] where political interests
are stimulated and political and organizational skills enhanced, and a contemporary commentator adds that 'a vibrant associational life . . . provides
poor and disadvantaged persons the capacity to relieve or redress the
injustices they face' (ibid.). In brief, the argument is that a good, citizen-
based fighting force requires patriotism, patriotism requires a vibrant
associational life, and vibrant associational life requires democracy (authoritarian regimes tend not to tolerate independent voices in civil society).
While the historical record does not always support this formula,[27] it does
have some usefulness for East Asian governments faced with the difficult
task of instilling a sense of patriotism in a relatively apolitical, family
oriented population.

CONCLUSION

This last section leads us to modify the central thesis of this paper – pro-
democracy forces relying on moral persuasion will most likely not succeed
by founding their political programme on our (alleged) essential interest
in personal autonomy, or by emphasizing desirable outcomes commonly
thought to result from democratic procedures, but a 'communitarian' argument for democracy, namely, the idea that democracy protects and facilitates communal ways of life, is worthy of special attention.

3 Democracy and Identity: The Paradoxical Character of Political Development

David Martin Jones

Asia is not going to be civilized after the methods of the west. There is too much Asia and she is too old. (Rudyard Kipling)

As much as the communists were intolerant, the democrats, particularly the liberal democrats, are intolerant. You risk excommunication if you question the wisdom of even the less fundamental of democratic practices. You will be branded and hounded by the democratic press and the fanatical democrats. (Mahathir Mohamad)

In the wake of the disintegration of the Soviet Empire both the American government and the American political science community have devoted increasing attention to the prospects for democratization in East and Southeast Asia. On the one hand, we have Francis Fukuyama (1992) reprising the theme that we have reached the end of an era of ideology and that the world can look forward to a dull but respectable liberal democratic end to history. The global tendency modernization theory holds, is inexorably democratic and Freedom House confirms this with impressively quantified data to show just how far democracy has been instrumentalized.

On the other hand, a number of East Asian commentators and politicians are either a little reluctant to embrace this apparently inexorable movement, or find that it conceals a suspicious, 'new found mission in the West to use the imposed category as an international merit test' (Chan Heng Chee, in Bartley *et al.*, 1993: 6–7). In part this is a matter of *amour propre*. Confining post colonial East Asians in an ideological straight-jacket of Western design seems to an increasingly self-conscious East Asian political elite to be at best patronising and at worst an insidious ploy 'to bring about instability, economic decline and poverty' (Mahathir Mohamad, *Straits Times*, 31 August 1993).

In order to resist the sugar coated bullets of western style democracy, moreover, a number of East Asian 'new thinkers' (Chan Heng Chee, in Bartley *et al.*, 1993; Mahbubani, 1994; Ogata, in Bartley *et al.*, 1993) with some support from Harvard management theorists (Vogel and Lodge, 1987;

41

Vogel, 1991) have advanced an alternative East Asian model of political development. They maintain, in fact, that East Asian economies have successfully modernized precisely because of traditional East Asian political and moral values. Thus, politicians as various as Lee Kuan Yew, Mahathir Mohamad, Suharto and Roh Tae Woo have either contested the universality of western concepts of democracy, right and law, or suggested that there are different, but equally valid 'Asian' understandings of these terms.

This East Asian undertanding of rule it is further contended is different from, but equally as effective, indeed, more effective, in an Asian context, than its western alternative. Such a view, often superficially construed as Confucian or neo-Confucian, is advanced to explain the stability, order and dynamism of the Pacific Rim that contrasts so vividly with the 'dying economies' and civil disobedience that have come to characterize the Anglo-Saxon world.

The increasingly rancorous debate about the nature of the new world order has not been helped by a worrying degree of conceptual confusion and linguistic incoherence. This in part stems from the ambiguity, promulgated both by an officially controlled East and Southeast Asian media and by a new generation of 'Asian thinkers' (*Asiaweek*, 2 March 1994) that dismisses 'decadent' western notions of democracy, while at the same time claiming that traditional Asian values also meet certain democratic requirements. Moreover, the fact that the arguments advanced in favour of a new 'Asian model' of democracy (see Chan, in Bartley *et al.*, 1993) often draw upon the modernization literature, whose 'capitalist democratic' (Dunn, 1991) conclusions they most decidedly want to contest, serves only to amplify this contradiction. In an attempt to clarify what cross cultural misunderstanding and journalistic inadvertence has rendered obscure, this chapter addresses a series of related questions: What is the political character of traditional East and Southeast Asian thought about virtue, law and rule? How and why have these traditional understandings been adapted or amended to the needs of rapidly modernizing East Asian polities and what are their implications for democratic development in contemporary East and Southeast Asia?

THE EAST AND SOUTHEAST ASIAN UNDERSTANDING OF RULE, RELATIONSHIP AND ROLE

What can be addressed, in the consideration of the orient, are not other symbols, another metaphysics, another wisdom . . . ; it is the possibility of a difference, of a mutation, of a revolution in the propriety of a symbolic system. (Roland Barthes, *Empire of Signs*, 1987: 3)

As we suggested in the Introduction a neglected, yet increasingly central feature of democratic theory assumes a public tolerance of articulated difference. Historically contingent communicatory democracies have traditionally 'been distinguished as free, or political since they are characterized by self-determination and the process of determination is by public talk'. (Minogue, 1987: 61). Such a political arrangement increasingly recognized both the supremacy of law as establishing the formal conditions for public speech and participation together with an autonomous civil society of uncoerced citizen activity.

Yet this understanding of isonomy and its concomitant implications for democracy, equality and political rule did not occur in a vacuum. It emerged in opposition to what Western political commentators traditionally depicted as an Oriental or Asiatic mode of rule. Moreover, the genealogy of Western commentary upon the East from Aristotle to Marx and Mill in the nineteenth century and Wittfogel and Weber in the twentieth, consistently depicted East Asian rule as tyrannical, decadent and corrupt (Springborg, 1992; Bernal, 1991). Such a characterization evolved in part in order to distinguish a virtuous rule of law from what Western political theorists for the most part came to consider a corrupting rule of man.

This western rule of law tradition stands in dramatic contrast with the dominant East and Southeast Asian traditions of governance. For in East Asian political discourse the question of what is good government has been traditionally answered not with good law but good men. As Lee Kuan Yew a contemporary East Asian 'man of prowess' (Wolters, 1982: 6) maintained in June 1991, political understanding in East Asia sprang from radically different historical and cultural experiences. The East Asian, consequently possessed a different 'map up here in the mind' (*The Economist*, 29 June 1991). Centrally, the traditional eastern preoccupation with the rule of virtuous men and what that implied for an East Asian understanding of authority, obligation and moral identity emanated from a complex blending of Hindic, Buddhist, Islamic and Confucian traditions. How, we might initially consider, did these traditions affect East and Southeast Asian understandings of rule, and, more pertinently, what elements in these traditions have been resurrected to serve the purposes of the modernizing Newly Industrialized Countries (NICs) of contemporary East and Southeast Asia?

THE CONFUCIAN, NEO-CONFUCIAN AND LEGALIST LEGACY OF EAST ASIA

The dominant political and economic orthodoxy, promulgated in academic and journalistic accounts of contemporary South Korea, Hong Kong, Taiwan and Singapore uncritically assumes that the apparently shared Confucian or neo-Confucian values of these NIC's plays a determining role in generating both economic dynamism and social and political order. It is our intention here to examine this political legacy, particularly those features that have been adapted to the needs of contemporary rule in East and Southeast Asia, and to assess their democratic implications.

In this context it is important to establish that like any political tradition, Confucianism is not without its ambiguities and incoherences. Indeed, Confucianism's curiously aphoristic character has lent itself to interpretations that differ fundamentally in their understanding of human nature, the role of education, the nature and character of authority and the extent of popular obligation. Among contemporary interpreters it has been variously considered the basis for an Asian liberalism (de Bary, 1983), irredeemably autocratic (Elvin, 1986; Levenson, 1965), an essentially religious doctrine (Fingarette, 1972) and an apolitical moral and educational programme (Tu, 1984; Cheng, 1991). As James Cotton observes, 'Confucianism' in an important sense connotes 'the history of Chinese political thought,' and this thought in China 'was appropriated by the regime in both a narrow and a broad sense' (Cotton, 1991: 120). Significantly, rather like Marxism, Confucianism constitutes an established 'legitimating theory, that is an entity which has only the appearance of a single and constant theory, but the actual content of which is there in order to excuse a set of (political, social and economic) practices which already exist' (ibid.). What then is the content of this theory and what are the political practices that it legitimates?

Confucianism as a language of moral association that evolves across time is essentially conservative. (Metzger, 1977; Munro, 1977) Its emblematic exponents stress the transmission of a wisdom located in the past, handed down and refined or adapted by subsequent hands. Both Confucius and subsequent Han, Sung, Ming and Qing neo-Confucian reformers shared an essentially conservative vision of a past golden age of virtue and attempted to apply this vision to reform the present.

The Confucian worldview further assumed a universe linked through the operation of *tao* – the way. The *tao* that informs heaven, earth and man affords an ultimately mystical, and clearly problematic composition of otherwise incompatible opposing forces: *yin* and *yang*; masculine and feminine; positive and negative. Moreover, to conform to *tao* is evidently the aim of both the superior man *jin zi* and of virtuous government in general. In order to guide this project, the Confucian further contends that such a perfectly ordered arrangement of virtuous rule and universal harmony had once existed in the golden age of *Yao and Shun*. Records handed down from that time, the *I Ching*, the *Book of Odes*, the *Book of History*, the *Spring and Autumn Annals* and *Book of Rites* preserved ancient practices and effectively memorialize a past utopia. Transmuted and transmitted through Confucius' oracular understanding, this traditional wisdom offered the seductive possibility of its recreation in the present.

In deepening their understanding of this project, subsequent writers in the neo-Confucian tradition, notably Mencius and Zhu Xi, lessened the import of rites as the critical indicator of the way back and emphasized instead the importance of principle *(li)* to which man and institutions should ideally correspond. In fact, principle offered a model to which the individual in his social relations and government in its management of the people conformed. Consequently, neo-Confucians came to maintain that when the way is present in the state, uniformity, harmony and the Mean *(chung)* naturally prevail.

In order to instrumentalize the mean of harmonious balance, neo-Confucians following Zhu Xi paid attention both to the relationship between the inner realm of mind *(nei)* and the outer realm of society *(wai)* and to an education in its codes of behaviour. For the Confucian, therefore, from Zhu Xi to Tu Wei-ming (1987) the central concern of the state, as of the enlightened individual, is didactic. Pedagogic tutelage established the way. As the Confucian classic, the *Great Learning*, explains:

> The ancients who wished to illustrate illustrious virtue throughout the kingdom, first ordered well their own states. Wishing to order well their states, they first regulated their families. Wishing to regulate their families, they first cultivated their persons. Wishing to cultivate their persons they first rectified their hearts. Wishing to rectify their hearts they first sought to be sincere in their thoughts. Wishing to be sincere in their thoughts, they first extended to the utmost their knowledge. . . . Their persons being cultivated, their families were regulated. Their families being regulated, their states were rightly governed. (Legge, 1893: 131)

Analagously, the Confucian critic of the Taewongan's autocratic reforms in nineteenth century Korea maintained that, 'if the king's mind is as clear as pure water, his desires will be purified and disappear and heaven's principles will flow when it comes to government orders and carrying them out . . . the way will be established without doubt' (Palliser, 1991: 191).

Given this understanding not only was it perfectly plausible that virtue could be instrumentalized and the people transformed, the success of the project could also be measured. Classically the Confucian state had three measurable functions: the increase of the population; the development of the economic life of the people understood in agricultural rather than mercantile terms; and the promotion of education. Consequently a formula for virtuous rule could be deduced, 'the ruler should first concern himself with his own virtue. Possessing virtue he will win the people. Possessing the people he will win the realm. Possessing the realm he will command revenue. Possessing revenues he will have resources for all demands' (Legge, 1893: 131).

It was the inculcation of virtue, rather than the rule of law, therefore, that transformed the moral and economic condition of the people. 'Guide them (the common people) by virtue', Confucius remarked, 'keep them in line with rites and they will besides having a sense of shame, reform themselves' (Confucius, 1979: 114). This subsequently came to require a scrupulous attention to maintaining precisely defined relationships.

Essentially, Confucianism posited five basic relationships: between Prince and Minister; father and son; husband and wife: older and younger brother; and friends. Correctly regulated they offered the corresponding moral possibilities of loyalty and respect, kindness and filial piety, mutual respect and separate duties, brotherly love and consideration, and truthfulness and trust. Didactic exemplars like the Duke of Wei and sages like Confucius and Mencius provided model guidance and a virtuous elite of scholar bureaucrats (*jin zi* or *yangban* in Korea) monitored or rectified these relationships to ensure that name and reality coincided. Thus the ruler constantly examined the practice of the five relationships and scrupulously attended to both his own and his kingdom's cultivation in order to maintain true social harmony and political balance.

The corollary required that subjects learn the politically correct behaviour. Broadly, there existed four 'people': scholars; farmers; soldiers; and merchants. Together with the 'five relationships' and the three 'bonds' or 'mainstays' (between ruler and ruled; father and son; husband and wife) they expressed the totality of moral engagements.

Such a meticulous concern for the maintenance of correct relationship had profound implications both for self-understanding and East Asian perceptions of freedom and law. As Needham (1978, vol. 1: 78) has shown, while European philosophy found reality in substance, Chinese philosophy found it in relation. When each person followed precisely prescribed roles there existed no space for either the equal participation of equal citizens or constitutional limits on the nature and extent of virtuous rule.

Consequently, it was not justice, but harmony and balance that permeated the Confucian collectivity. Thus, egoistic, rationally self-interested, competitive, individualism was early anathematized in both Confucian, Taoist and legalist thought concerning self-creation. As both Metzger and Munro have argued the idea of the self in both traditional and contemporary East Asia only has meaning in terms of a series of relationships. Although Confucianism acknowledged the individual, what ultimately the doctrine respected was 'his ability to become one in feeling with that ultimately benevolent nature and that heart of benevolence shared by all men' (Metzger: 42). In this neo-Confucian understanding the self solidified not as an autonomous agent, but in a network of larger relations. In such self-understanding there is no room for a private self or a realm of beliefs that ought to be protected.

Indeed, the central project of Confucianism that rectified the distorted outward appearance to the true nature of things could not tolerate the notion of a private or autonomous selfhood. Thus, as the Ming neo-Confucian, Wang Yang Ming contends,

> in the mind of the sage heaven earth and the ten thousand things form one body. . . . If one's task suited one's ability one spent all of one's life doing heavy work without regarding it as arduous . . . a single spirit flowed through everyone a common purpose and feeling permeated everyone and there was no distinction between other people and oneself, no gap between things and the self. (Metzger: 81)

Freedom moreover from this perspective does not involve active political participation, but a state of rest *wu wei* metaphorically conveyed in powerful images of emptiness and quietude. In particular, neo-Confucians as well as Taoists and Ch'an Buddhists from Zhu Xi and Wang Yang Ming to Yukio Mishima refer to freedom in terms of the still surface of a reflecting pond or an empty mirror. Thus, for Wang Yang Ming true freedom is balance where 'equilibrium is nothing but the principle of nature . . . one recognizes it when he has got rid of selfish human desires. It is like a bright mirror. It is entirely clear without a speck of dust attached to it' (Wang Yang Ming, in Chan 1963: 52). This image contrasts strikingly with the Greek myth of Narcissus, the foundational western legend of the narcissistic subject's pursuit of its desired object.

Political virtue, therefore, manifested itself in the correct performance of duties, governed by a code of responsibility and deference that established order and harmony. As Needham observes, to invoke one's rights was looked on askance. . . . The great art was to give way on certain points and so accumulate an invisible fund of merit wherby one can later obtain advantages in other directions. . . . Only when something has happened and been examined can responsibility be assigned. (Needham, 1978, vol. 1: 284)

Power thus could be acquired and ritualized; it accrued in symbolic performances in which the inferior subtly deferred to the superior.

Most importantly, as Lucien Pye (1985) observes, it was an understanding of power that was both paternalistic and non-instrumental. A liberal separation of public and private, constitutional limitation and the preservation of rights is quite litcrally inconceivable. Instead what counts in interpersonal relationships is *guanxi* or connections (Pye: 293–5). Such relationships are necessarily conducted in terms of face saving and face giving. Those who *give face* defer and press for favours from superiors who gain face from the subservient behaviour of the soliciting party (p. 295).

This East Asian social logic further denied any merit to the articulation of an alternative viewpoint or the need to consult or consider popular taste. Intcrest articulation created partiality, disharmony and chaos. The Confucian ruler instead sought unity and balance through impartially following and, when necessary, autocratically imposing the way. Balance hierarchically maintained denied the possibility of a doctrine of equal right or natural equality. For if one man exceeded his proper station, 'there will be disturbance throughout society'. Thus, when Duke Ching of Ch'i asked Confucius about government, Confucius replied, 'there is government when the prince is prince, and the minister is minister; when the father is father and the son is son' (Hsu, 1932: 223).

Bureaucratic in its prescription and paternalistic in its form Confucian rule is not, then, unconstrained. The *tien zi* exercises heaven's mandate in order both to rectify the people and promote their welfare. In order to achieve this he assiduously cultivates both himself as a model for his people and a scholar bureaucracy committed to the instrumentalization of virtue based on *jen* (benevolence) and *li* (principle).

This view of rule by good men through correctly ordered relationship, however, presented a worrying dilemma. How do you ensure the continuation of the virtuous condition after the death of the sage ruler? Confucian attempts to overcome this problem often seemed confused. Ideally, the continuity of virtuous practices would ensure the reign of virtue.

However, such a view also implied that the mandate of heaven need not be located in a specific hereditary lineage. Significantly, as Mencius pointed

out, Yao, the founding Emperor of virtuous rule, had his mandate transferred not to his biological heir, but to the most qualifed, Shun. Heaven,
Mencius tells us, gave the Empire to Shun. Moreover, 'heaven does not
speak, but reveals itself through acts and deeds' (Mencius, 1970: 143).
Such an understanding offers little practical guidance on the problem of
ensuring the continuity of virtuous government. Indeed, it illustrates a
worrying incoherence in Confucianism between what Schwartz terms an
inner and outer 'polarity' (in Nivison, 1959: 61). Inner self-cultivation
leading to personal self realization may not lead to an outer ordering and
harmonizing of the world. The tension between inner and outer, the sage
ruler and the actual reality of Ming or Qing, led in practice to a state or
political confucianism (Elman, 1987) that increasingly emphasized the
maintenance of the outer realm through a more draconic application of
punishment not only to rectify, but also to strengthen the ruler.

This pragmatic recourse to severity, problematically elided into an autocratic, amoral, legalising centralism. In the actual practice of Ming, Qing
or the Korean Yi dynasty (1392–1905) this recourse to law *(fa)* paradoxically derived from legalist criticism of Confucian virtue and a concern to correct the common people. Moreover, from this perspective, as J.
L. Duyvendak observes, 'the government itself . . . desires' the universal
application of laws and their publication to 'safeguard its own power'. It
assumes that rule will be efficient if subjects know exactly what severe
punishment non-observance of the law entails (Duyvendak, 1928: 81). In
other words, legalism applied by a Confucian bureaucracy did not constitutionally restrict government it instead enhanced its operational competence. Thus in Yi Dynasty Korea the law and the judiciary in fact became
one 'of the chief instruments of autocratic dominance' (Henderson, 1968:
242).

Consequently, law in East Asia constituted the model to which the
subject precisely conformed. It was bureaucratic or administrative in that
it specified precisely what each office entailed. As Han Fei Zi drily
remarked, 'the defining of everybody's duties is the road that leads to
orderly government, while the failure to define responsibilities accurately
is the road that leads to disorder' (Han, 1964: 115).

In order to monitor performance, the ruler of men supplemented
adminstrative law with technique, *shu*. The ruler's *shu* consisted in
controling a vast, impersonal, governmental machine. The ruler established the machinery and then permitted it to run by itself, reposing in
non-action, while above and below his ministers trembled and obeyed.
'From your place of darkness,' Han Fei Zi advised, 'take hold of the
handles of government carefully and grip them tightly.' Meanwhile, Shang

Yang observed that different dynasties achieved supremacy 'by different rites' (Duyvendak, 1928: 98). Hence, 'to try to use the ways of a generous and lenient government to rule the people of a critical age is like trying to drive a runaway horse without using reins or whip' (p. 98). The wise ruler 'creates laws, but a foolish man is controlled by them; a man of talent reforms rites, but a worthless man is enslaved by them'. The methodical ruler, thus, treated both traditional codes of behaviour *(li)* and morality with pragmatic circumspection.

Between the Confucian ethical project for instrumentalizing virtue and the legalist desire for the strong state achieved by legislative fiat there appears no basis for accomodation. Yet not the least remarkable feature of East Asian political identity is its capacity to accomodate opposites. Hence, from as early as the Han dynasty synthesis of legalistic and Confucian political thinking performed by Tung Chung-shu (Chan Heng Chee, 1993, in Bartley, *et al.*: 271–88), a bureaucracy theoretically imbued with a Confucian ethical code instrumentalizes a Taoist-legalist view of imperial power. Such a remarkable reconciliation of antithetic understandings can only be explained by the essentially syncretic nature of both Confucian and Taoist understandings of *tao*. If opposing forces of *yin* and *yang* mystifyingly find reconciliation in the Tao, then Confucian suspicion of *fa* and legalist criticism of *li* might equally prove ultimately compatible.

Moreover, although the Confucian principle of instrumentalizing virtue through a return to tradition, clashed with the autocrat's concern with bureaucratic order, in practice they shared certain basic assumptions about civil order (Dutton, 1992: chapter 1). Centrally, both the legalist concern for method and the Confucian pursuit of virtue agreed upon the need for constant rectification. Both required a strict correspondence between names and things. Moreover, Confucian political rationalism led to a cynicism in its political practice that supported order at the expense of virtue, a practice that ironically facilitated the legalist desire to perfect a bureaucratic machine. Pragmatically recognizing that the conventions of polite behaviour could never reach the common people, political Confucianism came to discriminate between the *li* of the self-cultivated superior man and the punishments *xing* appropriate for the ignorant masses.

Such accomodation, Levenson and others have suggested, favoured an increasingly autocratic style of rule in the Ming and Qing dynasties. Certainly, by the Qing period the Confucian bureaucracy seemed increasingly compromised by its need for imperial support. The autocratic Emperor in his remote forbidden city inhabited a realm beyond the reach of criticism, meanwhile the Confucian bureaucracy, instead of instrumentalizing the reign of virtue, paradoxically became its political target when that project failed. Somewhat differently, in Korea, the Confucian *yangban* bureaucracy remained in the ascendant, despite the Taewongun ruler's attempt in the 1860s to reform it. Nevertheless despite these local variations, by the late nineteenth century, political pragmatism, a neo-Confucian concern for an outer polarity of order together with syncretic habits of thought facilitated in practice an accomodation both of contradictory understandings from within the Confucian canon itself, but also of legalist and Taoist ideas that emanated from altogether different understandings of human behaviour. From the viewpoint of rule this 'Confucian' synthesis of Chinese thought offered a seductive dream of order, balance and harmony through the precise performance of ascribed roles that legitimated a virtuous cathedocracy measuring, asessing and monitoring every aspect of human behaviour. This bureaucracy without limit was in turn assessed by externally set standards governing prosperity, peace and public welfare.

Before we consider what elements of this understanding survived in the modernized and modernizing states of East Asia, we shall discuss the alternative notions of rule and political identity in *Nanyang*, the lands to the South of China that sometimes paid tribute to the Emperor of all under heaven but unlike Korea, Japan and Vietnam never fell directly under the influence of Chinese thought.

POLITICAL SYNCRETISM IN SOUTHEAST ASIA

The Southeast Asian cultures of Malaysia and Indonesia were largely untroubled by the Confucian or legalist political traditions of East Asia. Here a different vocabulary of rule and obligation affected the evolution of political identity. Historically, Buddhist and Hindic conceptions of power created a view of rule in which divine authority was concentrated in the body, or more precisely the phallus of the ruler. The kingdoms of what Coedes termed 'farther India' were profoundly influenced by Buddhist and Hindu ideas that considered temporal rule the reflection of a divine cosmology. The Sririjaya, Sailiendra, Majapahit and Mataram empires of Southeast Asia were conceived, as Heine-Geldern observes, 'to be an image of the heavenly world' (Heine-Geldern, 1956: 172). Javanese Kings, increasingly influenced by Hindu cosmology, played the part of Siva. Siva, as Wolters explains, was the sovereign deity who created the universe. 'Thus the overlord's close relationship with Siva meant that he participated in Siva's divine authority . . . he participated in sovereign attributes of cosmological proportions and his supporters could come to realize that obedience to their leader was a gesture of homage that implied religious rapport or bhakti' (Wolters, 1982: 11).

The fourteenth century *Nagarakartagama* depicted the Majapahit rulers as Sivaite incarnations and the king's lingam or phallus was worshipped at temple sites like Prambanan. The cult of the lingam 'was considered the seat of the divine essence of kingship' (p. 173). This phallocratic power mystically radiated forth from the ruler's capital temple site in the form of a mandala. As Wolters explains it: 'In practice the mandala represented a particular and often unstable political situation in a vaguely definable geographical area without fixed boundaries and where smaller centres tended to look in all directions for security' (Wolters, 1982: 17).

Mandalas would expand and contract in concertina fashion. Thus sometimes a mandala would encompass no more than a district on the island of Java. On other occasions when an exemplary 'man of prowess' endowed with a concentration of *semangat* or 'soul stuff' ruled, the mandala could extend over considerable areas. Thus, the mandala of the Majapahit in the fourteenth century comprised Java, much of Sumatra and other Indonesian islands. Indeed the Majapahit poet, Prapança, claimed that his ruler 'protected' most of mainland Southeast Asia. But as the mandala emanated from the *kraton* or palace in concentric rings, the ruler's authority faded the farther it reached, until it disappeared 'somewhere among the islands of the archipelago' (Steinberg (ed.), 1989: 85).

The Javanese view of history further reinforced the oscilating mandala of authority. Traditionally, the Javanese, like the Chinese, conceived history in cyclical terms. Javanese historical thinking depicted a cycle of ages moving from a golden age *Jaman Mas* through successively less happy epochs to the evil *Kaliyuga*. For Benedict Anderson this understanding subsequently attenuated to a sharp contrast between, 'the Jaman Mas and the Jaman Edan, the golden age and the age of madness'. Ultimately, the Javanese worldview was, 'one of cosmological oscillation between periods of concentration of power and periods of its diffusion' (Anderson: 34). For Anderson this conception of power explains two notable but apparently contradictory features of Javanese political psychology: its underlying pessimism and its susceptibility to messianic appeal (ibid.: 35).

It also explains the seminal importance attached in Southeast Asia to the man of prowess. Again as Wolters explains, 'the leadership of "big men" . . . would depend on their being attributed with an abnormal amount of soul stuff which explained and distinguished their performance from that of others in their generation and especially among their own kinsmen' (Wolters: 6). In Anderson's understanding the most obvious sign of the man of prowess was the ability to absorb and concentrate power and then project it 'like a laser'. Equally significant was 'the ability to concentrate opposites'. (p. 28) As with the Tao in China the classic iconographic symbol of this was the combination of male and female. This *ardhanari* image expresses 'the vitality of the ruler his oneness and his centerness. He is at once masculine and feminine containing both elements within himself and holding them in a tense electric balance' (p. 29).

The mystical ability to concentrate and unify otherwise centrifugal social tendencies facilitated a characteristically Asian syncretism that enabled the ruler to combine contradictory understandings from Javanese, Islamic and subsequently Western understandings without contradiction. In other words, what might appear contradictory to a functionalist political science is mystically resolved through the ruler's ascetic concentration.

This ability to contain opposites and absorb adversaries, further manifested itself in the ruler's *wahyu* (divine radiance) (p. 31)). The public visage of the ruler 'glowed' and offered a visual display of an inner creative and ultimately sexual energy. An energy that was often problematically transferred as the following apocryphal account vividly demonstrates:

> The story is told that the dead king's (Amangkurat III, d. 1703) manhood stood erect and on the top of it was a radiant light (*tjahja*) only the size of a grain of pepper. But nobody observed it. Only Pangeran Puger saw it. Pangeran Puger quickly sipped up the light. As soon as the light had been sipped the manhood ceased to stand erect. It was Allah's will that Pangeran Puger should succeed to the throne. (Anderson: 31)

This legend illustrates the central dilemma of Southeast Asian political thought, namely, who has the prowess to succeed the man of prowess? Given the traditional view of divine authority, power resided in certain signs and the possession of certain magical regalia rather than in a royal blood. Thus as Heine-Geldern observes, 'the deification of the king while raising him to an almost unbelievably exalted position with regard to his subjects, has in no way succeeded in stabilising government, rather the contrary' (Heine-Geldern, 1956: 175; Reed, 1993: chapter 4). Indeed, the theory of divine incarnation and even more so that of rebirth and of karma offered an easy subterfuge for potential usurpers. The problem was further exacerbated by the uncertainty of the rules of succession: 'sometimes the King himself chose his successor. Sometimes the ministers appointed a prince as king' (p. 175). Rather more unconventionally it might entail a swift act of necrophiliac fellatio. More often the crown fell to the prince who was quickest to seize the palace and execute his brothers. As Heine-Geldern concludes dynastic succession seemed notably unstable so much so that 'the empires of Southeast Asia from the very beginning were torn by frequent rebellion, often resulting in the overthrow of kings or even dynasties'.

Rule as a divine ritual, and the imminent fear of its dissolution into a *Jaman Edan* had important ramifications for Southeast Asian moral and political identity. Firstly, the emergence of men of prowess assumed relationships of dependency. The structure of traditional Malay/Indonesian society was inexorably hierarchic. A fundamental distinction emerged between the peasant *wong cilik* and the *priyayi* elite (Steinberg *et al.*: 87). Priyayi self-understanding. was in fact so status conscious that the language spoken by the Javanese elite, *krama*, was altogether different from the terse *ngoko* spoken by the *abangan* lower orders. This linguistic dualism in turn generated a pattern of dyadic self-understanding. A proper command of *krama* was an outward and visible sign together with a smooth appearance and a *langsat* complexion of an inward refinement and spiritual accomplishment. A priyayi was *halus* '(refined, able to control his emotions, attuned to God's will)' (Steinberg: 87) while *wong cilik* were *kasar* '(coarse, excitable, and little more aware than animals)' (p. 87).

A further feature of this concern for *halus* was a separation of the inner self the *batin* from the outer aspects of life *lair*. To order the inner life was a work of practice, meditation and self-regulation in order to achieve a cool heart. To preserve the *batin*, however, the external world of polite form required 'refinement, conformity and modesty' (Pye: 114). For Geertz, (1960) four major principles 'animate priyayi etiquette: the proper form for the proper rank; indirection; dissimulation and the avoidance of any act suggesting disorder or lack of self-control' (Geertz, 1960: 243). Such self-control of the inner and outer self was vital to preserve both the past and the self and avoid the fearful alternative of running amok in the Jaman Edan. This practice of self-enactment came therefore to value pretence or dissimulation, (*etak-etak*) in inter-personal behaviour. As Geertz explains, this form of 'proper lying' is not only largely approved it need not have any obvious justification (p. 246). In terms of an evolving political etiquette *etak etak* is particularly 'valued as a way of concealing one's own wishes in deference to one's opposite' (p. 246).

Such practices had important implications for Javanese government. In an intensely hierarchical society elaborately coded rituals of deference governed courtly and regional politics. Crowning this paternalistic hierarchy the man of prowess exemplified the *priyayi* ideal. In fact, it came to inform political practice in an elaborate process of decision making or *mufakat*. Decisions required extensive consultation and deliberation (*musyawarah*) yet avoided contention through the practice of the *priyayi* virtues of deception and self-concealment. This Javanese self-understanding and the practice of dissimulation actually facilitated *gotong-royong* (co-operation) and *musyawarah*, a procedure in which community mutual assistance and discussion led to harmony and consensus.

Thus the traditional Malayo-Indonesian language of politics elaborated both an autocratic and hierarchical view of rule, but one constrained by practices of self-regulation that evolved through time. Central to this political practice is a dynamic syncretism that assumes apparently contradictory ideas and policies can be reconciled by the man of prowess and his mystical technique. This syncretic understanding had important implications for the reception of Islam into the Malayo-Indonesian world.

THE ACCOMMODATION OF ISLAM IN SOUTHEAST ASIA

A remarkable feature of the Malay world of Southeast Asia from the fifteenth to the nineteenth century was its capacity to absorb Islam into essentially Hindu and Buddhistic political traditions. This is in part because Islam arrived in Southeast Asia as a consequence of developing trade links in the fourteenth and fifteenth century and in part because Islam itself adapted to local practices.

The more Islamised sultanates of the Malay peninsula, Kedah, Kelantan, Terengganu and Malacca, illustrate this process of accomodation. Thus, the Malaccan (1444–1641) sultanate inherited the older Sririjayan mandala that enveloped parts of Sumatra, the Malay peniinsula and the Riau archipelago. Surviving accounts of the instalation of Islamic rulers illustrate the facility with which Islam reinforced traditional, sacral and magical attributes of rule (Wolters 1982: 24–5; Reed, 1993: 251ff). Thus 'a ruler's ascent to the throne was marked first by ritual lustration, signifying exaltation from the ranks of his kinsmen and the creation of a new and larger personality. He was then equipped with the royal regalia (*kebesaran*) ... held to share in the supernatural qualities of kingship' (Steinberg: 78). Finally, a senior official of the court mosque uttered the Koranic text, 'Lo! we have set thee as a viceroy on the earth', to mark the ruler's position as defender and arbiter of the Islamic faith. Even in the late nineteenth century the staunchly Islamic ruler of Kedah carefully guarded the royal regalia and musical instruments which held his supernatural power (Gullick, 1991: 29).

In Java Islam was more obviously assimilated into local practices (Anderson: 69). As the religion of traders it developed its strongest hold historically in *pasisir* urban, commercial communities on the Javanese and

Sumatran coast. As Anderson observes, the Islam that arrived in Southeast
Asia had already been 'patrimonialized' sufficiently to fit the traditional
Javanese world view. Consequently, from the fifteenth century 'the rulers
assumed Islamic titles, kept Islamic officials in their entourage, and added
Islam to the panoply of their attributes' (p. 69). Thus, the early seventeenth century Mataram dynasty of Jogjakarta in its syncretic adaptation
of Islam oscilated between Javanese and Islamic titles for rule. (Steinberg:
84).

Equally illustrative of Southeast Asian syncretism was the continuation
of customary adat law. For D. G. E. Hall the most significant feature of
Islamization in Southeast Asia is the fact that 'Muslim law has not the
same sanction in Malaya and Indonesia as in other Muslim countries'
(Hall, 1991: 234).

Nevertheless, this reception of Islam was not unproblematic. As Steinberg
observes, the increasingly Islamized urban, trading communities gradually drew apart from the agrarian interior and introduced 'an abiding tension into Javanese culture' (p. 84). A tension that grew more acute in the
nineteenth century when a reforming Islam not only questioned colonial
rule, but also traditional, hierarchical and legal understandings. It is these
developments and their implication for democratization that we consider
next.

THE METAMORPHOSES OF TRADITION IN POST-COLONIAL POLITICAL DEVELOPMENT

We have so far outlined traditional East and Southeast Asian political
understandings that have implications we shall argue for the East and
Southeast Asian perception of political authority, democracy and identity
in an emerging new world order. What aspects of these understandings
survive therefore and how have they mediated the transition to modernity
in the East and Southeast Asian NICs or what the World Bank recently
christened the High Performing East Asian Economies?

The legacy is obviously a difficult one. Ultimately, traditional patterns
of rule failed. Thus in East Asia and particularly, Taiwan and South Korea,
the Confucian NICs we are concerned with, the traditional scholar elite's
failure to adjust to the emergence of global capitalism in the late nineteenth century had catastrophic consequences.

In the case of Taiwan, the failure of the Imperial bureaucracy to adjust
to the challenges posed internally by the Taiping rebellion (1864–5) and
externally by foreign pressure to open the Chinese market led to the

weakening of the Imperial Mandate and the formal cession of the island
to Japan by the treaty of Shimonoseki (1895). Japan's first colonial experiment left a legacy of efficient, but unenlightened rule (Copper, 1993: 22).
Under the administrative strategy devised by Goto Shimpei, Taiwan's economic infrastructure, public hygeine and education improved dramatically,
but at a cost. Economic growth served the colonial power and the efficent
bureaucracy imposed a legalistic regime characterized by harsh punishment especially for political misdemeanours (p. 24).

In Korea, the hermit kingdom's Confucian bureaucracy similarly failed
to come to grips with both the internal challenge posed by the peasant
rebellion of the *Tonghak* (1894–5) and the external challenge posed by
late nineteenth century colonial rivalry. This failure ultimately led to the
collapse of the Yi dynasty and formal annexation by Japan in 1910. The
Japanese applied the administrative techniques devised in Taiwan to their
newly acquired colony of Chosen. As Gregory Henderson observes, 'much
like French colonialism in Vietnam, Japan's dominion in Korea brought
both exploitation and modernization in a mixture that . . . can hardly be
unscrambled' (p. 111). Although Japan itself shared a Confucian heritage, its brand of aggressive colonialism suppressed traditional political
practices and directly imposed an efficient but anti-political Japanese bureaucracy together with a Japanese programme of modernization. Such
ordered bureaucratic rule enhanced a tendency already present under the
Taewongun (1861–6) reformation, transforming society into a seemingly
homogenous mass, in which 'nothing had been left that could obstruct
the central government, but, by the same token, nothing could shore it up'
(ibid.: 71). Ultimately, the colonial experiment left an ambivalent legacy
of efficient, bureaucratic management of the people as an exploitable and
mobilizable resource together with an inchoate desire for national self-
renewal characterized in China by the 4 May movement and in Korea by
that of 1 March 1919.

Somewhat differently, in Southeast Asia the Malayo-Indonesian world
was artificially divided into Dutch and British spheres of interest by the
Treaty of London 1824. Although the colonial regimes that emerged in
the course of the nineteenth century sought to accomodate customary arrangements, traditional elites came to exercise a vestigial authority at the
behest of their colonial masters. Such accomodatory practices had implications for the Islamic revivalism and popular nationalism that developed
in Southeast Asia at the end of the nineteenth century. It also facilitated
the reception of Marxist Leninism and the proliferation of a brand of East
and Southeast Asian communism that threatened not only European and
American colonies but also the traditional elites they had accomodated.

Nationalism, communism and revived Islam introduced a hitherto unknown mass activism into traditional political understanding and its already problematic accomodation with colonialism. Mass organization introduced powerful ideas of liberation through collective mobilization that clearly threatened not only colonial arrangements, but also traditional ideas whether of a neo-Confucian or of a Hindic–Buddhist provenance. The new ideological character introduced into East and Southeast Asian politics clearly organized itself around a democratic principle. However, this principle was essentially illiberal, constructing the people not as autonomous, diverse individuals, but as an active mass, organized to liberate both themselves and their inchoate nations from a perceived colonial oppression. In their attempt to create a new East and Southeast Asian man, moreover, these doctrines were essentially progressive and viewed not only the yoke of imperialism, but also the hierarchical aspects of traditional culture repressive impediments to the creation of a liberated post-colonial utopia.

The essentially ideological and forward looking character of revolutionary nationalism and communism, therefore, powerfully undermined the possibility of traditional or conservative revivals in both East and Southeast Asia. Moreover, at the same time, the new Asian consciousness while democratic and activist was also powerfully anti-liberal, a doctrine that both communist and nationalist leaders associated both with decadence and Western colonial exploitation.

Burgeoning national self confidence was paradoxically strengthened in the 1940s by the collapse of European colonial rule in Southeast Asia and the brief imposition of a Japanese imperium. The Japan led Greater East Asian Co-Prosperity Sphere (1942–5), although far more brutally exploitative than its European predecessor, nevertheless undermined the belief in any natural Caucasian superiority. Furthermore, the nuclear solution to the liberation of East and Southeast Asia in 1945 left in its fallout a political vacuum, one that the attempted reimposition of European colonialism after 1945 dramatically failed to fill.

The aftermath of 1945 ultimately entailed, in Pacific Asia, a stand off between two ideological versions of the new Asian identity constructed either around revolutionary nationalism or a Maoised version of Marxist Leninism. This political polarization, moreover, effectively dominated the conduct of Pacific Asian politics internally and externally until 1989 and continues to influence the debate on the possibility for democratization in East and Southeast Asia in the 1990s.

In the concluding part of this chapter we shall examine how traditional ideas received a conditional reinvention by newly established nationalist regimes in East and Southeast Asia. New regimes that nevertheless also wished to claim popular consent for their liberating rule and their modernization plans. It is to the paradoxical application of tradition to development in the East and Southeast Asian NICs of South Korea, Taiwan, Singapore, Malaysia and Indonesia that we next turn.

THE NEGOTIATION OF TRADITION IN MALAYSIA AND INDONESIA

I give witness
That this country is the country of officials and bureaucrats.
The priyayi custom of old times
Is patched up with new fancy touches,
The new princes ally with foreign *cukongs*. . . .
I give witness
That in the culture of officials and bureaucrats,
Philosophy is dead . . . distorted.
And appreciation of facts is controlled, replaced by official guidance.
Obedience is emphasised, doubts are regarded as sin, and questions become protests.

(W. S. Rendra, *Witness to Mastodons*)

It was through an emerging concern with the character of colonial rule and the need to assert an independent identity that a popular revived Islam demonstrated a concern for a more authentic Islamic practice. Out of this concern emerged the first organized mass movements in Indonesia. Primarily concerned with self-renewal, movements like *Sarekat Islam* for the first time mobilized the peasants and urban workers on a mass basis. This new mass organization also introduced a growing cleavage in Southeast Asia between the purer Islamic vision of the *santri* and the syncretic, traditional practices of the *abangan*.

When Sarekat Islam collapsed in 1923 it provided a powerful stimulus not only to the emergence of an Indonesian Communist party (Parti Kommunis Indonesia, PKI) but also for an indiginous nationalist movement, Sukarno's Parti Nasional Indonesia (PNI) (Lapidus, 1991: 767; Steinberg: 307). It was here that the notion of an *Indonesia Raya* emerged as an arrangement that potentially embraced the whole Malay world, or as the Youth Congress of 1928 put it, 'one nation – Indonesia, one people Indonesian and one language – Indonesian'. The very idea of Indonesia constituted in fact a great 'leap of the imagination' (Steinberg: 308) and also of language. Indeed, the major nationalist symbol 'was the transmutation of the Malay of the islands into the national language' (p. 309) or *bahasa*. The attempt to forge a new national identity in the 1920s and 1930s clearly involved both mass democratic participation and a radical break with a traditional self-understanding linguistically preserved in a high Javanese whose literature entailed not just the recording of the past, but its perpetuation (Wolters 1982: 111). In fact, the early and unstable years of the Indonesian Republic after 1945 were characterized by constitutional arrangements that facilitated the democratic emergence of different aspects or streams *aliran* of the emerging national consciousness, notably Islamic, Nationalist, communist and the revolutionary armed forces (ABRI).

The political contestation that emerged between 1950 and 1957 as a consequence of parliamentary democracy, however, clearly illustrated the lack of a shared understanding between the different aliran and alienated the army by gradually excluding it from the political process (Mahmood and Ahmad, 1990: 23). The instability of this inchoate parliamentary democracy led to a new emphasis on Presidential authority. Under Sukarno and particularly with Suharto, after 1966, the government promoted an ideology of guided democracy, *pancasila*, with clearly Orwellian resonances in which guidance increasingly replaced a facade of constitutional democracy. With the obliteration of the communist (PKI) *aliran* in the coup and counter coup of 1965, Indonesian rule assumed an increasingly autocratic character (Anderson and Mcvey, 1971). In the bloody transition from Sukarno to Suharto the armed forces (ABRI) came to occupy an increasingly prominent political role in Suharto's New Order. Its political, bureaucratic wing *Golkar* came to dominate the constituent assembly (Mahmood and Ahmad: 26) while former General Suharto assumed the role of paternal guardian of the republic. Under the slogan 'unity through diversity' the new order regime of Suharto used the state ideology *pancasila* devised by Sukarno to eliminate political opposition.

In this context of developing autocracy, Indonesian pancasila democrats found it particularly useful to reinvent traditional understandings in order to reinforce political stability. A 'new' traditional paternalism which in the context of the 1970s and 1980s also offered a prophylactic against the ever present internal and external threat of dissolution posed by the now anathematized communist *kaliyuga*.

The pretentious gold-plated linga mounted on a tall column that adorns the centre of Merdeka Square, Jakarta, close to the Presidential Palace from which Suharto's mandala now emanates, clearly symbolizes this rejuvenation of traditional authority. Moreover, the fact that Suharto magically reconciled the differences that threatened to undermine the infant Indonesian republic in 1965 made him peculiarly placed to exploit traditional under-standings of rule. As Pye explains, 'General Suharto, the Javanese mystic who succeeded Sukarno has come much closer to embodying the essence of Javanese culture. . . . Suharto has mastered the art of masking his feel-ings while at the same time calibrating them to such a fine point that he can choose his responses to stimuli with great delicacy' (Pye: 115). Similarly, Bresnan (1993) observes that Suharto significantly projected himself as Semar 'one of the most revered figures in the Javanese wayang' (Bresnan, 1993: 49) (2). From a humble East Javanese peasant background himself Suharto was able to draw upon Semar's image repertoire as 'the loyal servant . . . observant of his own lowly status, yet able to bend even the god's to his will; Semar the mystic restorer of peace to a divided land' (ibid.).

Under Suharto's enigmatic guidance, then, it is not entirely surprising that traditional relationships of dependency emerged in the increasingly bureaucratic and anti-political Indonesian state during the late 1970s and in the 1980s. The running of the influential Indonesian bureaucracy de-pends, Pye maintains, on *bapakism*, 'a relationship involving a bapak or father and his *anak buah* or children' (p. 117). The father assumes exten-sive responsibilities for his children and they in turn owe him the incalcul-able debt of *hutang budi*. This paternalistic guidance receives further support from traditional understandings of smooth behaviour and *gotong royong*. Suharto himself has been officially described since 1983 as 'bapak pem-bangunan – the father of development' (Vatikiotis, 1993b: 2).

Thus in the New Order's hierarchical bureaucracy a premium is placed on avoiding direct statements and on speaking elliptically (Pye: 308). This practice of self-concealment has profound implications for contemporary political behaviour. The Javanese continue to enjoy the use of symbolism and the represensentations of heroic archetypes derived from the *Ramahyana* depicted in the wayang kulit shadow plays, but their officials have a spe-cial appreciation of subtlety derived from the need for balance and har-mony in decision making. Great emphasis has been reattached to the practice of *mufakat musyawarah*.

Thus in contemporary Indonesian decision making, subordinates vigor-ously articulate their views, and 'consensus' is at last declared on the basis of the judgement of the principals. Participants understand that 'the opin-ions of subordinates are irrelevant exaggerations useful only for filling in time, while superiors must be more judicious in expressing their ideas'. Interestingly, this is not just because deliberateness and paucity of expres-sion connotes wisdom, but also because fewer words offer less oppor-tunity for conflict with other 'notables', a bureaucratic practice further facilitated by the traditional Javanese practice of *etak etak*.

This reinvented tradition means that not only intra-bureaucratic communication, but also that between rulers and people, is encoded in an elusive
wayang shadow play. Blunt language and clear expression of views are
viewed perjoratively as likely causes of embarassment for others if not
for one's self. Indeed, the Indonesian scholar, Ignas Kledan, has noted an
'increasing use of sanskrit words', in the course of Suharto's rule, notably,
'the use of feudalistic words like *bapak, berkenan,* and *memohon* to replace more democratic words like *anda, saudara, bersedia* and *meminta*'.
Such a vocabulary fits with the New Order 'emphasis on politeness in
political and formal relationships' (Vatikiotis: 112).

This revival of traditional practices has also paradoxically facilitated a
growing political managerialism that has provided both political stability
and since the 1980s achieved impressive economic growth. This has led
some commentators (Chalmers, 1991: Bresnan 1993) to assume the emergence of an incipient pressure to democratize. Yet, what seems to remain
the problem for the New Order just as it was for the old one, as well as
for the pre-modern rulers of Mataram and Majapahit, is who succeeds the
man of prowess when his wahyu begins to wane. Our analysis of future
Indonesian political development in Chapter 4 addresses the relationship
between economic growth, the succession issue and democratization.

ONE PARTY RULE IN MALAYSIA

Despite a different colonial experience and the relatively smooth negotiation of independence from the British Empire in 1958 analagous traditional understandings have affected the character of contemporary rule
in Malaysia. Here again an early experience of political democracy was
destabilized by the threat of communist insurgency and further exacerbated by inter-racial conflict in 1969. The outcome was the political marginalization of the large Chinese minority in Malaysia and the imposition
of a *bumiputra* policy designed to facilitate greater Malay participation in
the social and economic life of Malaysia.

In this context of what Southeast Asian writers like to term 'threat
perception', the constitution of 1957 has been modified to suit the needs
of the leadership of the United Malay National Organization (UMNO)
which has dominated government since independence in the Malay interest. Ironically, UMNO as a Malay organization, came to prominence initially as a successful campaign to defeat a British proposal for a centralized
Malayan Union in 1948 (Suffian *et al.*, 1979: 4). The complicated machinery of checks and balances that emerged in the federal constitution of

1963, reflected the wishes of both the Malays and their mostly aristocratic rulers to negate the possibility of centralization (Suffian *et al.*: 10).

However, one party dominance since then has significantly eroded a constitution designed to facilitate multipartism, the rule of law and federalism. Emergency provisions in the constitution were used to overthrow elected state governments in Sarawak (1966) and Kelentan (1977). The interracial riots of May 1969 and the introduction of Article 153 of the constitution that afforded special economic rights to the Malay majority together with the evolution of the thirteenth schedule of 1962 that gives electoral weight to rural and essentially Malay communities has further facilitated the political authority of UMNO in the ruling Barisán Nasionalis (BN National Front) coalition.

In order to tighten further UMNO's oligarchical grip on both Malaysian politics and also increasingly on the economy, the UMNO elite has had recourse to traditional values selectively chosen to support their political dominance and the leadership of a man of prowess. This tendency early evident in the treatment of the first post-Independence leader Tunku Abdul Rahman as *Bapa Kermerdekaan* has been intensified during the period of Mahathir Mohamad's leadership since 1981, a period also characterized by strident attacks on western values.

Synonymous with this revival of tradition is an increasing emphasis on paternalistic guidance, at the expense of political pluralism. A guidance facilitated by press controls and the periodic recourse to the harsh Internal Security Act (1960). The outcome has been therefore a reassertion in Malaysia of the idea of *gotong royong* and *musyawarah mufakat* in order to create a balanced and harmonious Malay dominated, but economically developed Malaysia.

Yet this selective use of tradition is further modified by Mahathir's desire to create an economically dynamic Malaysia through an untraditional mobilization of the Malay masses towards an utopian vision of a fully developed modernity. This desire to modernize Malaysia has important implications for the uses of tradition. Thus although Mahathir acts as a Southeast Asian 'man of prowess' it is paradoxically at the expense of the traditional rulers, the nine sultans who share the monarchy on a rotating basis under the federal constitution of 1957. Under the guise of attacking a corrupt and reactionary royalty, the federal power of the sultans has been consistently eroded.

Mahathir has sought in fact to forge a new Malaysian identity based on a strong, UMNO dominated, centralized state (Kahn and Loh, 1992: 58). Consequently during Mahathir's premiership (1981–) the constitution has become a movable feast. From an obscure *mamak* or mixed race

background himself, Dr Mahathir rose to prominence as an 'ultra' Malay
nationalist. As his 1970 excursion into political philosophy, the *Malay
Dilemma* (1989) indicates, eugenic ideas preoccupy the medically trained
doctor. His diagnosis maintains that environmental and hereditary factors
have bred in the Malays a feckless 'tidapathy'. This 'lassitude' subsequently facilitated their exploitation first by the British and since Independence by the 'unscrupulous' Chinese, who constitute a problematically
large minority of the population.

To cure Malay weakness, therefore, Mahathir prescribed more rigorous
govenment intervention. After 1981, he intensified the New Economic
Policy begun in 1971 that afforded Malay businessmen special treatment
and reserved governmental and educational places for indigenous or
bumiputra Malays. This Malaysian version of 'affirmative action' has
formed the cornerstone of Mahathir's political thought and recently received its apotheosis in his pretentious, thirty year plan, *Vision 2020*, to
create a fully modernized Malaysia.

To realize utopia, however, demands the severing of some traditional
bonds, both customary and constitutional, that hinder Malay progress while
reinforcing those that facilitate a centralized authority. In 1983, Mahathir
succeeded in removing the *Yang Di-Pertuan Agong's* monarchical power
of veto over parliamentary bills and in 1986 he succeeded in curtailing the
constitutional independence of the judiciary.

Similarly, in forging a progressive, new, but Malaysian identity, the
UMNO leadership selectively emphasises its historic Islamic roots in the
Malay sultanate. Yet although Islam is the official religion, its practice
is not allowed to stand in the way of development. As in Indonesia, the
Malaysian bureaucratic elite has great difficulty in syncretising the orthodox Islamic interest represented by PAS in Kelentan with its developmental goals.

Evident contradictions in Mahathir's vision are, however, effectively
suppressed by a subtle mixture of fear and bribery. The muzzling of
critical debate in parliament, and the strict licensing of the press have
effectively curtailed criticism of Mahathir's increasingly autocratic rule.
To ensure conformity, moreover, Mahathir has at his disposal draconic
internal security legislation that dates from the Malay emergency of the
1950s. In 1987, security forces launched 'operation lalang' arresting 106
people as 'security threats' including the leader of the largest opposition
party, Lim Kit Siang. Thirty three people were eventually detained without
trial for two years '*pour encourager les autres*'. As Chandra Muzaffar of
the Aliran Social Reform Movement observes, 'the parliament, the judiciary, and the royalty have been forced to surrender their powers gradually

to the UMNO executive ... to which everything else in the country is subservient' (Muzaffar, *Straits Times* 2 March 1993).

What emerges in modern Malaysia then is a selective use of tradition to facilitate centralization and economic development. The effectiveness of blending tradition with development, however, has created an increasingly technocratised and urbanised Malaysia. Elements of traditional practice are preserved in Malay villages and a moderate Islam is encouraged as the state religion, but government ideologues constantly revise traditional understandings to create an ersatz Malaysian identity in order to mobilize the population not towards a past, but actively towards a future vision.

Clearly these traditional practices and the way they have been attenuated and promoted for purposes of economic development and social control have important implications for a political democracy in Malay speaking Southeast Asia. As all debate in modernized and modernizing Southeast Asia occurs within a context of consensus seeking in which participants strive for the state of *halus*, nothing can be said that engenders confrontation. The result is a contemporary practice informed by the Javanese art of indirectness, calculated to ensure that one neither provokes another nor reveals one's own feelings.

Debate is further attenuated by the emergence in the twentieth century of what Geertz has termed aliran or streams in contemporary Javanese politics. Thus the most powerful ideological currents in Indonesia and Malaysia until the 1980s, communism, radical nationalism and Islam (both reformist and orthodox) all represent modes of explaining an increasingly complex and confusing world. The adepts of each of these aliran feel themselves to have acquired, through a process of politico-religious initiation, an esoteric, but comprehensive picture of the universe and its workings. From the perspective of communicatory democracy, 'the hermetic quality of the aliran' is problematic (Anderson, 1990: 57). They are distinguished by their lack of congruence, the rarity of intimate social contact, 'the virtually total absence of intellectual exchange and the sharp distinction between adherents and non-adherents'. Meanwhile a seemingly modern bureaucracy is oiled by 'money politics' and bapakism.

Authority and its container the man of prowess, then, continue to reconcile apparent contradictions in contemporary Southeast Asia. Things have a natural tendency to fall apart and it is the particular genius of the ruler Suharto or Mahathir to hold them together. The problem that the traditional rule of good men never solved, however, was how to ensure continuity. Much of the literature that addresses apparent democratization in Southeast Asia clearly misses the point. The apparent factionalism emerging in Indonesia between middle class technocrats and ABRI functionaries or in Malaysia between a thrusting urban 'vision team' and an otiose leadership is not concerned with political communication or argued debate but the problem of managing transition as the respective wahyus of Mahathir and Suharto begin to wane.

THE CONTEMPORARY RECREATION OF AN EAST ASIAN POLITICAL TRADITION

J. R. Levenson has famously argued that political Confucianism had not the wherewithal to adapt to the challenge posed by 'western' influence and the need to modernize (Levenson, 1965: 3). After the collapse of the Celestial Empire and the subsequent travail of modern East Asia an already ossified and increasingly contradictory political understanding, Levenson maintained, collapsed irrevocably under the weight of invasion and post-war Maoism. From at least the time of the May Fourth Movement, the Chinese intelligentsia showed a notable commitment to uprooting everything that smacked of a traditional understanding whether Taoist, legalist or Confucian. As both Mary Wright and Mark Elvin have observed, there was a remarkable absence in China of a creative conservative response to the challenge of either Marxism-Leninism-Maoism or modernity (Wright, 1957; Elvin in Yu, 1986). This failure left China spiritually and intellectually resourceless.

Analagously in Korea the failure of late nineteenth century Confucian rule to meet the Japanese challenge spawned, it is claimed, an inchoate nationalism that drew its inspiration from Western sources, most significantly the Christian churches (Henderson: 80–6) that grew in popularity in the course of the twentieth century.

In the course of the last decade, however, a number of Asian scholars, encouraged by attacks on liberal individualism from a business management provenance (Lodge, 1991) have assiduously promoted an alternative to Levenson's thesis of Confucian decay. They argue that the successful modernization of a number of East Asian economies in the last twenty years owes a significant debt to the survival of 'Asian' or 'neo-Confucian' values. In this interpretation, East Asian post war development derives from a Confucian ethical legacy which may be distinguished from the political programme of legalistic neo-Confucianism (Tu in Jiang, 1987; Tu, 1991; Cheng, 1991). Students of the East Asian economic miracle claim that the Confucian ethical practice of relationship, balance and harmony facilitated, 'a consensual – as opposed to a contractual – relationship between managers and managed'. Such a 'communitarian ideology' engenders in the view of Ezra Vogel and George Lodge, both competitiveness and order (Vogel, 1991; Vogel and Lodge, 1987).

This curious reversal of the Weberian understanding of China that claimed Confucianism prevented China in particular and East Asia in general developing the ethical resources to modernize has had important implications for the reinvention of tradition in capitalist East and Southeast Asia with Chinese roots notably in South Korea, Taiwan and Singapore. Contemporary neo-Confucian scholars like Tu Wei-ming and Chung-ying Cheng, bathing in the unaccustomed luxury of the new compatibility between Confucianism and entrepreneurial flair, have tried to draw a distinction between a failed Confucian political project and its still flourishing ethical legacy. In this view, neo-Confucian ethics, far from failing the challenge of modernity, have actually been central to the stability, rise in educational standards and economic vitality of contemporary East Asia. An argument apparently sustained by the recent World Bank report on the East Asian miracle (World Bank, 1993: chapter 4).

Clearly, such competing interpretations of the role of Confucianism in the East Asian miracle are irreconcilable. The only point of consensus would seem to be that both ethical Confucians like Tu Wei Ming and Chung Ying-Cheng agree with the view expressed by Levenson and J. K. Fairbanks that the resurrection of a specifically Confucian political project is untenable (Elman in Fu, 1987). A somewhat curious conclusion given the fact that Confucianism centrally maintained the ethical inseperability of the social and the political. What I wish to consider here, then, is what aspects of a traditional understanding of rule in either a neo-Confucian or a legalist guise, continues consciously or unconsciously to inform an East Asian attitude to rule?

Evidently, for a classical neo-Confucian, certain key elements of a moral understanding and vocabulary have been irretrievably attenuated. The idea of recreating the golden age of *Yao and Shun* and the hierarchical ordering and self-cultivation it entailed are no longer feasible or desirable in contemporary Seoul, Taipei or Singapore. The ideal of the sage creating rule based on virtue rather than law seems as far off now as it did to Wang Yang Ming. Contemporary Confucianism has then lost a crucial conservative element in its vision, the myth of the past and the prospect of its immanent recapture.

Lost, too, is an economic ideal based in its Confucian version around the scholar amateur *jin zi* and the virtuous, hard-working peasant or, in its Taoist–legalist rescension, a nescient village idyll. No one in Pacific Asia, the Khmer Rouge apart, would seriously subscribe to the classic Taoist or Confucian economic programme that either despises or forbids entrepreneurial activity. This is not a little ironic, given the apparent centrality accorded by management theorists like Vogel and Lodge to the Confucian roots of East Asian economic dynamism.

Nevertheless, vestigial traces do remain of a traditional understanding that have important ramifications for current East Asian governmental theory and practice. In both legalism and Confucianism there exists a concern with order, balance and harmony. If the world is ordered according to a principle, neo-Confucianism tells us, then the way will inexorably be established.

This understanding initially seemed irrelevant to the nationalist *Kuomintang* (KMT) establishing their rule in Taiwan after their failure on the mainland in 1949, or Syngman Rhee attempting to stave off the imminent collapse of South Korea between 1950 and 1953 or Lee Kuan Yew riding the tiger in unstable Singapore in the early 1960s. These 'first generation' rulers of newly formed East Asian states vindicated their rule in terms of 'nation building' rather than recreating a traditional arrangement. Indeed, politcal leaders in both South Korea and Singapore initially accepted political pluralism and multi-party democracy as a reflection of the popular will. Only latterly did the spectre of communism and the need for unity come to attenuate radically the possibility of political difference.

Thus the first Korean Republic (ROK), established in 1948 after thirty-five years of Japanese colonial rule had a democratic, presidential constitution modelled vaguely on that of the USA. The circumstances of the Korean war (1950–3) and the ultimate division of the peninsula into a communist State North of the 38th parallel and an American protected South undermined the infant democracy. In South Korea, the period 1950–60 witnessed an increasingly autocratic rule by Syngman Rhee. In the view of Gregory Henderson, Rhee's rule invoked the bureaucratic centralism and insecurity of the late nineteenth-century Yi dynasty (Henderson, 1968: 214). After student demonstrations in 1960, Rhee was replaced by a brief constitutional experiment (1960–1) which ended in a military coup. The coup announced a military presence in South Korean politics that lasted twenty-seven years initially under General and subsequently President Park Chung Hee (1961–79). Another brief attempt at constitutional democracy collapsed into a reassertion of military hegemony under Major General and subsequently President Chun Doo Hwan. As James Cotton observes: 'in South Korea the personal clique of Syngman Rhee gave way after the briefest of democratic interludes in 1961 to a group of middle level military officers united by common experience' (Cotton, 1992: 315). Only since 1988 has the prospect of open opposition and new electoral constraints on the ruling military bureaucratic elite emerged.

Central to political and economic development in South Korea, then, has been the role played by the military together with a centralized bureaucracy instrumentalizing industrial modernization. Although this autocracy was given a cloak of constitutional legitimacy by new and restrictive constitutions and strictly regulated elections in the period 1960–88, the regime increasingly relied on its capacity to achieve economic growth and distribute economic benefits without consultation. In this context, the fear of communism in the North provided a powerful incentive to suppress demands for greater accountability. In order to legitimate autocracy, moreover, Syngman Rhee and his successors consistently reinvoked Korea's traditional Confucian heritage. As Pye has pointed out Koreans possess the dubious distinction of being 'more Confucian than the Chinese' (Pye, 1985: 223). The reinvention of a Confucian legacy dating from the Yi dynasty, substantiated the new South Korean Republic's claim to be the legitimate vehicle of the Korean nation (Suh, 1983: 160–1). It also enabled both Rhee and subsequently Generals Park and Chun to give a Confucian credibility to their otherwise dictatorial practice. A Confucian concern with hierarchy further facilitated the technocratic management of a new professional cadre who inherited the mantle of the Yi dynasty scholar bureaucrats or *yangban*.

Consequently, the ageing Syngman Rhee insisted that the new Korea should be 'ruled not by laws but by superior men', (Cotton: 219) and the capacity of successive presidents to draw up new constitutions indicates a continuing Confucian suspicion of the rule of law. In 1987, President Roh Tae-woo introduced Koreans to their sixth constitution since 1948. This new rule of virtuous men facilitating efficient economic development, however, increasingly required the active participation of the people who were mobilised towards new targets. During President Park's regime (1961–79) the *Samil Dongnip Undong* movement was charged with, 'inculcating a national spirit . . . more fundamental than the national spirit of modern nationalism' (Suh, 1983: 60). At the same time, the Park regime made explicit efforts 'to inculcate into the Korean populace the Confucian value of *cheng hyo* (loyalty to the state, filial piety and harmony)' (Chowdhury and Islam, 1993: 32). This blend of military dictatorship, mass activism and Confucian morality mobilized the countryside and generated rural development. As Pye observes it, 'hit responsive chords among government cadres, who hope they can be shielded against criticism merely by displaying dedication; and at the other extreme it has appealed to the peasantry, who concentrate on the economic payoffs of its developmental drive' (p. 224). Such guidance moreover fitted a Korean self-understanding which emphasized social conformity and reflected in attenuated form the 'Confucian beliefs and values that have influenced Korea's past' (Kim and Young, 1990: chapter 3).

Yet the reinvention of this Confucian identity for the purposes of regime stability has not been without problems especially in terms of the transition from Yao to Shun or in South Korea's case from Park to Chun. The enduringly Confucian moral conception of leadership leads 'on the one hand to a strong emphasis on obedience and conformity and on the other hand, to irreconcilable political conflicts' (p. 67). A Confucian claim to rule is inexorably self-righteous, demands obedience and conformity and views opposition as unconscionable. Moreover, the other side of the reinvented Confucian dilemma requires any challenge to leadership to be posed in equally absolute moral terms. As Chong Yim Kim points out this has the effect of transforming all 'political conflicts into a . . . morality play' (p. 67).

Consequently, where opposition has emerged and since 1988 been constitutionally endorsed, politics as argumentative talk is rendered impossible by the practice of *ch'ijo* which considers an inflexible stance on matters of principle a supreme virtue. As Chong notes, 'leaders and informed citizens cling to the bigotry of a sense of self righteousness regarding their own political positions there is no room for compromise' (p. 67). Reinforced by personal, factional and regional ties or *inmaek* it leads 'power players to overestimate their own strength and underestimate that of their rivals' (Diamond *et al.*, vol. 3, 1989: 285). Clearly, such self-understanding premised on a moral certitude combined with the need for conformity and hierarchy makes democratization problematic.

A similar Confucian self-righteousness has had implications for political change in Taiwan. While Korea is the most culturally and racially homogeneous country in Asia if not the world, Taiwan was divided between the mainlanders, who arrived in 1949 like an occupying force and the native Taiwanese who between 1895 and 1945 had like Korea been part of greater Japan (Pye: 228–9). The immediate aftermath of the defeat of Chiang Kai-shek's nationalist Guomindang (KMT) forces on the Chinese mainland and the retreat to Taiwan had important implications for political development in Taiwan.

Fresh from defeat, nationalist rule was founded on a curious mixture of a 'sacred mission' (Tsang, 1993: 48) and the suppression of indiginous Taiwanese political aspirations. Moreover, the nationalist doctrine that the defeated KMT brought with them to Taiwan had itself grown out of an ambivalent response to classical Confucianism. As formulated by Sun Yat-sen and interpreted by the nationalist leader Chiang Kai-shek, nationalism embraced the *San Min Chu I*, the three principles of the people:

anti-imperialist nationalism, democracy and socialism (Spence, 1990: 338). Yet since Sun Yat-sen had provided for an undefined period of 'tutelage' that would follow the military consolidation of the nation, there was little need for Chiang to bother with the trappings of democracy. Thus on the mainland after 1928 and more successfully in Taiwan after 1947 a 'five power' constitution was established dividing power between the Executive, Legislative, Control, Judicial and Examination Yuan. In practice, however, the constitution concentrated power in the executive and the leader. After 1934, Chiang began to modify the democratic elements in Sun's philosophy and develop what Spence describes as a 'new unifying ideology', drawing in part from Sun's views on nationalism and socialism and partly 'on his own views of the central tenets of traditional Confucianism, especially with regard to the formation of a loyal and moral human character' (Spence: 414). Central to this new ideology was an activist mobilization of the masses that Chiang derived both from his admiration for German and Italian fascism and his German advisers (Spence: 414–15). In order to create the new Chinese political identity, Chiang launched collective campaigns against 'such antisocial or undisciplined acts as spitting, urinating, or smoking in public, casual sexual liaisons and provocative clothing' (ibid.: 415).

This vision of a renewed nation, inspired by a traditional respect for order and hierarchy, but driven by an active and unifying zeal to modernize, failed on the mainland. With some modification, however, the Guomindang philosophy was successfully translated to Taiwan where the small size of the island enabled the 'quasi-Leninist' KMT informed by Chiang's Chinese version of the leadership principle to mobilize both order and modernization (Clark, 1989: 121). One of these modifications involved an American inspired rural reconstruction programme that by 1953 accomplished a massive transfer of land to peasant farmers (Vogel, 1991: 19). Meanwhile, the former Taiwanese landlords 'became an astoundingly vigorous entrepreneurial class' (Pye: 229). Thus while the indiginous Taiwanese small businessmen came to constitute an economic elite, political and economic guidance remained in the hands of the KMT. In particular, their continuing Confucian paternalism enabled the party to plan effective economic growth through the bureaucratic direction of what Vogel terms 'super-technocrats' (Vogel: 24–5). The fact, moreover, that economic advance was 'relatively equally distributed' (Vogel: 40; World Bank: chapter 1) enhanced the government's increasing recourse to the Confucian ethical claim that it exercised guidance and rectification in the interest of the common people. This reinvented Confucian paternalism facilitated by a school based ethical programme in correct relationship formation was further facilitated by the *guanxi* relationships of dependency that exist between the KMT and the economic elite.

Nevertheless, despite its successful and at times autocratic mobilization of the masses towards export led growth and Confucian deference, the KMT has been under consistent pressure to tolerate increasing political opposition. In part this demand for greater Taiwanese participation in government is an inevitable consequence of the assimilation of mainlanders and Taiwanese as the first generation dies out. It also reflects the fact that there is a real political dilemma facing the Taiwanese. On the one hand, the nationalists, with some ambiguity, continue to maintain a traditional claim to be the legitimate rulers of all China, while on the other, the Taiwanese Democratic Progressive Party (DPP) have somewhat ambivalently proposed Taiwanese independence. The lack of an obvious solution to this dilemma together with the appointment of the indigenous Taiwanese, Lee Teng Hui, to the Presidency in 1988 has seen a considerable lessening of political control. The period after 1987 has significantly witnessed the abolition of martial law, the acceptance of open dissent and public demonstrations together with the institutionalization of an official opposition.

In spite of the greater access to information and the institutionalization of opposition, however, the KMT continues to maintain a paternalistic political dominance. Moreover, the practice of *guanxi* and the continuing concern with both hierarchy and mobilization towards political certainty through a successful reinvention of tradition means that the prospect of realizing a communicatory and tolerant multipartism remains fraught with difficulty.

Analagously in Singapore the rule of the People's Action Party (PAP) since independence has seen an intensification of the rule of the party and its leader Lee Kuan Yew at the expense of constitutional restraints. Regularly re-elected into power since 1959, the PAP has curtailed opposition on security grounds. The struggle for power with the proto-communist *Barisan Socialis* in the early 1960s together with its ejection from the Malaysian federation in 1965 left the PAP firmly opposed to mass, popular, participatory, 'democratic' politics in both principle and in fact' (Chew, 1994). To avoid participation, an ideology of survivalism and the spectre of communism and communalism have been regularly invoked.

This 'hegemonic' or 'one party dominant system' (Chan Heng Chee, 1993, in Bartley *et al.*; Lee in Mahmmood and Ahmad, 1990) has successfully modernized Singapore through a practice of bureaucratic state management. In the process, however, it has undermined the possibility of critical comment let alone political opposition. As former deputy premier Goh Keng Swee cynically observed in 1988, the most important prerequisite for Singapore's success was 'an efficient secret police' (Chew, 1994: 10). In the course of time, the PAP has effectively eroded the distinction between government and party and applied 'severe legal and political measures to combat the emergence and growth of a credible opposition political organization' (Lee: 59). In practice this means the PAP has undermined, or in their terms 'fine tuned', the 1963 constitution in the interest of what they deem to be more efficient political management. Thus in 1991 the PAP replaced the 'parliamentary system' with an 'elected president'. Elsewhere fine tuning permeates the legal process where lawyers ostensibly practice English common law, but without the presence of an 'inefficient' jury system. As the Minister for Home Affairs, Jayakumar, explained in 1992, the continuing application of Emergency Powers dating from the communist Insurgency of the 1950s enables the government to combat domestic crime more efficiently. Over 1000 Singaporeans enjoy 'preventive detention' under these emergency provisions (*Straits Times*, 7 August 1992).

Although since 1985 the government has approved interest groups, Nominated MP's and feedback mechanisms to allow what it euphemistically describes as 'constructive criticism', the fine tuning of the rule of law has severely curtailed political debate. Moreover, as the threat of communist insurgency and communal tension that initially legitimated the oligarchical dominance of the PAP has diminished, the PAP has had recourse to the inculcation of what it defines as 'national values'. The inculcation of these values, moreover, has occurred at a time when the technocratic efficiency of the bureaucratic state has realized a standard of living second only to Japan in East Asia (World Bank, 1993: chapter 1). To stave off a perceived, but as yet unrealized call for greater political freedom, the PAP technocracy has assiduously reinvented traditional values and inculcated them rather uncertainly into a multi-cultural population of Chinese and Indians and Malays. Central to this policy has been a critique of individual autonomy, an emphasis on community before self and consensus and harmony rather than contestation (Quah, 1990: 91–2). In order to inculcate such values the PAP between 1983 and 1988 devised a school based programme in Confucian ethics. Most effective, however, has been the inculcation of values through mass mobilization campaigns analagous to those devised by Chiang Kai-shek for China in the 1930s.

Indeed, in the political thinking of the island's founding father and current Senior Minister, Lee Kuan Yew, the recently developed Asian dragon cannot afford to allow its increasingly affluent citizens to create their own identity. Instead, the government does it for them. Just as the PAP intervened in the economy to generate impressive growth in the seventies and eighties, a variety of units, and programmes now seek to organize every aspect of the Singaporean psyche. Feedback units monitor what people think. Education units encourage the Singaporean to 'train up be the best you can be'. The Productivity Board's Quality Club encourages 'quality work' and the Family Planning and Social Development Units monitor the city state's eugenic progress. The continuing need to 'upgrade' Singaporeans means that a month rarely goes by without a campaign addressing some aspect of behaviour. The Orwellian MinDef's Psychological Defence Unit coordinates this transformative activity. The PAP's thirty years of uninterrupted one party rule, its stranglehold upon the media, combined with the 'intelligent island's' small size ensures a captive audience. Moreover, Lee Kuan Yew, as the founding patriarch, and current Senior Minister, is constantly on hand to offer correct guidance and paternal rectification. Psychological defence reinforces his reinvented understanding of tradition where citizenship consists in the precise performance of an alloted role in an unfolding master plan. Such political managerialism clearly has implications for any future democratization in the City State.

THE REINVENTION OF TRADITION AND THE PROBLEM OF DEVELOPMENT

The continuing concern with paternalism, dependency, balance and harmony in the East and Southeast Asian polities we have discussed clearly poses a problematic legacy for further political development. 'Consensus', as modernized Asian politicians describe the traditional pursuit of balance, does not require a pluralistic consultation of a multiplicity of interests, far less submission to popular taste. Politically, East Asian thought asserted the need for hierarchy and expertise. Rule was always the responsibility of a virtuous elite, or a man of prowess.

In the East Asian past it was the self-cultivated *jin zi* who rectified the people, while in Southeast Asia an elaborate indirect process of consultation enabled rule to proceed apparently by agreement or *gotong royong*. In its modern version, the professional expert replaces the *jin zi* and technocratically adjusts the people to their required role. In this elitist understanding there is a continuity of the view that harmony is achieved not by a proliferation of interests, but by each precisely fulfilling his ordained relationship or by subtly deferring to the requirements of *mufakat*. The harmonious, multi-function Pacific Asian polis still requires that when the wind of the managerial elite blows, the popular grass continues to bend.

Another traditional understanding lends credence to this emerging view of harmony based on precise adjustment to criteria 'objectively' defined by a managerial elite. Neo-Confucianism traditionally justified virtuous government because it created prosperity as well as harmony, while the Jaman Mas created by the man of prowess in Southeast Asia was a time of order, wealth and harmony. Conversely, it follows that if the efficient managers of the state sustain high levels of growth and prosperity, such rule is not only legitimate, but also virtuous.

A managerial science of East and Southeast Asian politics, then, draws sustenance from etiolated traditional languages of rule. These traditions are filtered through a managerial science that offers rational efficiency and then syncretized to suit the needs of contemporary technocratic rule. This emerging modern Pacific Asian identity has profound implications for the way in which East and Southeast Asian politicians assess 'western' understandings of the rule of law and communicatory democracy.

Centrally, as we have observed, Confucianism and legalism and Southeast Asian political thinking was hierarchical and autocratic. Concern for the welfare of the people is essentially paternalistic. It accomodates neither a popular right of resistance, consultation, nor any indefeasible individual right. Similarly, when legalism considers the people it considers them only as a managerial problem. In all these understandings, rule must be exercised firmly and efficiently. If there are to be laws they must originate from a single source and be enforced absolutely. There is no room here for politics as an essentially pluralistic activity, or for the notion that government reflects a popular will.

This Asian map of the mind also explains some of the confusion that occurs in Western attempts to grasp an East Asian attitude to law and its embodiment in a constitution. As we have observed, Confucianism had little regard for laws and considered them detrimental to the proliferation of a virtuous norm. The legalist, by contrast, enthusiastically embraced a notion of law that entailed a precisely defined code of conduct equally applied to all subjects. Meanwhile in Southeast Asia, nationalist movements reinforced traditional understandings of dependency and consensus and forged a new identity at the expense of 'colonial' understandings of the rule of law.

The traditional East Asian understanding of law, therefore, has nothing in common with Anglo-American jurisprudential thought and practice. *Fa* cannot accomodate legal right. It only provides for a precise regulation of duties. East Asian law neither reflected an idea of a transcendental natural law, nor a contract with mutual obligations enforceable by an independent judiciary. Consequently, constitutions can be rectified by the virtuous, a fact that explains the continual amendment and alteration of constitutions in East and Southeast Asia. Law is essentially administrative and alter-able at the behest of the virtuous ruler, evident in the use of martial law in Taiwan, the new constitutions that appear with nearly every change of president in South Korea, or the regular constitutional changes that occur in Malaysia and Singapore.

Indeed, the purpose of East and Southeast Asian managerial rule is essentially apolitical or anti-communicatory. In place of a legal under-standing that articulates a common and evolving association in terms of rules, we have law as a set of exactly prescribed performances with no opportunity for a creative interrogation of what these performances might actually entail. Central to this technical and rationalistic interpretation of law in East Asia is the Confucian and legalist preoccupation with *xing ming*, the rectification of names. Rectification provides the device for per-petually adjusting laws to the new circumstances of development or mod-ernization. In the contemporary practice of the Pacific Asian multi-function polis this is now termed 'fine tuning' and 'proactive' pragmatism. Such fine tuning legalism further recognizes no limit to its operation. Such an understanding of rule and the self-understandings it seeks to manage denies both an autnomous realm of activity or a value in civil society.

Continual management, however, must be shown to benefit the people. A residual paternalistic concern with benevolence or the welfare of the masses survives. This concern moreover has been intensified by the fact that the post-independence parties claimed both to represent a national past, but also to overcome the past failing of tradition by creating a new and progressive Asian identity. Such concern appears democratic, but clearly it is not a 'Western' understanding of democracy. Only the skilled tech-nocrat can plan 'the next lap' (Government of Singapore, 1991) of devel-opment. The people need to know their new responsibilities and they may 'feedback' their views. They also need to be reminded constantly of their new identity as morally reborn vehicles of an ill defined national mission. Nevertheless there remains a clear divide between the technocratised man-darinate and the common people.

In this emerging Asian understanding of democracy, it is the people who are accountable and not the party. Thus, when the people fail to endorse their technocratic elite correctly, rectification can swiftly follow. In Singapore, this might require errant constituencies losing their bus routes or nurseries and failing to have their housing estates upgraded, as hap-pened after the 1991 election when an unprecedented four opposition MPs were returned to the eighty-one-seat parliament. Analagously in Malaysia, the continuing independence of the federal state of Sabah and its reluct-ance to accept UMNO guidance means that its infrastructure has been massively neglected. The Asian understanding of democracy, then, like the understanding of law offers a resource for rule. It in fact enables a more complete mobilization and management of the people. Certainly, in the understanding of Southeast Asian rulers like Mahathir and Lee Kuan Yew and, even in more democratic Northeast Asia, democracy and autocratic rule are potentially syncretized and rendered compatible.

A traditional preoccupation with rectification modified by managerial science has, therefore, spawned a new technocratic understanding of rule. The legalist view of law, *fa*, as a precisely defined set of rules mechanically administered, conduces to the notion of government as managerial technique. While the understanding of *shu* methods and *shih* circumstances offers a legitimation for adjusting definitions, rules or names to changing political needs. Indeed, it has generated a new East Asian vocabulary in which voters 'feedback' to the state managers but never challenge their expertise. Continual 'fine tuning' bureaucratically rectifies law to meet new circumstantial exigencies. Feedback, fine tuning and consultation inexorably lead to a new harmony or 'consensus'. Meanwhile, the modernized version of benevolence requires that technocratic rulers adopt 'proactive' measures to ensure the pragmatic adjustment of policy to economic targets.

Consequently, in the modified East and Southeast Asian understandings that permeate contemporary bureaucratic practice, the government remains veiled in an arcana. An arcana of techniques couched in a technocratic language, but which ultimately derive from a vestigial understanding of *shu, fa* and rectification or *musyawarah and gotong royong.*

A traditional sensibility, thus, informs rule in the modern Pacific Asian state. However, under the influence of powerful ideological understandings of the mid-twentieth century these traditions serve the paradoxical purpose of furthering progress. This drive to realize an ill-defined new Asian identity requires continual and evidently democratic mass mobilization towards short term moral, social and economic objectives. This syncretic combination of managerial planning, progress and tradition has subtly reinforced a moralistic form of rule in which the dependency and security offered by the man of prowess offers a certain solution to the anxiety created by the constant need to compete.

The unresolved problem of how to manage generational change remains, however, in these increasingly neurotic political arrangements. The concern for order and the emphasis on dependency and self-concealment present clear difficulties for an institutional or communicatory management of change. It is to this problem and the management of political and economic change that we turn in subsequent chapters.

4 Democratization and the Myth of the Liberalizing Middle Classes

David Brown and David Martin Jones

In the East and Southeast Asian newly industrialised countries (NICs), or to use the preferred acronym of a recent World Bank Report, High Performing Asian Economies (HPAEs), it appears that political development occurs in the wake of economic modernization. Arbitrary rule gives way to constitutional and institutional procedures and restraints, and competitive elections replace the military coup as the favoured means of legitimating leadership transition.

Writers imbued either with a modernization or a Marxian view of development assume that these changes are a consequence of the creation of a vocal, articulate and increasingly self-confident new Asian middle class. Thus, tied to the evidence of increasing democratization is an assumption of proliferating interest groups, and the concomitant liberties of the press, of assembly, and of association that a diversified modernity increasingly demands. Indeed, a literature has emerged claiming to demonstrate this process of bourgeoisification in the NIC's. Thus, for instance, in South Korea after 1987 an increasingly self-confident middle class brought an end to an 'authoritarian cycle' of rule (Diamond et al., 1989: 292), in Taiwan the success of 'democratic transition . . . has been largely attributed to the political entrepreneurship of the new opposition' which is 'essentially a middle class movement' (Cheng, 1989: 474). Indeed, the Taiwanese middle class has become 'politicized and powerful' (Robinson, 1991: 2). Meanwhile in Southeast Asia, democratic 'revolt' in Malaysia stems from 'a type of middle class politics' (Savaranamutu in Rupesinghe, 1992: 50), Singapore's 'considerable middle class may be (an) extremely important precondition for political liberalization' (Rodan in Hewison et al., 1993: 104) and in Indonesia a 'middle class has grown larger and is demanding more public information' (Chalmers, 1991: 121). In this understanding while 'authoritarian states with developmental features' provided the necessary stability for economic development, they eventually came to constitute 'formidable opposition to (capitalist) democratization' in East and Southeast Asia (Porter in Held, 1992: 366). As *The Economist* characteristically sums up this dominant orthodoxy: 'In Asia, authoritarian governments may find it easier than democratic ones to haul countries out of poverty, but once Asian countries are thus hauled out, they too will want more freedom and democracy' (29 June 1991: 18). Moreover, it is the burgeoning middle class, itself the Frankensteinian creation of the 'bureaucratic authoritarian' NIC, that becomes its democratic nemesis.

Yet at the same time as modernization and Marxist proponents of market driven change towards capitalist democracy in Pacific Asia admit, the role played by the liberalizing middle class is a 'problematic' one. Problematic, because it does not play the role that Marxist, neo-Marxist and modernization theorists claim that the middle class historically plays. Thus in South Korea, Dong Won-Mo finds that the middle class is highly sensitive 'to a stable social order' (Dong in Cotton, 1993: 89). Analogously, in Taiwan, in the 1970s the middle class was 'apolitical' (Robinson: 36). Moreover in the 1980s 'the middle class support for the opposition quickly levelled off after the regime committed itself to political liberalization and embarked on an accelerated democratic transition' (Cheng: 8). At the same time in Southeast Asia, Hewison *et al.* note that although their concern is with the emergence of 'bourgeois' or what we would term communicatory democracy, they nevertheless 'do not propose that the bourgeoisie, the middle class and democracy go together naturally in all historical situations' (Hewison *et al.*, 1993: 6). In Malaysia, Harold Crouch discovers that the middle class had 'ambiguous political consequences', operating confusingly both as democratizing agents and supporters of continuing authoritiarian rule (Crouch in Kahn and Loh, 1992: 40). In Indonesia Robison finds that the emerging middle class, while threatening 'the pact of domination' that maintained the Suharto regime (Robison, 1989: 52–74), also maintain an Indonesian version of a 'Bonapartist state' (in Hewison *et al.*: 41). In this view not only is the concept of the 'middle class' ambivalent, but the explanatory usage of the term becomes increasingly obfuscatory. For if the middle class is both increasingly central to the continuity of an illiberal politics and the main agent of liberal 'democratization' the term has as much intellectual rigour as a rubber band.

This conceptual incoherence, while particularly evident in the analysis of political development in Pacific Asia, is no means confined to that discussion. Indeed it has its roots in an evolving European discourse about the political role played by capital and the capitalist class. In the early modern era, the growth of a mercantile middle class came to connote the emergence of a virtuous and autonomous civil society. European thinkers classically came to identify an urban middle class with political or constitutional rule. The virtue of this polity stemmed directly from the communicatory participation of its active, free and essentially middle class citizens (Pocock, 1977: 203).

However, in the course of the nineteenth century 'aristocratic' liberals like Mill and De Tocqueville (Kahan, 1992) challenged this view. They identified the emergence of an anti-liberal urban middle class that sought democratically to impose a common uniformity. Such a middle class tyranny, Mill interestingly averred, might, instead of facilitating liberal diversity, advance 'the Chinese ideal of making all people alike' (Mill, 1970: 203).

Subsequently, twentieth century social scientists attempted to reconcile this middle class intolerance with pluralist democratic outcomes. Thus, by the time Seymour Martin Lipset writes *Political Man* (1960) and Almond & Verba discover *The Civic Culture* (1963) middle class, egoistic, self-interest has become a dynamic phenomenon in a developmental process leading from tradition to a modernized, bureaucratic and rational condition. Thus twentieth century political science transformed the nineteenth century aristocratic liberal suspicion of the Renaissance virtuous middle class citizen into an objective, value free tool of social analysis.

This already problematically transvalued understanding of middle class virtue was then applied to Asia. At the same time as nineteenth century European thinkers grappled with the political implications of the expanding middle class, they nevertheless assumed that it was its absence in Asia that explained its political and economic backwardness (Springborg, 1992: 18–20). Max Weber's *The Religion of China* (1951) apotheosised this understanding. Significantly, from this apparently objective perspective, as Bryan Turner shows, 'the absence of civil society in oriental society constitutes the basic theoretical postulate of the case for oriental despotism' (in Springborg: 19). From this problematically Eurocentric political science viewpoint, a damning caricature of traditional Asian political practice was established. A subsequent generation of political scientists most notably, but by no means exclusively, of the modernization school, naturally inferred that the appearance of a middle class signals the emergence of a civil society that will inexorably terminate a servile, asiatic despotism or, in the language of this seemingly neutral science, 'authoritarianism'.

Clearly, the transfer of an ambiguous understanding of middle class dynamism to the process of democratization in East and Southeast Asia is problematic, especially if dependency has positive advantages both for the rulers and the growing middle class that rapid growth has created in the NICs. Instead of the middle class acting as a motor of change, this chapter poses by contrast an anxiety ridden middle class whose emergence constitutes a managerial problem rather than a threat to the reinvented tradition of Asian political rule.

TECHNOCRATIC MANAGEMENT AND THE DEPENDENT MIDDLE CLASS IN PACIFIC ASIA

Clearly the successful modernization of the NIC's owes nothing to democracy, but much to the enlightened practice of virtuous rulers whose foresighted appreciation of export led growth mobilized a disciplined and increasingly educated workforce towards developmental targets. The harmonious and balanced polity in the Asian model is one where each group knows and appreciates its defined social duty. Problems arise only where duties are unspecified or where an emerging group, the middle class for instance, has no clearly specified dyadic relationship with the virtuous rulers. The very success of this developmental strategy, then, poses a dilemma. How do you ensure a smooth transition to the next generation of state managers, and how do you contain the new and supposedly articulate and entrepreneurial middle class that efficient rule creates? How, in other words, do you manage political development?

It is to these questions that virtuous rulers in both Northeast and Southeast Asia have addressed themselves with interesting consequences for what is sometimes referred to as the Asian model of democracy and the problematic role played by the middle class. In order to elucidate the problem we shall discuss the role of the middle class in South Korea, Taiwan and Singapore, by any standards effectively modernized economies; and also their role in the less modernized, but nevertheless high performing Southeast Asian economies of Malaysia and Indonesia.

The effective modernization of the three Confucian capitalist states was heavily indebted to an East Asian political tradition of rule by good men. The virtuous practice of the South Korean, Taiwanese and Singaporean ruling elites relied to a very large degree upon the Confucian values of consensus and harmony, hierarchy and duty that Vogel and Lodge (1987) consider the efficacious legacy of a communitarian ideology. At the same time, the virtuous rulers had to pursue policies that mobilised the people towards progressive values. In this endeavour, a Confucian political culture expedited a managerial political rationalism committed to planning and instrumentalising export led growth. The virtue of this technocratized Confucianism consisted essentially in its ability to manage proactively the successive stages or 'laps' of economic development. Yet, its very success created a problem that potentially conflicted with the hierarchical assumptions of the technocratized *jin zi* of South Korea, Taiwan and Singapore.

Meanwhile in Malaysia and Indonesia traditional practices of *musyawarah* and *gotong royong* have facilitated the emergence of a politically dependent, *bumiputra* middle class. This has been done through an affirmative action policy (implicit in Indonesia, explicit in Malaysia) that promotes indigenous Javanese and Malays into the state and para-state sectors, while at the same time facilitating the economic development brought about by multinationals and local Chinese businesses which exist in clientelist arrangements with powerful politicians. This technocratic management of ethnic division and the successful creation of a *gotong royong* economy of mutual cooperation, itself created problems in the 1980s and prompted calls for deregulation, which indicated not a promise of liberalism, so much as a strategy to preempt and prevent liberalism (Chalmers: 112).

Inculcated with modernization theory in their American graduate schools, the super technocrats in Taiwan and South Korea, the next lap visionaries in Singapore, the technocratic 'Berkeley Mafia' in Indonesia and the 'vision team' in Malaysia knew that modernization had created or is creating a middle class. They also learnt that the middle class form the engine of future democratization. If the liberalizing impact of the new middle classes has not always been immediately evident in the Asian NICs it must according to the model be imminent. Despite their often expressed fear of westernization and the western preoccupation with democracy, managerial rule necessarily took cognizance of this potential. State technocrats therefore initiated proactive strategies to manage the middle class. They either initiated competitive inter-party, presidential, or intra-party elections; or established new ground rules for the articulation of interests by societal groups. These initiatives presented obvious benefits to a technocratic ruling elite for they seemed to promote elite legitimacy as initiators of democratization, while at the same time coopting potential opponents by incorporating them within manageable state institutions and establishing pacts between the middle class and the state. But the extent to which the incumbent regimes have managed to remain in control of the democratization process has varied. It is these variations and the evolving relationship established by the elite with the new middle class that we now explore.

REGIME INITIATIVES IN SINGAPORE

During the 1970s the People's Action Party (PAP) ruled Singapore by a policy of autocratic exclusion embodying principles both of Confucian paternalism and meritocracy. 'Survivalism', state ideologists maintained, constituted the only method to prevent the collapse of the small, fragile, resourceless society.

However, by the early 1980s the regime came to view this strategy paradoxically as a potential source of insecurity and uncertainty. Firstly, the age of Lee Kuan Yew, the founding father of the tiny island republic, implied the potential for unstable leadership succession. There were no mechanisms to facilitate 'leadership renewal'. Secondly, successful industrialization had created a middle class whom, it was assumed, would ultimately embrace liberal values, and reject state paternalism. Equally worryingly, Singaporean society appeared to be increasingly westernized, while the outcome of competitive meritocracy had spawned a politically alienated Malay underclass. Finally, the need for a high-tech revolution implied the need for new mechanisms of consultation with the private sector.

After 1981, these issues prompted the PAP leadership to adopt a new strategy of corporatist participation. They began to devise organizational channels for political discussion and competition in order to give both the regime, and Singaporeans, an enhanced sense of certainty, identity and security. These channels included: the introduction of nominated MPs to promote controlled debate between PAP and non-PAP viewpoints; and the wider use of parliamentary committees and committees of inquiry on a range of policy issues like religious harmony and an elected presidency. These devices, it was held, served both to promote political debate, provide constructive criticism and enhance 'bonding' between people and government. Similarly, the PAP has taken various initiatives to institutionalise the articulation of ethnic interests, particularly through group representation constituencies (GRCs) and the introduction of officially sanctioned Malay (Mendaki), Indian (Sinda) and Chinese (Chinese Development Association) interest groups. Finally, the PAP invited controlled political discussion through the creation of a feedback unit, 'informal dialogue sessions' and 'walkabouts'. The 'Next Lap' (1991), the manifesto of the 'new team' that replaced the first generation of leaders in 1991, outlined the central features of this strategy; and the new Prime Minister Goh Chock Tong's 'caring and consultative' style of rule revealed shortly before the elections of August 1991 apparently emblematised it.

These initiatives have certainly maintained stability and continuity by legitimating the leadership transition (a transition facilitated by the fact that Lee Kuan Yew continues to hold cabinet office as Senior Minister), and by providing arenas for the controlled articulation of criticism of the PAP. The drop in the vote for the PAP, from 75.5 per cent in the 1980 general election, to 61 per cent in 1991, and 59 per cent in the 1993 presidential election has not been destabilising. Thus, faced with the assumption that the growing middle class would espouse liberal values and demand political participation, the PAP regime chose not to exclude and suppress it, but rather to accommodate and coopt it, by offering expanded channels for participation.

Clearly, this does not constitute the development of a liberal democracy. Instead the democratization process in Singapore is an endless search for certitude and reassurance through the proliferation of new rules, institutions and safeguards. Democratization thus involves the expansion of political participation and consultation within the limits defined by the state, a procedure which as we shall see offers therapeutic reassurance to the middle class.

REGIME INITIATIVES IN TAIWAN

If Singapore's democratization is taking the form of inclusionary incorporation, the process in Taiwan has been somewhat different. In Taiwan the erosion of the KMT's corporatist system, and the security and state managed growth it provided, has impelled the state technocrats to try to resolve the problem of regime legitimation by creating new political rules and relationships.

As Daniel Metraux points out, the KMT provided Taiwan 'with strong authoritarian rule from the late 1940s to the mid-1980s' (Metraux, 1991: 63). Central to this rule was a Confucian paternalism, or, in terms of the three principles of Sun Yat-sen as modified by Chiang Kai-shek: a period of political tutelage that concerned itself with the 'principle of livelihood' which 'makes the nurture of the people its aim' (p. 37).

Although the 1947 constitution had provided for multi-partism, the suppression of indigenous Taiwanese aspirations in February 1947 and the continuing threat posed by communist mainland China, led after 1950 to the reaffirmation of the KMT's traditional role as a charismatic party with a historical mission to 'complete national reconstruction' (Cheng, 1989: 477). The political dominance of the KMT was 'based on several so-called temporary provisions that were attached to, but actually superseded, the Constitution in the name of the national emergency arising from the confrontation with the communist regime on mainland China' (p. 477). This continuing external threat legitimated the introduction of temporary provisions and the passage of emergency decrees which instituted a martial law regime. This concentrated power in the hands of the president, although in accordance with Sun Yat-sen's five principles, space was found for executive, legislative, judicial and examination and control *Yuan* or branches. The President was indirectly elected by the National Assembly consisting of members of the legislative and control Yuan and Mainlander delegates appointed for life to 'represent' mainland constituencies, thus perpetuating the fantasy that the President represents all China (Copper, 1993: chapter

4). The KMT further legitimated its autocracy through its claim to represent the historic legacy of the Chinese people and its Confucian virtue, illustrated by its paternal concern for the people's educational and material welfare. The latter claim was to some extent vindicated by its impressive educational record and its effective nurture of the people evident in its land reform policy and its effective technocratic management of export led growth (Vogel, 1991: 29–30).

In order to develop tutelage and nurture, the KMT evolved a 'quasi-Leninist' regime (Cheng, 1989: 471). There was organizational parallelism between the party and the state: party organs controlled administrative units at various levels of government as well as the military via a commissar system (p. 477). In 1988 the *Asian Wall Street Journal* observed, 'all major government decisions are first made by the KMT's 31 member Central Standing Committee . . . [and] the cabinet rubber stamps decisions handed down by the KMT leaders . . .' (6 July 1988).

Nevertheless, external factors, most notably the loss of United Nations membership in 1979 and the credibility gap faced by the nationalist regime in maintaining its historic claim to the Chinese mainland increasingly confronted the KMT leadership with a serious political and strategic dilemma. In the course of the presidency of Chiang Ching-kuo (1977–88) and more dramatically during the current presidency of Lee Teng Hui (1988–) growing uncertainty about the claim to the mainland has forced an otherwise rigidly autocratic KMT to admit the existence of irreconcilable political alternatives that require debate.

The problem that confronts the KMT's neo-Confucian pursuit of moral certitude is that (as Brown explores in Chapter 5) there exists two clearly competing ideas of nationalism. 'The old KMT line holds that Taiwan is the last remaining base of the ROC and their vision of Taiwan as an essential part of the mainland is very real. Many native Taiwanese, however, have no dream of returning to the mainland . . . their goal is an independent Taiwan, a Taiwan which is not the Republic of China but a nation in and of itself with no outside territorial claims' (Metraux: 63). The growing recognition of this dilemma forced the KMT after 1987 to permit the articulation of political alternatives. Martial law was lifted in July 1987 and tacit permission granted for *dangwai* 'outside' or opposition parties to operate openly.

The KMT thus reluctantly embarked on a policy that tolerates political opposition. Under Lee Teng Hui's technocratic guidance, the KMT moved from an autocratic paternalism to gradual technocratically managed reform as an always problematic strategy to retain its virtuous guidance of Taiwanese affairs. Both Presidents Chiang and Lee assumed that some democratization was inevitable in order to allay future demands by the emerging middle class (Robinson, 1991: 41). This strategic accommodation, moreover, has been remarkably successful in coopting some of the most popular issues advanced by the main indigenous opposition Democratic Progressive Party (DPP) in order to maintain and to increase the legitimacy of its rule (Clarke, 1989: 140–1).

Ironically, the character of the opposition has facilitated the remarkable success of this strategy. The DPP which favours Taiwanese independence is significant mainly for its uncertainty and insecurity. As the *Far Eastern Economic Review* observed, 'catapulted from obscurity to national prominence by grabbing 23 per cent of the vote in the last island wide elections in 1987, it remains fractious and lacks direction' (23 June 1988).

The problem for the KMT then, as we shall subsequently explore, comes not from any middle class pressure for political pluralism but from its own uncertainty about how to proceed in the emerging new world disorder. An uncertainty that ill suits paternal guidance and creates a neurotic anxiety in the middle class to find certitude in new institutional arrangements.

THE REGIME INITIATIVES IN SOUTH KOREA

As Gregory Henderson has observed, 'Korea's post war years can be viewed as a series of attempts to find in various governmental forms the sense of a viable whole that society had lost' (Henderson, 1968: 148). Traditionally, government constituted a 'great vortex summoning men rapidly into it, placing them briefly near the summit of ambition and then sweeping them out, often ruthlessly'. (p. 31) Postwar strategies for rule characterized by increasing centralization and autocracy punctuated by often violent and intransigent resistance reflected this traditional pattern.

Thus from 1961 to 1979 the military dictatorship of Park Chung Hee maintained order by means of repression and a manipulation of tradition. This repressive strategy allied with effective bureaucratic planning engendered both rapid economic development and a growing middle class who were successfully mobilised to vote for the Park regime in 1963, 1967 and 1971. An atomized 'mass' society, as Henderson depicts it, supported autocracy so long as it maintained 'economic growth, social stability and security from external threats' (Han in Diamond *et al.*, 1989: 277). However, the Park regime resorted increasingly to arbitrary measures during the Yushin period (1972–9), and by the time Park was assassinated in 1979, his regime appeared capricious and despotic and had generated widespread opposition.

In 1980, Major General Chun Doo Hwan projected himself into the unstable centre of the Korean political vortex. Chun staged a coup against his senior officers and used the armed forces to suppress demonstrations, arrest opponents, and infamously massacre hundreds of unarmed civilians at Kwangju in April 1980. In order to legitimate his rule Chun subsequently attempted to coopt the opposition. This involved introducing some of the institutional forms and practices of democracy.

Chun began with a new (1981) constitution, approved by the curious device of a referendum held under martial law that forbade any debate of the constitutional proposals. The new constitution was only slightly less restrictive than the earlier Yushin Constitution (1972), but it did contain the provision that the president should be indirectly elected by an electoral college, and could stand for one seven year term only (see Henderson in Kim and Young, 1990: 36).

Prior to the restricted elections to the National Assembly (March 1981), the government, in a classic corporatist manoeuvre, unilaterally created several political parties: one government party, the Democratic Justice Party (DJP), and seventeen opposition parties designed to divide opposition into small, defeatable segments. Nevertheless, despite this tactic, the governing DJP only managed 35 per cent of the vote which nevertheless translated into 55 per cent of the seats. This pattern continued in the second election held in 1985. Confronted by mass demonstrations, however, Chun offered concessions that would subsequently democratize the constitution. Yet, when the opposition groupings briefly united under Kim Dae Jung and Kim Young Sam, to form the Reunification Democratic Party, the Chun government responded characteristically with increased surveillance and legal harassment. Chun stifled debate and dissent prior to the Olympic Games (1986) and, reneging on his earlier promise of constitutional reform, nominated his friend, retired General Roh Tae Woo, to succeed him.

It was this arbitrary action that brought the urban middle classes on to the streets in June 1987. Faced with massive unrest, General Roh announced that constitutional reforms would after all take place, including for the first time direct and open presidential elections. This decision sought to guarantee, 'political tranquility, a smooth transition, a legitimate government, [and] a peaceful Olympic Games' (Henderson, in Kim and Young, 1990: 39). Thus it was the search for certainty and order, rather than freedom, which lay behind these concessions, a fact seemingly confirmed both by the middle class demonstrators who, 'took to the streets to demand democracy [but] they also chanted "order"' (*New York Times*, 13 March 1989) and the election results of December 1987, which returned Roh Tae Woo as president.

The new (1986) constitution specified that the directly elected President could hold power for one five year term. Power was further constrained by a directly elected National Assembly. Roh Tae Woo took office in February 1988, and National Assembly elections followed in April. Once more, the results confirmed support for Roh, and his Democratic Justice Party (DJP).

After the elections, political reform continued. The government attempted to curb nepotism and corruption, and remove the judiciary and the armed forces from the political arena. Nevertheless the pattern of student demonstration and police suppression continued. The government also maintained restrictions upon both the media and the political opposition. Ideological crime under legislation dating from the 1950s remains a criminal act.

In a bold attempt to break the cycle of conflict and achieve a new harmony in 1990, the ruling Democratic Justice Party sought to ensure its continued dominance by merging with the largest opposition group, Kim Young Sam's Reunification Democratic Party, to form the Democratic Liberal Party (DLP) as a potentially unbeatable coalition. Kim Young Sam was subsequently designated the DLP candidate to succeed Roh Tae Woo. The result of the December 1992 Presidential election was a victory for Kim Young Sam who became the first civilian president since 1961. He began his term in office with new initiatives against the corrupt and arbitrary use of power and assisting the retreat of the military from politics.

Clearly, these events can not be interpreted simply as facade democratization from above. Even if they began like this, countervailing forces ensured that the outcome differed from the intention. Evidently the new middle class wants political change but are they motivated by a desire for freedom or by a continuing search for security and certainty?

REGIME INITIATIVES IN MALAYSIA AND INDONESIA

In Malaysia, the character of rule has depended upon on an 'unequal alliance between the elites of the Malay and non-Malay (mainly Chinese) communities' (Crouch in Hewison *et al.*, 1993: 136). In practice government has taken the form of a Malay (UMNO) dominated multi-communal Barisan Nasionalis (BN, National Front) coalition. On the peninsula, the Malays constituted 56.5 per cent of the population in 1985 and the electoral dominance of the multi-communal BN coalition has been assisted by weighting the electoral system in favour of the Malay community (Hewison *et al.*, 1993: 137). At the same time, areas of commerce and industry not controlled by foreign capital have been left largely in the hands of Chinese traders and businessmen, so that since racial riots in 1969 the Chinese community (32.8 per cent of the population) has been politically impotent, but economically powerful. To redress the ethnic economic imbalance since 1971 UMNO has introduced a series of economic plans in an attempt to increase the indigenous Malay or *bumiputra* participation in the economic life of the country.

Since 1981, under the abrasive leadership of Mahathir, the government strategy has been one of increasing centralization that vests power in the party rather than in parliament or bureaucracy. The BN government, moreover, has frequently invoked the fear of inter-ethnic strife to modify the constitution in an authoritarian direction. In addition, the Internal Security Act, the Sedition Act and government licensing of the press has limited and deterred political debate.

UMNO's oligarchical management of communal tension and growing political centralization, nevertheless, did not inhibit the modernization of the resource rich state. In the course of the eighties economic growth created an increasingly urbanized Malay middle class economically dependent upon the state for employment and patronage. This economic growth together with the emergence of a Malay middle class has in turn generated growing tensions within the UMNO leadership itself about future strategy.

Factionalism within UMNO is not an entirely new phenomenon, however. The resignation of the founding father of Malaysia, Tunku Abdul Rahman, in the wake of the 1969 communal riots, evidenced a growing divide between a traditional aristocratic Malay elite and more forceful modernizing Malay Nationalists in UMNO. These divisions became increasingly apparent with the rise to power of the Malay 'ultra' Mahathir in 1981–2, culminating in the defection of the aristocratic wing of the party led by Deputy Premier Razaleigh in 1988 to form a new Malay opposition party, Semangat 46. More recently, increasing tension within the UMNO elite took the form of an uncharacteristically confrontational leadership battle for the Vice-Presidency of the party. Challenged by the 'new generation of leaders' led by the 'thrusting young Turk' Anwar Ibrahim, the incumbent, Deputy Premier Ghaffar Babar, felt constrained to 'step down' to avoid the 'humiliation' of defeat in the party ballot (*Straits Times*, 3 November 1993). Growing conflict between Anwar's Vision Team and an ageing Mahathir increasingly undermines the reinvented traditional conciliatory practice of *musyawarah*. In part these are generational tensions illustrating the problem of managing leadership transition, but they also reflect emerging differences about realizing Mahathir's vision of a fully modernized Malaysia and the role that a new Malay middle class will play in this process.

The very success of the strategy of modernization has ironically created problems of choice that cause elite fragmentation. As Professor A. B. Shamsul observes, it is increasingly evident that there is a growing conflict within UMNO between the 'politically savvy' pro-business team led by Anwar and the UMNO stalwarts whose support is 'rooted in the Malay villages' (*Straits Times*, ibid.). Moreover, even within the new vision team there exists a rift between an economic camp of young Malay corporate entrepreneurs and a 'political group centred around the Islamic based Abim' which remains Anwar's most 'trusted think tank' (Shamsul, *Business Times*, 29 November 1993). This burgeoning factionalism within the UMNO elite forms the context both for an emerging pluralism reflecting a necessary expansion of consultative and participatory mechanisms and, as an almost accidental by product, potential democratization.

In Indonesia the New Order of Suharto came to power in 1965, 'in what must warrant as one of the bloodiest inaugurations of a new regime anywhere in the world' (Vatikiotis, 1993: 34; Pilger, 1994). In these circumstances the military counter coup that placed Suharto in power presented a significant legitimatory problem, exacerbated by the fact that 'election to public office was not well grounded in the political ethos of Indonesia' (Bresnan, 1993: 87). The Independence constitution of 1945 had provided for an elected parliament, a People's Consultative Assembly (*Majelis Permusyawaratan Rakyat*, MPR) consisting of directly elected and nominated members meeting every five years to choose a President with extensive executive authority. The only experience of open elections in 1955 were, in first President Sukarno's view, 'premature' and caused instability, prompting him to introduce an autocratic, guided democracy in 1957. The removal of Sukarno in the still confused events of 1965–6 (Anderson and McVey 1971, Bresnan, 1993: 86–8) led his successor, the hitherto anonymous Major General Suharto, to revive the constitution of 1945 but to amend it or syncretise it with the paternalistic thinking that informed guided democracy. Under this New Order, the MPR elects the President every five years by unanimous agreement on a single candidate. In practice as Vatikiotis explains, 'a consensus on who should be unanimously proclaimed sole candidate, and therefore the successful candidate, is arrived at well before the MPR meets' (Vatikiotis, 1993b: 25). Under this arrangement Sukarno in 1991 embarked upon his sixth term as president.

To ensure that the revived constitution functions harmoniously and avoid the *unhalus* contentiousness of 1957 and 1965, the democratic element was interestingly refined in the 1970s 'by a series of initiatives carried out under the direction of general Ali Moertopo' (Hewison *et al*.: 43). As Robison describes it, 'a selected number of the old political parties were permitted to reform and compete electorally under strict government control' (p. 43). The centrepiece of this state management strategy, however, was the creation of linked functional groups or *Golongan Karya, Golkar* a state sponsored political party. As Bresnan shows, 'the core group was an army sponsored labour federation, composed of twenty five organizations of workers and officials of government run firms and plantations' (Bresnan, 1993: 96). Moreover, 'with the resources, both political and financial of the military, the presidency and the state bureaucracy' (Hewison *et al*., 1993: 44) Golkar consistently won large majorities in all of Indonesia's elections held since 1968.

This corporatist management was further facilitated by a state ideology of *Pancasila*. Under legislation passed in 1985 subscription to *Pancasila* was made the 'sole basis' of political participation (Bresnan: 232). This ideology enabled the New Order to legitimate paternal guidance and dependency as a 'mechanism that achieves the common will of society through consensus under the tutelage of a state in the possession of its own officials' (Robison in Hewison *et al*., 1993: 44).

This paternalistic management strategy also extended to the economic sphere. To avoid the deracinating implications of 'free fight capitalism' (Taubert, 1991: 123) state bureaucrats exercised a strategic grip over the economy which facilitated not only 'the authority of the state over the market', but also enabled the creation of clientelist alliances between the state technocratic corps (*Korpri*) and corporate capitalist clients (Robison in Hewison *et al*., 1993: 45). These policies laid the basis for rapid industrial and urban growth in the 1970s facilitated by the successful exploitation of the country's oil reserves (Vatikiotis, 1993b: 35).

Thus Vatikiotis observes that 'the hallmark of Suharto's New Order has been the totally successful extension of state powers to all corners of society'. The effective distribution of state largesse, moreover, has enhanced dependency in an already paternalistic society. Through welfare programmes like 'Inpres' the President assumes direct responsibility 'for the welfare of his people and guarantees grass-roots support for his mandate' (Vatikiotis, 1993b: 96).

Yet, the success of the New Order technocrats' paternalistic management of the archipelago's political economy poses the regime with difficulties in managing further development. As Bresnan observes, the very effectiveness of Indonesia's New Order, 'has involved an increase in the number, variety and complexity of private groups ... and is now greatly complicating the process of public policy making' (Bresnan: 294). The difficulty of managing this emerging pluralism is further exacerbated by the problem of managing the succession to Suharto. The unwanted dilemma and the absence of constitutional mechanisms to manage it has created increasing political tension. This is evident both within the military, concerning their role as guardians of the republic (culminating in the recent election of the first civilian head of Golkar), within the bureaucratic elite in managing economic development and political transition, and among middle class intellectuals and students about the possibility and character of rule post Suharto. This anxiety has created a climate of 'openness', an uncertain atmosphere in which previously depoliticized voices are now invited to articulate their concerns in order to find a new consensus. 'Openness' and debate becomes the uncertain response of corporatist management to an unwanted dilemma.

TECHNOCRATIC MANAGEMENT AND THE MIDDLE CLASS CULTURE OF DEPENDENCY IN PACIFIC ASIA

The strategic initiatives of the regimes we have discussed reflected the assumption that the burgeoning middle classes were likely to demand increasing liberalization. Indeed, at different times in South Korea, in Singapore and Taiwan the recently arrived middle class seemed to be acting in the way that modernization theory outlined.

In East and Southeast Asia, however, the traditional and reinvented values are those of dependency rather than autonomy, and moral certitude rather than tolerance. Moreover, in all the cases we have discussed large sectors of the new middle classes are dependent upon the state for their employment, either as public servants, or as employees of state-supported companies (the *chaebol* in South Korea, the government officials of the New Order in Indonesia and the large public sectors in Malaysia and Singapore). In addition, the urbanized middle classes are frequently dependent clients of the personalized patronage networks through which state resources and benefits are distributed. Thirdly, the influence of East and Southeast Asian traditional cultures and of the developmental technocracy of their strong states, has combined to produce middle classes with a corporatist or clientelist mentality, motivated by deference or loyalty to whichever leader can best offer protection.

Moreover, this reinvented dependence does not accept mere political acquiescence, since leaders or patrons who promise new certainties require their middle class adherents to demonstrate an active mobilization towards a new goal and a future harmony. Traditional understandings of virtuous rule reinvented for contemporary consumption further give rise to the perception that the only alternative to consensus is unwanted conflict between right and wrong, good and bad. There is, in such an understanding, little space for tolerant debate, or a loyal opposition.

The managerial techniques of contemporary corporate capitalism further reinforce this 'political culture of intolerance' (Kuo and Myers, 1988: 129) by postulating an economic rationalism in which management, entrepreneurship and administration may be pragmatically acquired through more efficient instruction. It is the relationship between this illiberal middle class culture and democratization that we next explore.

THE MIDDLE CLASS CULTURE IN SINGAPORE

The exclusionary corporatism of the bureaucratic-authoritarian state in the 1970s gave way to a strategy which seeks to widen the network of participation. In dealing with the emerging middle class the move towards an inclusionary corporatist strategy has been apparent in the coopting of professionals into the decision making process.

The government thus presents itself as the expert management of a consensual polity while at the same time promoting and mobilizing participation towards clearly identified goals. This activist style receives its legitimation from a Singaporean middle class that is neither traditionally Asian nor Western liberal, but anxiously syncretic. Uncertainty about identity facilitates a middle class culture characterized by an absence of critical awareness, creativity and self confidence. This in turn, enhances recourse to the certainties of management by experts, that offers a neurotic middle class the reassurance that the interventionist regularities of scientific management provide.

The idea of scientific management, therefore, appears neutral, modern and objective. It is value free rather than Western. At the same time, it appeals to an Asian notion of virtuous bureaucracy. In the managerial vocabulary of Singapore politics, therefore, the elite consists of 'experts' guided by 'pragmatism', while the electorate's role is to 'endorse' and 'feedback', never to oppose. Managerial science and inclusionary corporatism ultimately support a technocratic vision of harmonious balance and state managed consensus.

It is this idea of balance and consensus which in fact justifies a melange of often contradictory and shifting political goals. Moreover, once pragmatism has also been depicted as a virtue, it becomes difficult to distinguish the harmonious balancing of extremes from the incoherent admixture of incompatibles. Apparent contradictions in policy go unmentioned, because the rational bureaucracy follows the way and in the *tao* all contradictions disappear.

However, the promiscuous mixing of the languages of liberal entrepreneurialism, technocratic management and Asian values has generated conceptual ambiguities that intensify anxiety about both personal and political identity. Yet, the significance of this linguistic incoherence is that it does not pose a problem either for the PAP, the Singaporean middle class or the Singaporean intelligentsia. Partly, this is merely the result of limitations on public political debate in Singapore with its state controlled media and strict licensing of foreign periodicals. Nevertheless this does not occasion any obvious resistance from the middle class who on any scale produced by modernization theorists should by now be demanding alternative sources of information.

The middle class capacity to absorb and in fact endorse the linguistic ambiguities of political discourse stems from the survival strategy of *kiasuism*. *Kiasu*, from the Hokkien 'scared to lose', is a culture which effectively legitimates otherwise anti-social activity provided the progenitor can maintain conformist anonymity. The attitude of the state managers towards *kiasuism* is significantly ambivalent, on the one hand, condemning it for undermining communitarian values, yet at the same time implying that it might also constitute the essence of a distinct and interesting Singaporean identity.

Moreover, the selfishness which characterizes *kiasu* behaviour does not stem from any arrogant self-confidence, but rather from its absence which makes fear of failure the dominant concern in a competitive and regulated society. This middle class culture actively enhances the corporatist managerial claim to expertise. Both the middle class fear of the future and its deracination from past tradition facilitate the PAP's claim to technical expertise and political certainty. Shifts in strategy and goals are not a problem provided they are stated in suitably absolutist terms. Indeed, the neurotic anxiety of the *kiasu* could not tolerate a free choice. This lack of confidence, moreover, welcomes the activist PAP style of politics. Indeed, the active response to the mass mobilization campaigns which characterize Singaporean political life offers a group conformist solution to the doubts about individual identity. The anxious desire for authority, and the conformism it ineluctably entails, legitimates the government's claim to reflect and articulate a communal consensus. Conformism is thus raised into a political and moral virtue. Furthermore, the government's pursuit of technocratic efficiency and the accumulation of ever increasing wealth reconciles the *kiasu* pursuit of material self-interest with *kiasu* unself-confidence, since it offers state-managed capitalism without the risk of entrepreneurial individualism.

The Singaporean middle class consists of professionals who in their education, background and outlook are both specialized and dependent. In part this reflects the influence of an education system which encourages, 'rote learning, cramming, lack of creativity and the breeding of obedient technocrats and bureaucrats' (Ho, 1989: 686), it also reflects the fact that they rely to a very high degree on careers in state or para-state sectors. Their narrow specialism on the one hand implies a lack of interest in wider political issues, but on the other a strong regard for their own and other's expert knowledge. As professionals they have interests and perceptions which are relevant to technocratic 'good government'. Nevertheless specialization combined with a *kiasuist* calculation produces a managerial rationalism that continually requires rules, consultation, and endless feedback. Neither the western model of progress towards liberal democracy, nor the Asian model of traditional paternalism serve to explain the role of Singapore's middle classes in its political development; rather, it is the linguistic melange of its managerial corporatism which engenders a middle class culture characterized by anxiety and uncertainty, and which sustains the development of a Singaporean neurocracy informed by continual proactive mobilization.

Singaporean culture, depicted by its government as embodying the Asian virtue of 'community before self', turns out in fact to be characterized by precisely the opposite 'virtue' which prioritises the neurotic self over the ambiguously manufactured community.

MIDDLE CLASS CULTURE IN TAIWAN

Taiwan's rapid and equitable industrialization has transformed its social structure, creating in thirty years a heterogeneous, and urban middle class that constitute, on some estimates, 35 per cent of the population (Robinson, T., 1991: 40). Numerous discussions of Taiwan's politics have recognized that this development is central to an understanding of the democratization process (Clark, 1991; Robinson, T. 1991; Copper, 1993). However, this discussion has tended to elide social pluralism into political pluralism, political pluralism into liberalism, and liberalism into democratization, and in so doing misconceived the character of the democratic transition.

We must begin by recognizing that the authoritarian KMT system was stable and effective so long as it provided security and certainty, particularly for the growing middle class. From the early 1950s onwards, the middle class were locked into the KMT's patronage machine either as state employees, or as clients coopted into the main middle and local levels of the party through personalised factions. Moreover, as the professional and business middle classes expanded during the 1960s and 1970s, their proliferating interest associations had only limited autonomy and functioned as 'transmission belts' for policy implementation or support mobilization. This system was coherent and stable, providing the *guanxi* (connections) through which the middle classes could attain the security which their Confucian education in moral certitude required.

The coherence of this corporatist system began to crumble in the 1980s. Its unravelling left the recently arrived middle classes 'in search of an identity . . . politically immature . . . [and] also socially unsure' (Metraux, 1991). The decline of the KMT corporatist machine and of its clientelist network arose in part simply because the extent of social diversity and mobility made corporatist controls increasingly difficult, and personalised political networks increasingly fragile (e.g., Cheng: 161; Hung: 63). In part also, it arose out of the loss of certitude among the KMT elite about how to deal with their leadership renewal crisis, and the problem of Taiwan's identity in relation to the Mainland. This emerging fragility was further exacerbated by what Kuo and Myers describe as a culture of intolerance which gives ethical credence to government provided it delivers public goods and behaves morally and responsibly, but often holds government to impossible 'standards of perfection' (Kuo and Myers: 130). This Manichaean view of rule allows 'very little tolerance for those in power to make mistakes' or to appear uncertain.

From this perspective then, the rise of autonomous 'social movements', the growth of political opposition notably the DPP, and the articulation of dissent within the KMT after 1988, constitute an anxious search to resolve a burgeoning sense of insecurity. An anxiety clearly manifested in the behaviour of the Taiwanese businessman Mr Lu described by Jonathan Moore in 1988. Thus:

> businessman Lu is typical of Taiwan's emerging middle class which has grown in the past decade with the country's economic boom, but is very much in search of an identity in the face of political, cultural and social pressures. . . . Whatever its size the middle class has yet to find a political voice. It does, however, have certain traits in common with middle classes in other countries; it is politically pragmatic with an overriding interest in preserving the status quo. . . . Thus Mr Lu might approve of Taiwan's political opposition DPP . . . but at the

same time they see the ruling KMT as the best choice for a stable government. (*Far Eastern Economic Review*, 23 June 1988)

This *parvenu* social group is not only politically immature, it is also socially unsure and its members are 'not always able to express themselves adequately'. An inadequacy allied with practices of deference and dependence has actually reinforced KMT dominance strikingly in recent local prefectural elections (*Far Eastern Economic Review*, 2 December 1993).

Thus although as Tung Jan Cheng and Stephen Haggard have noted, 'the newly emergent opposition . . . is essentially a middle class movement' (Cheng and Haggard (1992): 3), their goals are not altogether foreign to moderates within the KMT party, with whom they occasionally form tacit alliances. Given the continuing insecurity of the middle class and their Manichaiean perception of the KMT's paternal guidance, democratization, but not necessarily pluralism, offers a problematic escape from their modernization predicament. Democratization, in fact reflects a continuing search for certainty through new rules, procedures, institutions and constitutions.

MIDDLE CLASS CULTURE IN SOUTH KOREA

The major socio-economic change in South Korea has been the rapid growth of the urban middle class. Estimates of its size vary. However recent analysis suggests it has expanded from approximately 34 per cent of the population in 1984 to 40 per cent in 1988 (Dong, in Cotton, 1993: 75).

The search for order, certainty, and security constitutes the abiding political concern of this group. Yet whereas autocratic military rule used to provide security, by the late 1980s its increasing arbitrariness led the middle class increasingly to espouse the cause of democratization.

The middle class unrest that precipitated Roh Tae Woo's promise of constitutional and democratic reform in 1987, was evidently a response to the arbitrary, corrupt, and repressive behaviour of the Park Chung Hee and Chun Doo Hwan regimes. Yet shortly afterwards, they voted for the same Roh Tae Woo because of their yearning for stability.

This 'sentimental' behaviour of the South Korean middle class has been noted by several observers (Ilpyong Kim in Kim and Young, 1990: 60). Those who demonstrate violently against autocrats like Rhee, Park and Roh subsequently regret their behaviour and pay respect, in Roh's case even electing him President.

However, little has been made of the implications of this incoherent behaviour for Korean democratization. During the mid-1980s, for instance, the South Korean middle class was, in Choe Jai Hyon's phrase, 'fragile', 'silent' and 'timid' (Dong in Cotton 1993: 85). Similarly, Sung Joo Han observed the middle class was 'still too insecure about its economic and political status to opt decisively for political freedom and democracy' (Diamond *et al.* 1989: 281). Indeed, as Kim Kyong Dong has explained, prior to 1987, 'the role played by the entrepreneurial-management sector as far as the process of political democratization has occurred has been passive if not negative' (Chalmers Johnson in Cotton: 103).

Yet, apparently, the 'democratic revolution' of 1987 was essentially a middle class revolution. By 1987, this apparently passive bourgeoisie had suddenly become politically self confident actively demanding democratic reform. This schizophrenic shift from passive dependence to militant activism can only be explained by the fact that such activism itself constituted a search for reassurance.

In 1987 the middle class perceived that authoritarian military rule no longer offered security. It demanded 'democracy' because it offered the promise of an orderly leadership transition through the new certainties of constitutional rule. As Dong Won Mo noted, 'at present [1991], the Korean middle class appears to be more concerned about issues of democratic constitutional order and the rule of law, than with issues of distributive justice and class cleavage' (Dong in Cotton, 1993: 90). It was certainly true, as Dong goes on to note, that the middle classes were incensed in 1987 by the torture of individual students.

This did not, however, mean the conversion of the South Korean middle classes to a liberal respect for constitutionally protected rights, but rather that such incidents of state violence (like the 1980 Kwangju incident) dramatically and symbolically illustrated the immorality and uncertainty of personalist, arbitrary rule. In fact such behaviour demonstrated the failure of corrupt rulers and demanded Confucian admonition traditionally administered by scholar students and the resolution of predicament through constitutional certainty.

This shift from political passivity to political activism and its resolution in new constitutional certainties reflects the Confucian roots of the apparently modernized middle class's political culture. South Korean society is characterized by extreme social conformity. Indeed, 'there are probably no other societies in which social conformity is stressed as strenuously and at times as harshly as in Korea. . . . The strident norms of social and political conformity are shaped, in a large measure, by Confucian beliefs and values that have influenced Korea's past' (Chong in Kim and Young, 1990: 61). Moreover, this group conformity values an inflexible moral stance.

Since all political leadership necessarily entails moral virtue, any opposition to the ruler is phrased as a non-negotiable moral challenge. This leads to conflict conducted in terms of moral absolutes, rather than to negotiation, political disagreement and argumentative compromise.

The lack of a bargaining culture rigidifies political cleavages and often leads to an irreconcilable polarization. In cultures where actions are judged on their 'form' rather than on their substance, where taking an inflexible stand on matters of principle, called *ch'ijo* in Korean, is a supreme virtue, where leaders and informed citizens cling to the bigotry of a sense of self-righteousness regarding their own political positions, there is no room for compromise solutions (Chong Lim Kim in Kim and Young, 1990: 50).

A further relevant feature of Korea's political culture is its clientelism. Reinforced by the experience of military autocracy, common bonds of kinship, locality, training or personal contact form the basis of factions where individuals coalesce around patrons who offer both protection and prebends. There is, moreover, no space for compromise among factional rivals, since such behaviour offers little reward. Consequently, 'political parties especially are notable for their factional strife, for parties in truth are collectivities of individuals who have banded together to enable a leader to attain and maintain power and reflective advantage for his followers' (Jacobs, 1985: 26).

The Korean legacy of being more Confucian than the Chinese has in fact created a political culture in which, 'the Koreans first idealize authority to such a degree that they fancy their rulers should be paragons and second assume that they could escape all their personal travails if only their rulers would behave correctly' (Pye, 1985: 230). This legacy gives a discontinuous quality to political change in Korea. As John Oh has suggested, while 'the legal and institutional superstructure' appears increasingly democratic and modern, the substructure or culture remains 'debilitatingly deferential' (Oh, in Kim and Young, 1990: 37).

However, such cultural attributes are intrinsically antithetical to democracy only if democracy is defined in communicatory terms. Behavioural values develop in the context of, rather than preceding, political actions, and the Korean value of *ch'ijo* has clearly been sustained or exacerbated by the autocratic character of recent Korean history. But it is a culture which is also perfectly compatible with the confrontational electoral politics of the contemporary scene.

Thus although there has been a radical pressure for democratization, the self-understanding that informs this radicalism is clearly not conducive to the emergence of a liberal form of democracy characterized by orderly competition, tolerance and compromise. Instead there appears something like 'patrimonial democracy' (Jacobs: 52). A form of democracy where plural political groupings form on the basis of personalist factions rather than as issue-oriented parties and where political disagreement takes the form of confrontation rather than debate, with decisions reached either by majority vote, or appeal to the decision of the patrimonial ruler and where political participation occurs through the manipulation of conformist clienteles by competing patrons, rather than through any autonomous activity.

Ironically, while the military regimes and their technocratic advisers premised their democratic initiatives upon the assumption of middle class liberalism, middle class cultural values remain distinctly illiberal. The *ch'ijo* mentality of the middle classes does not, however, imply political acquiescence. The implication is rather that they actively seek new certainties and new patrons who can resolve their problems.

This may not result in a particularly stable or effective form of democratic politics, but the tension between a *ch'ijo* middle class and democratic procedures is probably no more fundamental than the tension between liberal individualism and democratic majoritarianism in the West. The politics of democratization is always problematical.

The Middle Class in Indonesia and Malaysia

The central feature of politics in Malaysia has been the ability of UMNO both to manage communal differences and promote an increasingly Malay national identity through a bumiputra affirmative action policy, the ideological manipulation and reinvention of a Malay past as a *Rukun Negara* and the promotion of a progressive Islamic *agama*. To develop and deepen a Malaysian identity, however, has required both the manipulation and management of non-Malay minorities and the mobilization of the Malays away from their rural indolence into a thrusting, forceful, brave, new, urban world.

This has entailed both the creation of a new Malay middle class and an increasingly centralized one party state. Thus by the 1980s UMNO had been particularly successful in expanding not only the size of the middle class but also the bumiputra element within it (Savaranamutu, in Rupesinghe, 1992: 48–9). At the same time, as Harold Crouch observes, this burgeoning middle class has actively supported an increasingly authoritarian and interventionist state. Indeed, this is not surprising as the Malay middle class employed either in the state bureaucracy or in businesses with UMNO links, are its main beneficiaries. Such arrangements, moreover, reinforce classical ties of dependency and facilitate UMNO's rule by *musyawarah*, where the realignment of dependency arrangements both within UMNO and the wider business community negates the possibility of open disagreement.

Although Rupesinghe has identified a middle class 'revolt' and a propensity to democratization among middle class groups, notably lawyers and professionals, in the 1980s (pp. 59–60), the fact that most Malays support the notion of 'Malay dominance' and the promotion of a Malay culture as a political weapon (Vatikiotis, 1993: 113) indicates continuing support for an UMNO paternalism. This paternalism in turn reinforces a traditional need for dependence, harmony and balance. Moreover, much of the Islamic opposition to UMNO has come from aspiring and established middle class groups who have turned to the Islamic religion as a way of resolving both their occupational and their emotional insecurities (Muzaffar, 1987). The uncertainties and insecurities of the middle classes have indeed been reflected in the proliferation of factional rifts and opposition groupings, but the government has managed to maintain its dominance by actually increasing the state management of politics and business through a subtle use of press control, patronage and the judicious use of the Internal Security Act.

However there remain potential challenges to Mahathir's rule. The emergence of the new Malay vision team, the potential conflict between the requirements of Malaysian Islam represented by ABIM and a growing Malaysian entrepreneurialism, together with the need to offer greater representation to minority communities in order to manage more effectively the emerging vision, all pose problems for UMNO's continuing domination of Malaysian politics. Elite uncertainty promotes a new dilemma for the dependent Malaysian middle class, a dilemma resolved only in an anxious search for a new balance. Any prospect of democratization in Malaysia stems therefore not from any middle class demand, but from the managerial problems created for the UMNO elite by their successful management of modernization.

Analogously in Indonesia as the bureaucracy expanded and the power of the state grew in the course of the 1980s, not only did the general welfare improve, but the state effectively expanded its role as the 'great provider' (Vatikiotis: 109). Thus in the 1980s, 'everything from patronage to rice emanated from the state'. (p. 109) As Vatikiotis has shown, 'in true corporatist fashion the state has worked assiduously to ensure that all social activity is coopted. This is usually done either by providing patrons in the form of a minister or senior government official or by granting an association a representational monopoly and enforcing compulsory membership for all those engaged in the activity concerned' (pp. 110–11).

This hierarchical ordering of New Order Society and the establishment of channels of corporate control drew heavily upon and reinforced a tradition of political dependency. As we have seen, Javanese tradition in an attenuated form has served as a vital resource for New Order ideologues. This manipulation of traditional understandings, moreover, clearly addresses the anxiety of a people dislocated by rapid growth and urbanization. Nowhere is this neurotic dependency more evident than in the behaviour of the middle class, the major material beneficiaries of New Order paternalism. As Bresnan (1993) shows, this was the class that clearly prospered from the paternalistic 'management of the nation's affairs. It had a stake in the economic and social progress that had been achieved. It had a stake in the status quo, in continuity' (p. 280). Significantly, most of 'this middle class belonged to the civil or military service. In some Indonesian cities and towns, government employment provided jobs for as much as 25 per cent of the labour force. . . . Soeharto reduced the size of the armed forces over time, but he vastly increased the civil service' (Bresnan: 278–9), which after 1967 grew faster than the rise in population. Bresnan somehow concludes from this that a middle class 'growing in its economic independence of the government' has liberal democratic 'political implications for the future' (p. 280).

Nothing, in fact, could be further from the truth. For this state employment essentially provided the middle classes with

> a means of plugging in to a secure well being. Young Indonesian graduates strive very hard to obtain their . . . civil service registration number, even though salaries are abysmally low. . . . As well as a regular salary, the bureaucracy provides its four million employees with rice, housing transport to and from work, and comprehensive medical care. In return, rigid conformity and total commitment to the government's policies are demanded. (Vatikiotis, 1993b: 109)

Such a *politique* reinvention of the Javanese practice of *gotong royong* and *etak etak* helped to intensify an apparently enlightened paternalism. Indeed, as James Mackie noticed in 1989 the character of the New Order had become 'increasingly exclusionary rather than participatory' (in Vatikiotis, 1993b: 98). An arrangement that suited a docile, pessimistic and dependent middle class. The traditional political practice of consensus building that Sukarno revived to foster national consciousness, had by 1990 become 'the only acceptable mechanism of decision making' (p. 94).

However, the very effectiveness of this corporatist arrangement has recently begun to generate stress within the New Order's technocratic elite about the management of transition and further development. The government's attempt to exclude potential critics has begun to give way to a concern to include and perhaps tolerate alternative viewpoints in order to bring about a new and more effective consensus. This has taken the form since 1990 of the call for more 'openness'. In this context, the bureaucracy and the army (ABRI) have each begun to articulate different approaches to future political development. Within ABRI a dissensus rather than a new consensus is emerging about its *dwifuncsi* (dual function). While Vice-President General Sutrisno continues to see the army as the 'stabilizer' of society, others suggest that openness requires the gradual withdrawal of the military from political life. Increasing ABRI uncertainty demonstrates not openness but a loss of direction for the guardians of the republic.

Meanwhile in the bureaucracy and universities appeals for openness while widespread have only created ambiguity. Clearly, on the one hand, the new openness offers a means of widening the circle of participation and generating greater stability through a new agreement, on the other, the lack of direction that openness permits creates unwanted anxiety. Thus it is uncertain whether the recent call for openness from the previously depoliticized Islamic party, Nadhlatul Ulama, constitutes a potential threat to stability or a possible basis for greater consensus. Equally, student protest against the anti-Islamic national lottery in December 1993 and student leaders' claims that 'we have been cool for 15–20 years, but now we're thinking of democracy' (*Far Eastern Economic Review*, 9 December 1993) seem to presage instability rather than a 'refreshing' reinvigoration of 'national stability' in what Suharto describes as 'the take off era' (Vatikiotis, 1993b: 97).

In order to manage the insecurity engendered by uncertainty about how to begin a conversation about change, a traditional syncretism characteristically re-emerges. Thus Amir Santoso, an Indonesian political scientist, commenting on the uncharacteristic recourse to the 'voting mechanism' to elect the leadership of the National Youth Committee (KNPI) observes that traditionally, Javanese are suspicious of democracy because the losing side would suffer frustration and loss of face, 'which our culture considers demeaning to the highest degree' (Santoso, *Jakarta Post*, 10 November 1993). 'This sense of shame, often prevails over the wish to apply democracy'. By inculcating a spirit of 'sportsmanship', Santoso piously hopes, the worrying transparency of elections might be accommodated with the continuing Javanese need for 'smoothness' and harmony.

Evidently, then, in Indonesia, too, the elite has embarked on an ambivalent policy of extending the circle of political participation in order to renew and intensify a sense of harmony and balance, a harmony attenuated by the very success of corporatism and rendered problematic by the collapse of old certainties and the fading power of Suharto's wahyu. Here once again an intensely conservative and anxious middle class is faced with an unwanted dilemma. They seek resolution through an ambivalently 'open' and less 'primitive' political culture that offers, in Vice President Sutrisno's view, a more effective method of managing 'differences' in order to create a new 'consensus'. (*Sunday Times* (Singapore), 19 December 1993).

CONCLUSION

The vocabulary of political science conventionally presents the democratization question in terms of the power relationship between state and civil society. Its positivism expects the project of modernity to strengthen and pluralize civil society, or in its Marxist version engender a liberally disposed capitalist middle class. The outcome, democratization, thus comes to connote the state's increased responsiveness to societal pressures and the emerging political diversity in turn reflects the increased pluralism in civil society.

However, the evolving political practices of East and Southeast Asia confound this assumption. In East Asia the puzzle is, why did democratization take so long and why has there been more democratization than liberalization? How is it that the democratized polity still leaves the one party dominant system strong enough to ensure the continuation in power of the incumbent DLP in South Korea and the KMT in Taiwan?

In Southeast Asia the process of change is even more illiberal. For although the regimes in Indonesia, Malaysia and Singapore have modified their autocracy, they do not seem to be moving in the direction of a constitutional, communicatory democratic practice. Indeed, the reinvention of certain traditional understanding militates against the rule of law and open debate in these intensely conservative political arrangements. Yet, the dominant paradigm in both its modernization and Marxist variations demands a move towards greater accountability or 'bourgeois liberalization'. This lack of fit between model and practice has occasioned a conceptual breakdown resolved only by a sterile recourse to describing illiberal but softly authoritarian regimes as 'anomalous' or by an equally confusing appeal to an Asian culture of communalism, deference and dependency that in an unspecified way inhibits democratization.

Our analysis instead proposes, firstly that democratization in East and Southeast Asia is misleadingly conceived if it is presented as a process of weakening the strong authoritarian state. In fact, during the 1970s and 1980s authoritarianism in East and Southeast Asia became too fragile a basis for rule, partly because of socio-economic change and partly because of the ongoing problem of elite transition in East and Southeast Asia. Thus democratization actually constitutes a conservative response by incumbent elites faced with uncertain times in order to amplify political control through new 'intermediations' with civil society, thus rendering it more visible. The extent to which the incumbent state elites manage this process depends not on the autonomy of the middle class and the relative strength of civil society, but instead upon the cohesion of the managerial elites and the felicity of their initiatives in defining what they consider legitimate interests.

Secondly, and relatedly, a shared continuity in East and Southeast Asian understandings of power is its magical capacity both to harmonize, balance and, particularly, in the case of Confucianism, to transmit an ethical understanding. Consequently, all seek access to power or a relationship of dependence offering security and certainty. Power, therefore, is necessarily concentrated at a personal or geographical centre. This means that any alteration in the distribution of power should not automatically be thought of in Pacific Asia as progress from rule by good men to rule by law and the institutionalization of constitutional procedures. Rather democratization here really represents the unintended institutional by-product of a politics of generational transition and the desire to preserve rather than to change. In other words, democratization is the sometimes problematic and often transitory institutional arrangements and accommodations that eventuate from the search for new 'men of prowess' to replace a worried ancien regime.

Moreover, crucial to an understanding of the political role of the middle class in East and Southeast Asia, is the fact that it is not only the state managers that require a leadership principle. The psychology of the middle class desires the certainty that virtuous rule provides. This anxious pursuit of dependency relationships is daily manifest in the personalized factionalism of the ostensibly communitarian politics practiced in East and Southeast Asia. Hence democratic political participation actually involves an anxious pursuit by societal groups, particularly the middle class, for clientelist access to those individuals who actually or potentially distribute state largesse.

Consequently, we argue, liberal or communicatory democratization is not occurring in East or Southeast Asia. Nevertheless an Asian model of democratization is taking shape. Given the Asian understanding of leadership as the power to wrap clientelist followers in a consensual blanket, the 1970s assertion of depoliticized authoritiarianism became increasingly troublesome. Especially as this entailed potential or explicit confrontation with groups in civil society rather than balance and harmony. As we have seen conflict symbolises imminent dissolution in East Asian political thought. Consequently, in the course of the 1980s East and Southeast Asian states devised a number of managerial strategies not only to facilitate the strength and legitimacy of the state and the authority of the leaders, but also to assuage the anxieties of emerging urban middle class groups and thus render them both more visible and more manageable.

However, the state managers are not always able to initiate and control the process of change. Indeed, they may be themselves weakened or divided by the actual or impending absence of the man of virtue. Thus democratization in East and Southeast Asia necessarily entails a tense relationship between, on the one hand, a strategy of inclusionary corporatism by the state management and on the other, the problematic emergence of factions among the state elites and the consequent erosion of the effective transmission of power. The variation in the political practices of the various East and Southeast Asian NICs reflect their management of this transition. In other words, it is political technique reflected through a paradoxically conservative weave of tradition and national development that explains differences in the process of democratization rather than differences in culture *per se* or differences in the apparent autonomy and strength of their illiberal middle classes.

The generally passive and illiberal character of the middle class is equally evident when we examine the political economy of Pacific Asia and its capacity to endure strong state guidance. It is to this that we turn in the next chapter.

5 The Political Economy of Democratization

Kanishka Jayasuriya

In the burgeoning literature on transition to democracy, two competing research programmes may be identified: that is *structural*, and *process-oriented* explanations.[1] These two programmes adopt distinct methodological stances – analysts adopting structural explanations tend to be historical and comparative, whereas those working with strategic explanations tend to focus on short-term events. The *structural* explanation envisages democratic transition as the outcome of long-term forces that are in turn shaped by specific economic and social structures. In contrast, the *process-oriented* viewpoint adopts an agent-centred orientation built around the role of strategic choices confronting government and opposition leaders in the crafting of democracies. As with any craft, the end product depends on the skill, vision, and choices of the major actors.

The 'research programme' outlined in the work of O'Donnell *et al.* (1986) provides a useful illustration of the conceptual structure of the strategic arguments. They argue that the high degree of uncertainty of social and political action means that, at critical junctures, individuals and groups of actors have the potential to play a decisive role in political outcomes. It is suggested that:

> Hope opportunity, choice, incorporation of new actors, shaping and renewal of political identities, inventiveness – these and many other characteristics of the politics of transition stand in sharp contrast to the mode and tone of politics in the periods preceding the breakdown of democratic regimes. (O'Donnell *et al.* 1986: 19)

In the Latin American context, these theorists emphasize the role of *foundation pacts*[2] in shaping the initial move towards democracy. Much of this literature, while being informative and insightful on political development in individual countries, consists of a series of case studies rather than general explanatory statements applicable in a range of cases. No doubt, choice is an important factor in the explanation of democratic transition, but choice is always contingent. It is the understanding of this limited contingency that should be the purpose of social science explorations of the nature of this democratization process. Further, political theories of transition remain fixed upon the interaction between regime actors and agents in civil society. While this is an important aspect, it is but one trajectory of democratization. We wish to argue that, in East Asia, the major impetus for democratization comes from *within* the state rather than from civil society. In this context, political theories of democratization have somewhat limited utility for an understanding of East Asian democratization.

This chapter argues that democratization is an effect of the increasing relative autonomy of capital from political elites, caused in part, by the policies of economic reform pursued by East Asian states. Democratization is an attempt to renegotiate a new relationship between these political elites and capital. Central to this approach is the understanding that 'democratization' is not about the empowerment of civil society, but rather reflects a renegotiation of the relationship between political elites and capital.

According to the structural perspective the process of democratization is closely associated with increased political participation. As O'Donnell *et al.* (1986) point out:

> Democracy's guiding principle is that of *citizenship*. This involves both the right to be treated by fellow human beings as equal with respect to the making of collective choices and the *obligations* of those implementing such choices to be equally accountable and accessible to all members of the polity. (1986: 7)

Marshall's evolutionary account[3] of citizenship identifies the linear development of legal citizenship which encompasses the right of property, free expression and a range of civil liberties, political citizenship covering political rights in a democracy, and the citizenship of welfare which entitles a citizen to certain resources. Pivotal to Marshall's account is a conception of citizenship as a gradual extension of the right of entitlement to social, political, and economic resources to those groups who lack access to market power. These entitlements, as Esping Anderson (1985) points out, arise out of class conflict within civil society.

The argument is that the movement towards realization of a democratic order needs to be located in actors and social movements in civil society – civil society being an area of human activity which was primarily directed at the satisfaction of needs that required an association greater than the family.[4] As Cotton argues:

> implicit in the understanding of man as [necessarily] a member of civil society, therefore, was the belief that it was not the legitimate business of the state to interfere in the operation of civil society unless those operations were in clear conflict with the task of the state. (1992: 321)

The logic of this argument is that democratization is a concession to *civil society*; it reflects the growth of civil society, or rather, the self-consciousness of key groups and classes, and the weakening of state power. In short, for the advocates of this viewpoint, democratization is both a cause as well as a consequence of a 'weak state'. A great deal of the recent Latin American and Southern European literature, as well as earlier studies of European transitions to democracy, steadfastly maintained that the political fault lines in these societies were determined by the control of social and economic resources by private actors outside the state. The state was a political arena to which different groups sought access. Further, it was assumed that the interests of the actors were formed independently of the state.[5]

In this vein, political economy places great emphasis on the relationship between economic structure and resultant class structures and coalitions. The classic study in this regard is the work of Barrington Moore (1966),[6] who argued that the construction of parliamentary democracy is crucially dependent on both a relatively even balance of power between the Crown and aristocracy, and a dominant urban bourgeoisie at odds with a rural dominant class. Therefore, he identifies the presence of a strong bourgeoisie along with market-oriented rural labour controls, as central to the emergence of parliamentary democracy.[7]

The primary assumption of these structural arguments is that there is both a common logic and an inexorable movement towards a democratic order. In this teleological argument which most recently finds echoes in the work of Fukuyama, democratization – be it in Western Europe in the nineteenth century or in East Asia in the last decade of the twentieth century[8] – is a product of a gradually awakening civil society.

The problem with this argument is the presumption that industrial development is essentially similar across different historical periods. Gerschenkron's study (1943) of late economic development underlined the importance of understanding different strategies and models of industrial development. There was no single linear route to industrialization. It follows that the role of the state in economic development varied considerably, depending on the timing of industrialization.[9] Late industrialisers, such as Germany, were characterized by a vigorous and active state shaping industrial development. Kurth (1979) pointed out that the political position of industrial sectors will be significantly influenced by the timing of their development. For example, he notes that in the textile sector in Britain the manufacturers were economic and political liberals because their sector developed without state support; and therefore, that political liberalism had a strong social foundation. However, in Prussia and the East where industrialization was late:

the textile manufactures would not be strong enough relative to the agrarian upper classes to impose their political vision on the rest of society. The new 'infant industry' in the East was highly vulnerable in the domestic market to competition from the older established textile manufacturers in the West, and accordingly the Eastern manufacturers were highly protectionist in regard to international trade policies. These features of the textile industry diminished its liberal impulse and impact. (Kurth, 1979: 8)

In Prussia, the political ramifications of the industrial process ensured that though liberalization had strong intellectual roots, it was poorly anchored in social foundations. The ramifications of this argument for the study of regime change are two-fold: first, the dependence of private actors on the state precludes the formations of independent interests outside of the state; second, the state itself is an actor with its own interests rather than an arena to which contending social actors seek access. The process of late industrialization points to the importance of understanding the role of the state in the dynamics of regime transition.

The studies of Gerschenkron (1943) and Kurth (1979) on late industrialization suggest that democratic transition needs to be understood in the context of what Touraine (1988) calls 'a mode of development'. A mode of development refers to the fact that each sequence of industrial development brings with it its own distinctive style of political and economic regulation (Munck, 1993).[10] These regulatory patterns, in turn, determine specific patterns of social and political action. In other words, there is a correspondence between a mode of development and types of social and political action.

The East Asian model of development is distinguished by three features. First, the state has been extensively involved in the economy as both a regulator and a controller of key sectors of the economy. As a result, the independence of private economic actors has been considerably constrained. Second, the East Asian economies have been heavily export or outward oriented. In South Korea, for example, exports as a percentage of GDP increased over 10 per cent from 27.3 per cent to 37.5 per cent between 1979 and 1984, while in Taiwan exports formed 54.6 per cent of GDP in 1979. However, as Bradford (1990) rightly notes, the outward orientation of the East Asian economies was not similarly matched by domestic liberal policy. In East Asia, the state plays a major role in export promotion, while at the same time, limiting the penetration of imports in the domestic economy. In other words, a liberal external economy corresponds to a regulated domestic economic structure. It is this unique capitalism that enabled East Asian economies to exploit the advantages of the post-war trading system without incurring concomitant domestic changes. Finally, the East Asian economies are characterized by a *productivist* emphasis where consumption has been suppressed. In this regard, automobile density is a useful indicator of the extent of domestic consumption because the dominance of the automobile sector influences broad patterns of energy usage, family savings, etc. Further, as Fajnzylber (1990) notes, 'it is such an important core industry that it is linked to key service sectors'. While the newly industrializing countries (NICs) have become significant exporters of automobiles, their domestic markets are small in comparison with other economies of similar size. In this context, Fajnzylber observes that 'while South Korea has become a leading exporter of automotive products, its domestic automobile industry imports only one tenth to one fifteenth that of the Latin American NICs' (1990: 338).

This suppression of domestic consumption has, in turn, required the exclusion of distributional and consumption issues from the political arena. Cumings (1987), in his path-breaking work on Northeast Asian political economy, emphasizes how the colonial legacies of both Korea and Taiwan significantly influenced the development of a strong state. He points out that:

> In Korea and Taiwan, the colonial power emphasized not only military and police forms of control, but also development under strong state auspices. This was particularly true after the Depression, when Japan used a 'mighty trio' of state organization, central banking and *zaibatsu* conglomerates to industrialize Korea and parts of Manchuria. (1987: 53)

Cumings argues that the colonial state therefore stood apart and above society, substituting for domestic classes that would otherwise have played a leading role in industrial development. Japanese colonial rule therefore fostered state–society relationships which were a mirror image of Japanese relationships. The distinctive character of East Asia therefore lies in the fact that

> it was the state that conceived modernization as a goal and industrialization as a means, that gave birth to the new economy in haste and pursued it unrelentingly as an ambitious mother her child prodigy. And though the child grew and developed its own resources, it never overcame the deformity imposed by this forced nurture. (Landes, 1965: 54)

This state oriented industrial model of development in turn suggests that the tracks of political division in these societies are likely to be between political elites and private capital. Those accounts of democratic development, centring on the bourgeoisie, the middle class, or the working class as the historical bearer of democratic values, are implicitly based on patterns of industrialization where the market, the state, and civil society are clearly differentiated. The point about capitalism in a late industrializing context is the blurring of the boundaries of the market, the state and civil society. The dependence of private actors on the state makes it unlikely that interests can develop autonomously within civil society as assumed by most 'structural' theories.

LATE INDUSTRIALIZATION AND REGIME TYPES

In proposing that the process of industrialization in East Asia was heavily state driven, it may be argued that this conforms to the familiar pattern of late industrialization. Nevertheless, the East Asian case is distinctive because late industrialization, as Robison *et al.* point out, 'was characterized by rapid and large scale investments in capital goods industries, the establishment of industrial cartels and the active intervention of state and industrial banks' (1993: 23).

This pattern had a deep and lasting impact on the nature of democratic outcomes, primarily through its impact on civil society. While early industrializers such as England had an assertive and self-confident bourgeoisie, a strong civil society and 'weak' constitutional state, later industrializers were characterized by both a weak bourgeoisie and a strong state, making a democratic transition difficult (Moore, 1966; Mooers, 1991). Marx astutely observed that, in France, the bourgeoisie won out in order to 'humble the people. In Germany it humbled itself, in order to keep the people from winning. All history shows nothing more ignominious and mean spirited than the German bourgeoisie' (quoted in Mooers, 1991: 104).

German exceptionalism[11] increasingly proved to be the norm in many late industrializing countries that lacked a strong capitalist class. If this native bourgeoisie were insufficiently developed to carry through this task, then other social forces could be called upon to accomplish what was required (Mooers, 1991). In most cases where extensive state intervention was required, this 'revolution from above' began to dominate increasingly social and political life.[12] The combination of a strong state, weak bourgeoisie, and strong landed aristocracy inevitably produced some variant of authoritarian capitalism in late industrializers. However, the point that needs to be reiterated is that the rapid growth of capitalist economic practices led to the emergence of independent social forces in civil society that challenged the dominance of the absolutist state. As capitalism gave birth to a civil society that encroached on the state, even the absolutist Prussian state increasingly became an arbiter of competing economic interests rather than an autonomous actor.

Herein lies one of the major differences between 'late' industrializers such as Germany and 'late-late industrializers' such as Taiwan and Korea; in the latter, civil society remains limited and circumscribed. In accordance with the late industrialization model, the state has proved to be the motor of economic growth in these societies. However, the role of the state in economic development in East Asia has been more extensive and pervasive than in the paradigm German case. In East Asian economies like Japan, South Korea and Taiwan, the state has fostered the creation of a 'market' economy. Unlike conventional late industrializers, this new group of industrializers is heavily dependent on the state and the sustenance of an export oriented mode of development. The blurring of the boundaries between state, civil society and the market that has occurred in these East Asian countries makes these countries markedly distinct from the paradigm German late industrializing model.

The East Asian mode of development suggests the imperative for democratic reform is likely to be located in the changing relationship between political elites and capital. 'Statist'[13] industrialization policies followed by East Asian governments required an exclusionary corporatist type of political and economic arrangement that allowed little or no room for the autonomy of capital. However, changing international and domestic conditions undermined these arrangements by increasing the autonomy of capital. In this context, political reform in East Asia is about the renegotiation of the compromize between state and capital. It needs to be emphasized that this is a renegotiation of the terms of dependency rather than a growth of an independent capitalist class. In short, the process of democratic transition is about political management of intra-elite conflict rather than about the development of political citizenship. Of course, this theme of elite disunity figures prominently in strategic explanations of democratic transition. However, the argument presented here differs from these explanation on two counts: first, inter-elite conflict is played out within the state; second, the causes of elite disunity are to be found in structural changes in the economy.

Furthermore, the dynamic of this relationship is not played out between state and society; rather, it unfolds *within* the state. Analysts of democratization in East Asia need to pay greater heed to the changing architecture of the state rather than to the extension of political participation suggested by conventional theories of democratization. As Rueschemeyer *et al.* argue, 'democratization represents first and foremost an increase in political equality' (1992: 5).[14] To view democratic transition as an increase in political equality is to overlook the extent to which liberalization is an outcome of conflicts between the political and other elites. Democratization, from this perspective, refers to the 'opening up' of the state, the renegotiation of the previously clientalist relationship between political elites and capital. It should therefore be distinguished from the notion of liberalization as a means of redrawing the boundaries between state and society. Implicit in this latter, liberal, democratic perspective is the idea that liberalization is the consolidation of political citizenship. In East Asia, the process of liberalization is about the changing *architecture* of the state, not the expansion of the political community.

The late industrialization perspective on democratization places great emphasis on the changing relationship between state and capital. For Barrington Moore, it was the weakness of capitalists as a class that explains authoritarian political outcomes for Germany. More recently, Hewison *et al.* (1993) have argued that the changing relationship between state and capital provides an important clue to answering the puzzle of regime transition in Southeast Asia. In other words, as capital increases its structural power in the economy, it demands more economic and political reform.

In the East Asian case, this account is rendered problematic because capital is so dependent on the state that it has no capacity to act independently. In fact, it may be argued that capital itself is part of the state. In other words, the boundary between public and private power remains to be clearly demarcated. In this context, a key contention of this chapter is that the relationship between political elites and capital occurs within the state. The references to dominant political elites and capital is meant to underscore the argument that the relationship is one between capital and one segment of the state. Indeed, the diminution of the influence of political elites is reflected not in the weakening of the state in relation to civil society, but in the internal *reconstitution* and *restructuring* of the state. From this standpoint, democratization refers to the opening up of the state rather than its retreat from economic and social life. In a similar manner, economic liberalization – while it may usher in a degree of market reform – does not imply any departure from existing consumption and trade patterns.

Similarly, we propose that the state to a large extent shapes the nature of political competition after the democratic transition. This is achieved in two main ways. One is through the determination and structuring of the political institutions of democracy. As the recent 'new institutionalist' literature (March and Olsen, 1984) suggests, the design of institutions has a considerable bearing on the behaviour of political actors. The other manner in which the state shapes the rules of the democratic game is through the legitimacy it gives to certain collective groups and identities. Thus, it may be suggested that democratic politics, arguably, increases the level of political participation; however, to be meaningful, political participation requires the representation of interests, and this is contingent on the development of political identity. Accordingly, the language of politics deployed by the state disrupts the formation of certain types of political identities, and facilitates a form of political competition where the major political differences are those based on the personality of leadership and regional loyalties. In East Asia, therefore, not only is the process of democratization regime initiated, but also the 'rule' of the democratic game is to a large extent, shaped by the state. We next turn to look at the nature of the compact between capital and dominant political elites in East Asia.

EXCLUSIONARY CORPORATISM

Schmitter's (1979) oft-quoted definition of corporatism as:

> a system of . . . singular, compulsory, non-competitive hierarchically ordered, functionally differentiated categories, recognized or licensed (if not created) by the state and granted a deliberate representational monopoly within their respective categories in exchange for observing certain controls on their selection of leaders and articulation of demands and supports (1979: 13)

places emphasis on the nature of corporatism as a system of interest representation. Within the corporatist literature, it is useful to distinguish between societal corporatism that originates from 'below' and state corporatism that is imposed from 'above'. In the East Asian case, we are dealing with examples of state corporatism rather than societal corporatism because 'interests' are organised and regulated by the state. Even, within the category of state corporatism it is possible to distinguish degrees of exclusiveness determined by the extent of symmetry between the political elites and other actors within corporatist arrangements (Stepan, 1985). Our argument would suggest that in East Asia there is a shift from exclusionary to inclusionary state corporatism.

From an East Asian perspective, there are obvious obstacles to the use of the concept of corporatism as a system of interest intermediation. The notion of any independent interest outside the state – let alone interest intermediation – is highly problematic in the absence of strong differentiation between society and the state. Notwithstanding these limitations, corporatism is useful as a means of denoting the relation between capital and political elites in East Asia. In our formulation, corporatism signifies the compact between capital and political elites, and integral to this pact is the exchange of political and economic resources between the two parties[15] (Presworski, 1985). These exchanges, in turn, underpinned the process of export oriented industrialization that generated the economic 'miracles' of East Asia.

The process of capital accumulation generated by these strategies of economic growth provided legitimacy and revenue for state elites. The revenue was especially important in that it enabled East Asian political elites to make side payments to those social coalitions that underpinned the various authoritarian regimes. For example, in Taiwan, public sector pay and conditions were extremely generous because these groups provided support for the KMT (Cheng, 1990). Similarly, in Korea, the state provided price support as well as trade protection for key agricultural commodities and rural groups. These supports enabled the state to provide rural capital with an economic subsidy and protection in return for political support, thereby enabling the creation of a societal coalition that underpinned the authoritarian Park regime (Cheng, 1990), and the autonomous South Korean state.

This compact was realised through the designation of an institutionalized process of consultation. In Korea, this was facilitated through the development of 'deliberation councils' and discussion groups (Jones and Sakong, 1980). In addition, the government extensively used Trade Associations to gather information about industry conditions as well as to disseminate information about world markets (Jones and Sakong, 1980). In Taiwan, there was less institutionalized cooperation between the state and business, but the latter was increasingly incorporated into the policy making bodies of the KMT which was the site for this cooptation. Chu argues that:

> above the local level, the KMT controlled and demobilized all modern social sectors through pre-emptive incorporation of business and professional association, labour unions, state employees, journalists, intellectuals, student and other targeted groups. The KMT also captured the rents created by natural monopoly of governmental procurement

at the national level and used them to cushion the economic security of their loyalist mainland followers. (1992, 179)

While these modes of institutional cooperation – albeit of a clientalist kind – played an important role in the compact between state and capital, the primary dynamic of the relationship between the two groups lay in the structure of economic incentives provided by the state. As previously indicated, in East Asia the state is not an actor outside the market, facilitating economic activity, but 'is a member of the most important internal organization inside the system' (Lee, 1992: 189). In the parlance of neoclassical institutional theory, the relationship between the 'private' and the public sector is one of principal and agent. In the Korean context, this relationship between political elites and capital has been aptly described as one between a senior and junior partner (Jones and Sakong, 1980). More generally, it could be suggested that the relationship between political elites and capital is a clientelistic network held together by the exchange of political and economic resources.

Three major mechanisms by which the state (principal) influences the behaviour of private enterprise (agent) can be identified. These are: *administrative guidance, supply of bureaucratic services*, and *control of credit*.[16] 'Administrative guidance', a term originating in the Japanese context, refers to the support given by the state to certain select enterprises, (Johnson, 1982). It points to the preferential allocation of bureaucratic support to industries and enterprises perceived as winners in the international marketplace. As in Japan, both Taiwan and Korea adopted an anticipatory industry policy that enabled the growth of industries such as electronics and ship building (Wade, 1990). A good example of this form of administrative guidance is the strategy pursued by Korea in the 1970s to deepen its industrial base by moving the economy into industrial areas such as machinery, transport equipment, and chemicals. Haggard points out that the key to this plan was the fact that 'specific projects were negotiated with the large industrial groups, usually acting with minority foreign equity partners or under licence protection, and fiscal incentives were extended to the new industries' (1990: 131–2).

Although administrative guidance in Taiwan was considerably less heavy handed, it has, as Wade (1990) argues, played an important role in Taiwan's industrial development in a range of sectors such as textiles, artificial fibres, metals, autos, and plastics. Thus, he argues that the 'Taiwanese government has been rather active in leading the market in some industries some of the time' (1990: 27). In a similar way, business associations did not assert themselves as political actors in the policy making process; the

KMT sought to encourage clientalistic relationships between business and the state. As Chu points out, 'Economic officials administered an array of powerful policy instruments in bank credits, protectionist measures, fiscal incentives and market order regulations with a certain degree of selectivity among large-scale firms' (1992: 136).[17]

The second mechanism of state influence over capital is the supply of bureaucratic services. These services include the provision of information about market conditions, and active intervention to help enterprises secure licences to compete in international markets. More importantly, it includes the central supply of services such as science, technology, and in general, research and development that most export oriented enterprises would otherwise find difficult to generate internally. For example, in Taiwan, the government owned Electronics Research and Service Organization (ERSO) develops and markets semiconductor designs and production. It was given the responsibility of locating a foreign partner to develop this technology (Wade, 1990). Similarly in Korea, the State has been active in assisting firms to acquire information about international markets. The provision of such bureaucratic services provided the state with a source of control over capital.

The final and probably the most important mechanism is the control of credit. By resort to this mechanism, the state directs private enterprise to control inputs into the production process. The control of credit has been of singular importance in Korea where the control and allocation of credit has been the major instrument of state power over the chaebols. In this regard, Eckert notes that, through

> their ownership or subversion of all of the country's banks, their power to set interest rates, and their approval and guarantee of all commercial loans and investments from foreign countries, the more economically oriented regimes of Park Chun Hee and Chun Doo Hwan were able to direct capital toward targeted industries and to insure corporate cooperation with their various five year developmental plans. (1990–1: 122)

This has proved an effective method of dealing with imperfections in the capital market. Stiglitz (1989) has pointed out that the information assymetries present in capital markets usually mean that credit and equity rationing are inherent features of these markets; such problems are likely to be accentuated in developing economies because the 'institutional framework for dealing with these capital market imperfections are probably less effective, because of the small scale of firms within LDGs and because the institutions for collecting, evaluating and disseminating information are likely to be less well developed' (Stiglitz, 1989: 200–1).

Of course, from this perspective, East Asian strategies of financial repression are functional institutional responses to the resolution of the collective action problems faced by private enterprise, in this case, access to credit.

More important was the fact that this control of credit allowed the Korean state to exercise significant political leverage over chaebols. As Eckert states, 'such state control over the financial system has of course also left little practical room for political dissent from the business community' (1990–1: 122). A striking example of this leverage was the refusal of the Chun regime to approve the bailout of the Kukje group, a refusal widely attributed to the failure of the group to make a political contribution to the regime (Eckert, 1990–1; Clifford, 1988). Whatever the reasons for its demise, the bankruptcy of the group demonstrated the ability of the state to assert control over major industrial groups in Korea.

In Taiwan, state control of the financial system was considerably less repressive than in Korea. Nevertheless, the extent of control, was quite significant. Shea and Yen cite the example of Taiwanese financial authorities who 'often ordered financial institutions to expand or restrict their loans to certain activities, industries or borrower groups to promote economic growth, stabilise the economy or equalise the availability of bank loans' (1992: 223). Furthermore, as the government controlled and owned most of the major banks in Taiwan, it had access to a powerful lever by which the activities of private enterprise groups could be controlled.

In summary, the economic growth strategies of the East Asian economies and their pursuit of export oriented industrialization have been founded on a complex relationship with private business. This could be characterized by a notably exclusionary corporatist arrangement between political and corporate elites – a relationship that includes all the features of a clientalistic exchange relationship. However, the much vaunted economic success of these strong states began to undermine the sources of state strength, while at the same time enhancing the autonomy of corporate groups. This process will be examined in the next section.

CHANGING RELATIONSHIP BETWEEN POLITICAL ELITES AND CAPITAL

To a large extent, the roots of state autonomy and the strength of political elites, which were central to capital accumulation, lie in the external security dilemma faced by both Korea and Taiwan. Whereas in Taiwan, the ruling KMT was constantly in a state of military readiness for war with

China, in Korea, the militarisation of society occurred as a 'consequence of the Korean War and its armed truce aftermath reached its political demorsement with the 1961 coup that brought General Park Chang Khee to power' (Burmeister, 1991: 201). As Cumings (1989) points out, Korea was able to translate its external weakness into a source of internal strength; and the same argument could be applied to Taiwan. The development of a garrison state enabled state elites to insulate themselves from external political constraints. However, the changing international environment in the 1980s, with the end of the cold war, following the dramatic collapse of the Soviet Union, made the Korean Peninsula less central to the international security system. While tension with North Korea remained high, state elites found it increasingly difficult to conjure a siege mentality. Likewise, but in a slightly different way, the strong emphasis placed on economic development by the People's Republic of China (PRC) made an external threat to Taiwan less likely. In fact, as tourism and trade with the PRC increased, Nationalists increasingly sought engagement, not confrontation, with the mainland. As Winclar suggests, this has 'reaffirmed the centrist domestic consensus that for the foreseeable future, neither unification nor independence is feasible' (1990: 227). In both states, therefore, the decline of external threats reduced the capacity of decision-makers to insulate themselves from domestic forces.

Apart from the geopolitical roots of state autonomy, East Asian export oriented strategies were also rooted in the specific context of the postwar international political economy. The hegemonic role of the USA in the international political economy opened up a lucrative export market that the newly industrializing economies (NIEs) were able to exploit. In many ways, the NIEs and Japan were able to gain a free ride on the Bretton Woods system without the concomitant domestic cost. Ruggie (1982) has drawn attention to the fact that international trade in the post-war period went hand in hand with a social and economic structure that ensured domestic stability, economically and socially. Nevertheless, this provision of domestic stability entailed significant domestic social and economic costs for advanced industrial states. The post-war Bretton Woods system was underpinned by a set of domestic bargains in the advanced industrial states, thereby allowing these countries to participate in the trading system, while at the same time, permitting these states to protect vulnerable domestic groups through a social safety net. However, without such a safety net the NIEs were able to expand at the expense of other industrial nations, or, in other words, 'free ride' on liberal democracies. As a consequence, Japan – in the 1950s – and the NIEs – in the 1970s – were able to benefit from the post-war free trade system without incurring the costs of domestic stability. Especially pertinent in this regard is the fact that the post-war financial system of fixed exchange rates enabled East Asian states to maintain a devalued exchange rate.

The collapse of Bretton Woods[18] and the decline of US hegemony created increasing problems for those countries pursuing export-oriented developmental strategies. Especially important in this regard is the development of 'new protectionism' in areas such as consumer electronics, where East Asian economic strength was particularly strong. In addition, these pressured the USA to pursue an increasingly activist trade policy towards East Asia, thus forcing economic liberalization. Hamilton and Kim point out that 'The growing trade deficit between the USA and several East Asian nations, including Japan, South Korea, and Taiwan, prompted the Reagan administration to press these markets to open to US goods and financial' institutions (1993: 117).

In addition to these external factors, aspects of domestic economic strategy began to encroach increasingly on the ability of the state to manage domestic economic affairs. In Korea, the easy access to credit provided by the state led to a rise in the debt of the chaebols, increasingly limiting the ability of the state to manage the chaebols.

Paradoxically therefore, the swelling debt, while permitting state political control over Korean business, limited the ability of the state to move against these industrial companies. The irony of state strength was such that over a period of time, the very conditions which facilitated the existence of a strong state led to its enfeeblement.

Much of the now extensive literature on the NICs (Haggard, 1990; Gerrefi and Wyman, 1990) focuses on the dominant economic policy paradigm that was based on extensive state planning and intervention. Primarily due to the second oil shock of 1979, both Taiwan and Korea were forced to embark on a policy of structural adjustment (Hamilton and Kim, 1993). Structural adjustment, in this case, refers to efforts to make the economy more responsive to market signals; and this required considerable economic liberalization. However, it needs to be pointed out that, although both countries pursued adjustment programmes, the impact in Korea was more substantial owing to the greater statist orientation of the Korean political economy.

Structural adjustment in Korea was marked by macro as well as micro economic reform. In the macro area, a tight fiscal policy was demonstrated by the fact that the rate of growth dropped from 21.9 per cent in 1981 to zero in 1984. This fiscal restraint was supported by an equally stringent monetary policy implemented through strict controls over the supply of credit to the private and the public sector (Moon, 1991).

In the area of microeconomic reform, the Korean government actively pursued a policy of deregulation of the financial sector and shifted industry policy towards a non-discretionary policy regime. Given the important role of finance in Korean state intervention the most notable of these macroeconomic reforms was the move to deregulate gradually and open up the financial system. This involved

> liberalization aimed at greater bank autonomy in determination of credit allocation, in part through the privatisation of state-owned commercial banks, policy loans and administrative guidance over bank portfolios, have been reduced, though the government still exercises influence over banks through its ability to appoint key personnel. (Moon, 1991: 61)

These financial reforms, accompanied by the liberalization of capital markets in Korea and Taiwan resulted in a departure from the previously dominant statist policy paradigm. Although this shift in policy was not dramatic, it nevertheless signified a substantial policy movement from previous patterns. The implementation of these policies of economic liberalization increasingly limited the ability of the state to direct capital. Additionally, as the autonomy of political elites within the state declined, the assymetric clientalistic relationship (exclusionary corporatism) with capital became less sustainable.

DEMOCRATIZATION AND ECONOMIC CHANGE

The key feature of this transformed relationship was the increasing autonomy of capital in relation to political elites. This was mainly because economic reforms – arising from liberalization – had significantly reduced the ability of the state to influence the behaviour of firms and industrial enterprises. These enterprises in turn, were demanding not only greater political autonomy but also further measures to liberalize the economy.

In Korea, the chaebol provided services that were usually provided by the state. For example, many of the chaebols established non-bank financial institutions that 'enabled the chaebol to circumvent the state's regulation for severely limiting ownership of banks by the chaebol' (Hamilton and Kim, 1993: 118). Even in the provision of research and development, and international marketing, the chaebol was increasingly able to provide these services internally. The major effect of these changes was to enhance the autonomous capacity of these enterprises, and thereby, the autonomy of capital in relation to dominant political elites.

With this increase in independence came demands for further economic liberalization, but as Hamilton and Lee point out, these were essentially calls for the removal of restrictions on the freedom to trade, but without any commensurate desire on the part of business to reduce protectionist barriers.[19] To facilitate this process of economic reform, business in Korea has increasingly sought political reform to ensure restrictions on the political capacity of the state to intervene in the market. For example, statements made by leaders of the Federation of Korean Industry (FKI) suggest that business will use its economic power with more frequency 'to push the ruling party into giving more control of the economy to the private sector' (Eckert, 1990–1: 129).[20] Further, the greater autonomy and financial independence – created by economic liberalization in general and the modest financial deregulation – has led to demands for greater representation of capital in the formulation of economic policy.

In Taiwan, economic reforms have unleashed a similar dynamic of enhanced economic autonomy for corporate groups, which have facilitated calls for democratization. Illustration of this trend is Lo's contention that, in Taiwan,

> the government attempted to deregulate the financial market, [and] industrialists, and business people financially supported corporations to apply for licences for new private banks. In fact, the licensing of private banks was reportedly the outcome of negotiations between government officials and powerful business groups refresented in the law-making Legislative Yuan. Clearly, the lobbying activities of big business accelerated the liberalization of the government's outdated and conservative financial policy. (1992: 383)

Put simply, the rapidly developing capitalist system was beyond the ability of the state to monitor and control. As Cheng notes:

> the ever expanding civic and economic associations are simply beyond the capacity of the KMT to monitor, much less to control . . . there is a limit to which the regime can penetrate internationally oriented organizations, such as the Junior Chamber of Commerce, the Lions clubs, and Rotary clubs. (1990b: 482)

Clearly, in Taiwan, as in Korea, economic liberalization had fostered demands for greater economic autonomy as well as illiberal democracy, albeit – as we shall see below – a distinctive pattern of East Asian democratization.

Despite similarities on this score between Korea and Taiwan, it needs to be emphasized that state intervention in Taiwan was based more on indicative than command oriented planning. Taiwanese private economic structure has been built around networks of small to medium sized family enterprises (Hamilton and Biggart, 1991). In contrast to Korea, these enterprises have always maintained a degree of political independence from the state. But at the same time, state control of this sector through its large public sector companies has been quite extensive. As Nuzmazak points out, the state had the ability to 'intervene in the economy by manipulating the prices of basic materials and energy as it did during the two oil crises' (1991: 996). Therefore, the reforms in Taiwan tended to diminish the capacity of the state to intervene in the market place, and thereby the independence of corporate groups has been enhanced.

THE CHANGING ARCHITECTURE OF THE STATE

Apart from giving greater autonomy for private enterprise, economic liberalization led to considerable diffusion of power within the state. As the role of the state in the economy was increasingly transformed from development to a regulatory function, established agencies such as the Economic Planning Board (EPB) became less central to the formulation of economic policy. As the objectives of economic policy focused more on macro rather than micro economic goals, state institutions such as central banks began to exert greater influence on the direction of economic policies. The effect of these changes was to make power within the state less centralised in a group of core economic agencies. These agencies, by and large, relied on the use of coercive economic sanctions against an array of economic agents.

With the shift towards the provision of macro economic stability, and more particularly, regulatory functions, the coercive sanctions of these economic agencies had limited utility because in most cases regulation required the compliance of those affected; this compliance in turn, needed to be secured by negotiation rather than by sanctions. In such a shift, however, the language of bureaucratic authoritarianism becomes less relevant, while the language of democracy could well facilitate this shift from the coercive to the regulatory function of the state. Simply put, as the economy matures, the state needs to invent new forms of economic governance. These new forms of governance go beyond exclusionary corporatist or clientelist arrangements, and require explicit recognition of the representative demands of the corporate sector. By providing for the representation of capital, greater political reform may be one means of effecting this compliance.

There is a danger that the emergence of these governance structures will be perceived by societal actors as a growing societal encroachment upon state structure. Indeed, some recent works on the political economy of business associations in East Asia (Laothamatas, 1992; Doner, 1991) have argued that conventional models of bureaucratic politics need to give way to a more complex understanding of the relationship between state and societal actors. In other words, the conventional bureaucratic politics of Southeast Asia have become increasingly embedded in society. Indeed, Laothamatas argues that 'organized business has played a substantial role in instituting or shaping a new strategy and the associated policies to bring about economic development' (1992: 15). The point we wish to make is rather different; that is, that the process of economic liberalization reflects a diffusion of power to a multiplicity of access points. From this point of view, conflict within the state is a reflection of the bargaining that occurs between different sets of societal and state actors.

For example, in Taiwan, the struggle over political succession and the scope of political reform, between the 'mainstream' and 'conservative' factions within the KMT led to the cooperation of allies outside the state (Chu, 1992). In East Asia, several state agencies and institutions have enlisted the political support of various societal actors in the pursuit of different bureaucratic objectives. In Taiwan, during the 1980s, a number of institutionalized structures for business involvement in policy making was established. For example, the Industry Policy Advisory Board, under the Ministry of Economic Affairs, established working units in a range of industrial sectors (Chu, 1992). Further, a number of policy review groups were established which enabled the state to enlist the support of the private sector in the pursuit of its high technology objectives. This process of state-business consultation signified a move from exclusionary clientalistic relationships to more inclusionary corporatist ones.

Similarly in Indonesia, the emerging conflict between civilians – or rather, technocrats – and the military has compelled both groups to coalesce with outside actors.[21] Liddle points out that:

> The role of rule of law, as a political issue in the Third World, is typically associated with human rights activism. In Indonesia, however, its most influential proponents today are in the business community and in the government itself, making it a prime candidate for coalition between powerful New Order elites and not so powerful pro-democrats. (1992: 458)

Another example of such coalitions is the area of tax policy where both economic technocrats and the business community seek a greater degree of predictability (Liddle, 1992). In the Indonesian context, both cases illustrate the way in which the language of political reform becomes synonymous with technocracy.

Robison's work on the conflict between ABRI and President Suharto once again highlights the fact that political reform – albeit highly limited – arises from conflict within the state. He points out that: 'ABRI clearly sees the competing bourgeoisie, embodying the integration of conglomerate wealth and bureaucratic authority, as an amalgam of power likely to further marginalize its own institutional position' (1993: 252).

The major point to highlight is that one of the consequences of economic reform has been a gradual shift in power within the state, from the previously dominant ABRI, to the technocrats. In this conflict, both groups have enlisted the support of societal actors. It remains however, a conflict within the state.

The shift towards an inclusionary form of corporatism was most evident in the Thai case. A notable feature of this form of corporatism was the establishment of the Joint Public and Private Sector Consultative Committees (JPPCCs). In theory, The JPPCCs, provide a basis for the identification and resolution of significant economic problems in consultation with the business community. In practice, however, the JPPCCs have been more concerned with the reduction of bureaucratic regulation and taxation (Laothamatas, 1992); they have, therefore, essentially pursued an agenda of economic deregulation. In this respect, the JPPCCs have enabled business interests and associations to play a more active role in the formulation of economic policy. Laothamatas argues that in Thailand the government–business relationship has moved from one of clientalism to a corporatist arrangement,

> where government leadership has coexisted with the political autonomy and effective policy role of business associations. Increasingly an interaction – cooperative or conflictual – between two relatively equal parties, not a domination by one party over the other is the building block of the emerging liberal corporatism. (1992: 160)

Laothamatas's description of Thailand as 'liberal corporatism' is somewhat overdrawn. The state remains the dominant partner by its ability to grant recognition to business associations. Nevertheless, the JPPCCs reflect a move away from clientalistic relationships. More importantly, for our argument, the JPPCCs were used by technocratic state agencies to enlist support for their economic reform programme. Technocrats, in economic agencies such as the National Economic and Social Development Board (NESDB), were able to gain the support of business through organisations such as the JPPCCs. From this point of view, the growth of JPPCCs reflects tensions within the state rather than an empowerment of civil society. Conventional wisdom would have it that Thai politics in the last decade and a half has been one of a constant battle between authoritarian military and the democratic civilian leadership. Our account would suggest that this needs to be reinterpreted as a conflict within the state. As in Indonesia, technocrats have appropriated the language of democracy. Indeed, in a curious way, O'Donnell's account (1979) of bureaucratic authoritarianism has been neatly inverted in Asia where technocratic decision making is enhanced by the expansion of formal democratic procedures.

Indeed, the declining power of central state agencies allows for a greater plurality of power within the state enabling excluded capitalist elites to exercise a greater degree of political influence, illustrated by a shift from an exclusionary to an inclusionary corporatist form of governance. The emergence of these structures of economic governance should not be read as an encroachment of society on the state. Rather, it is a reflection of tensions within the state leading state actors to seek allies outside the state. Under these conditions, democratization may reflect a conflict within the state apparatus where societal actors are coopted in the pursuit of the objectives of some state actors. Viewed in this light, democratization is not about the broadening of state social linkages, but rather about the diffusion of power within the state.

In both East and Southeast Asia, electoral politics has enabled capital to use representative institutions to penetrate the state. The expansion of electoral politics has enabled business to invest in politics by financing individual candidates or parties, or in certain cases, running for election. In Taiwan, for example, Chu argues that 'the diversified business groups suddenly became the most sought-after patrons of elective politicians and local factions' (1992: 142). He notes, for example, that in the Legislative Yuan of 1989–92, 38 of the 101 democratically elected members had public ties with at least one business group. Those business groups previously unable to penetrate state directed clientalistic networks, began to invest in individual candidates. The business bias[22] of the electoral system in Taiwan is further exacerbated by the fact that the electoral system based on the Japanese multi-member system tended to diminish the authority of the party and increase the power of the individual candidate. The candidate centred nature of the electoral system has, in turn, facilitated the growth of business influence in politics. A similar story of business influence on electoral politics seems to be unfolding in South

Korea, illustrated recently by the presidential candidature of the founder of the Hyundai chaebol. In Thailand, important businessmen such as Boenchu Rochansathian have always been active in politics. In response to recent military intervention in Thai politics, business groups and associations have responded by backing 'pro-democratic' parties. Additionally, the fact that the cost of a parliamentary seat in Thailand – estimated at 30–500 bahts per vote – depending on the intensity of competition (Maisrikrod, 1992) has meant that business is the only group capable of running or financing candidates for public office. It is estimated by the Thai Interior Ministry that business representation increased from 37 per cent in the 1988 election to 41 per cent in the 1992 election (Maisrikrod, 1992). Further, following the 1992 election, business played an even greater role in parliamentary elections through such organisations as the 'Businessmen for Democracy Club'. As Maisrikrod notes, 'this kind of participation goes beyond running for a seat, but includes giving more financial and intellectual inputs to political parties' (1992: 48). These examples of the role of business in national elections – particularly in more electorally advanced countries of South Korea, Taiwan, and Thailand – suggest that electoralism is a process by which capital is able to influence a distinctive arena within the state.

In both South Korea and Taiwan, as well as in Thailand, the growth of the legislature has limited the power of the executive. In Taiwan, the Legislative Yuan has become an arena for increasingly tripartite bargaining between bureaucrats, political elites, and law makers. As Chu (1992) points out,

> An immediate consequence of the politicization of economic decisionmaking is that the cabinet can no longer force its way through the Legislative Yuan. Economic officials must be ready to compromise over the content of legislative proposals and the timetable for their implementation. (1992: 145)

The point is not that representative institutions have become the most influential part of the state even in Taiwan and South Korea. In these countries, though the executive is powerfully dominant, there is a plurality of political arenas *within the state*, which are dominated by various elite groups. Electoralism, in this perspective, reflects conflicts within the state and not a broadening of political participation.[23] As Anderson has argued: 'under different historical circumstances electoralism has quite different meanings' (1992: 57). In fact, effective political management lies in the coordination and regulation of these different elite groups and arenas.

This emerging picture of East Asian electoralism, characterized by business dominance, is further facilitated by a party system with weak social foundations. In both the Taiwanese and Korean cases, party identification is best predicted by personality, regional, and in the Taiwanese case, sub-ethnic loyalty. In both, cases, social structural influences are non-existent, and as such, the nature of this emerging electoral and party system departs from the accounts of the origin of Western European party system (Lipset and Rokkan, 1967). Parties in East Asia are loose organizations where individual politicians have a degree of autonomy.[24] This autonomy, sometimes enhanced by the electoral system, such as the Japanese system of a Single Non-Transferable Vote (SNTV) in use in Taiwan, enables corporate actors to exercise preponderant influence.

An equally important indicator of the changing organisation of the East Asian state is the emergence of a new generation of technocrats who increasingly occupy key positions within the state. Unlike political elites, these technocrats have different aspirations and interests. For example, in Taiwan, the gradual process of democratization has been related to the shift of policy making power from the KMT to government technocrats. Winclar argues that economic success 'has made government technocrats themselves increasingly assertive. Though the party has always claimed to set the general direction of government policy, it has never had the staff to specify the details' (1992: 237).

The KMT, as a quasi-Leninist party, played a strong role in policy formulation through party organs such as the Central Policy Committee; however, the restructuring of the KMT, from being an ideological to an electoral party, has diminished the influence of these policy organs within the KMT (Yu-Shan, 1989), while at the same time, increasing the role of governmental technocrats in the formulation of economic policy. From the point of view of the technocrats, any limitation of the power of political elites only served to enhance their role and strength within the government.

Political change therefore, is not about expanding the influence of civil society on governmental processes; it reflects instead a fundamental restructuring of the state. This suggests that the process of democratization in East Asia reflects a redistribution of power within the state, rather than a diffusion of power within civil society. Economic liberalization, by opening the state to multiple actors, provides a multiplicity of access points for elite groups. What is distinctively East Asian in this process is that the pressure for reform is in the domain of the state rather than in civil society as conventional wisdom would have it. However, it would be misleading to assume that this process has no societal foundations.

COALITIONS AND REGIMES

It is clear that economic reform helped to reshape the coalitions and constituencies that had been the basis of the export-oriented development
strategies pursued by East Asian states. Korea again provides a good
example of the manner in which the politics of structural adjustment transformed the coalitions that underpinned both export-oriented development
and bureaucratic authoritarianism. The coalition that sustained the Park
regime coalition consisted of both big capital and the rural sector. The
clientelistic relationship between industrial capital and the state is also
evident in the operation of rural economic policies, particularly because
the political support of the rural sector was vitally important for the Park
regime. Thus, we find that the rural sector was subsidised by an extensive
price support system as well as the *saemaul* movement which was aimed
at the creation and renewal of rural infrastructure. The political rationale
of the movement was to build a local political base for the ruling party.
In addition, to the saemaul movement, Korean government introduced the
New Agricultural Policy (NAP) which was designed to promote industrial
decentralization. However, economic reform rapidly dissolved these coalitions as economic reform forced the rural sector to confront the threat of
increased foreign competition and the reduction of price support (Kim and
Joo, 1982; Cheng, 1990b). In similar manner, decentralization policies
were abandoned. Cheng points out that 'the rural coalition was costly and
difficult to sustain. Grain subsidies were a heavy burden for a regime with
constant deficits in domestic and international payments' (1990b: 107).

The latter part of the Park regime, and also the ensuing Chun regime,
therefore, had a very narrow and limited constituency. As Moon argues,
'By the very nature of the reform however, the Chun regime failed to
develop the new coalition that could replace the old one. . . . As a result,
the Chun regime ended up a naked power without a corresponding social
support base, which in turn facilitated its collapse' (1991: 65).

In Korea, the dissolution of these coalitions threatened the domestic
social foundations which were so important in securing state autonomy. In
this context, if economic reform is to be politically sustainable, new social
coalitions supportive of these policies must be found. In both Taiwan and
Korea the rapidly growing urban middle class provides such a source of
support for these reform policies.

For a party such as the KMT, economic liberalization presented constraints as well as political opportunity. It was constrained because economic liberalization – be it externally or internally driven – limited the
ability of the state to intervene in the economy; it was also constrained by

its ability to disperse patronage to various groups. On the other hand, economic reform provided the KMT with an opportunity to build links with new groups and actors such as those sections of the new middle class that could provide the basis for a new societal coalition that could underpin new modes of economic regulation. These new coalitional partners wanted access to positional goods (education, status) as well as to material goods (subsidies, loans). Economic liberalization enabled greater access to them. However, in order to build this coalition, the KMT needed to embark on a strategy of political management and cooperation.

STATE AND DEMOCRATIZATION

To reiterate, the central thesis being advanced in this essay, there is a complex interplay between economic and political reform; complex because it differs from the simple Barrington Moore type of argument that places the historical burden on an assertive bourgeoisie in conflict with a landowning aristocracy. In contrast, we have argued that the dynamic of democratization is to be located in the changing relationship between political elites and capital. The 'statist' economic strategies that propelled East Asian economic development were based on, to use Stepan's (1985) term, a highly 'exclusionary' corporatist or clientalistic relationship between state and capital. This political exchange remained highly assymetrical as political elites dominated this clientalist exchange, and at best, capital remained a subordinate partner in the relationship. However, changing international and domestic economic and political conditions forced many of these states to pursue policies of limited economic reform. A major consequence of these reforms was the reduction in the autonomy of political elites and a corresponding strengthening of private capital within the state. In this regard, of special importance have been policies of partial financial deregulation which limited the capacity of the state to regulate the growing financial autonomy of private capital through the provision of alternative sources of capital. The initial programme of economic reform therefore led to demands for further change in modes of economic regulation and a greater role for capital in the formulation of economic policy, leading to a more inclusionary form of corporatism. In other words, this process entailed a renegotiation of the clientalist arrangements between political elites and capital. However, in contrast to Barrington Moore, this remains a process of renegotiation rather than an assertion of independent class interests. For this reason, renegotiation is not about the changing balance of state–society relationship, but a process of mutual adjustment within the state.

Consequently, political change represents, not a move towards liberal democracy, but rather, a shift towards a more polycentric corporatism. As dominant parties and dominant political elites lose ground, corporate, and one might add, technocratic elites, gain. As relative autonomy of private capital grows it is likely to result in a renegotiation of its relationship to the state as well as to the regime of economic governance under which it functions. Democratization therefore represents a search for mechanisms to manage intra-elite conflict, and perhaps more centrally, to provide for representation of various elite interests. In this context of the changing architecture of the state, the multiplication of political arenas within the state is the key to understanding political change in East Asia. We have sought to illustrate this by examining the growth of inclusionary corporatist relationships, the cooptation by technocrats of capital in struggles over the distribution of state power and resources, and finally the growth of business influence in national legislatures. Democratization, on this argument, therefore, represents the competition for influence and resources between different elite groups. The main thrust of our argument is that – unlike a strategic emphasis on elite disunity and conflict – the sources of elite disunity are broadly structural. Unlike Western Europe where the drama of democratization was enacted in civil society, in East Asia it takes place within the theatre of the state.

CONCLUSION

Presworski's recent work (1985) suggests that capitalist democracy was based on a system of economic compromise between capital and labour mediated by the state. Carroll summarizes this argument:

> Arising out of the crisis of this 1930s this system recognized consent around a general interest in national consumption as the motor for production. This Keynesian revolution allowed social democrats to claim a greater interventionist role for the state while justifying their retreat from struggles over production as such. State power became a means not of socializing production but of 'nationalising consumption'. (1990: 394)

For Presworski, although the terms of the compromise between labour and capital can be (and has been) renegotiated, there is no strategic alternative to such a compromise in a capitalist democracy.

In East Asia, social compromises are equally important in understanding the nature of the process of political reform. Our analysis suggests that democratization represents a renegotiation of the terms of the relationship between political elites and capital; it represents the increasing relative autonomy of private capital. This differs from the Presworski argument that in Western Europe, the electoral system enabled the participation of labour which in turn required significant political concessions from capital in order simultaneously to sustain a capitalist economy and a democratic polity. In contrast, in the East Asian case, political reform has mobilised private capital which has sought a greater political role and a less interventionist state in the economic sphere. However, unlike the late industrialization argument, this renegotiation is played out within the state rather than between state and society. It reflects a process of mutual adjustment within the state. The Moore thesis suggests that the strength of capital as a class is the primary causal factor in the emergence of liberal democracy. In East Asia, we argue that 'markets' are so heavily dominated by state power that there exists no basis for the emergence of a capitalist class autonomous of the state. Therefore, capital is only able to gain greater influence within existing state structures. It follows that 'liberalization' in East Asia concerns political management of elite differences rather than the assertion of autonomous interests of civil society. It is for this reason that East Asian democracy is likely to be a different kind of beast to that of liberal democracy. Much of the literature on democratization held together by a notion of convergence neglects this point.

In East Asia, unlike in Western Europe, the predominant role of state power in economic development has meant that major political cleavages are not between labour and capital, but between dominant political elites and capital. Nevertheless, this is not a zero sum relationship. In Korea, political restructuring allowed the chaebol to come under greater public scrutiny and thereby allow public officials greater leverage to discipline errant companies. Further, democratization enabled public officials to anchor state autonomy in the safer and more secure harbour of electoral legitimacy as well as in new coalitions that included significant sections of the new middle class.

6 Democratization and the Renegotiation of Ethnicity[1]

David Brown

INTRODUCTION

There is a pervasive notion that the emergence of a national identity must precede successful democratization. Sometimes, the argument is that 'the vast majority of citizens in a democracy-to-be [must] . . . have no doubt or mental reservations as to which political community they belong to' (Rustow, 1967: 35). Sometimes, it is argued that democracy presupposes a community which is not divided into a few large ethnic segments, and which shares a common culture (Diamond *et al.*, 1989). More frequently, the community which must precede democracy is depicted both as the political nation and as the cultural nation.

Since democracy refers to some form or degree of 'rule by the people', it might seem reasonable to assume that there must exist a 'people'; a community with a shared national consciousness which can provide the foundation for the transition to democracy. Moreover, since the 'nation before democracy' argument can cite such proponents as Aristotle, J. S. Mill, and Rupert Emerson, the French Revolution and Mazzini, it is one which must surely be taken seriously.

The 'nation before democracy' argument has indeed attained something of the status of conventional wisdom. In A. D. Smith's words, 'national identity everywhere underpins the recurrent drive for popular sovereignty and democracy' (Smith, 1991: 143). A recent work on democratization by Georg Sorensen confirms that 'national unity . . . must be in place before it is possible to conceive of a transition towards democracy. . . . Democratization demands a settling of the national question: Who are the nations that are going to democratize?' (Sorensen, 1993: 41). Samuel Huntington has recently reiterated the view that 'the preferable overall process of development for a country is first to define its national identity, next to develop effective institutions of authority, and then to expand political participation' (Huntington, 1984: 211). But the idea of 'nation before democracy' is not just an assertion or a preference with a long pedigree; it has been developed in a series of arguments which may be briefly outlined.

1   The Plural Society Argument

The observation that ethnic attachments sometimes manifest themselves in the form of mass irrationality directed against 'enemies' identified solely by their different language, religion or physiognomy, has engendered the argument that the ethnic bond must be an irrational manifestation of a genetic or instinctual attribute; or at least a primary emotional tie to the kin, the homeland and the 'way of life' into which individuals are born and from which they can never, without grave damage, escape. If ethnicity were indeed such a primordial bond, then a multi-ethnic society would necessarily constitute a 'plural society' in which the constituent ethnic communities, each ethnocentrically defending its distinctive values and lifestyles, 'meet but do not mix'. Such a society would clearly lack the 'normative consensus' necessary for the democratic politics of tolerant consent, and so must, perforce, be held together by some kind of force. This argument, formulated with varying degrees of sophistication, has been repeatedly attacked for its intellectual shallowness and ambiguities, but it survives intact, not least because it appears to fit at least some of the facts.

2   The Modernization–National Integration Argument

For the mainstream of nineteenth century European nationalists, the shift from empire to nation-state was proclaimed, not as an end in itself, but rather as a first step towards a liberation from oppression which would culminate in democracy. To be sure, there could be nations which were absolutist and authoritarian, but there could not be democracies which were not nations. This strand of European nationalism was elevated into a theoretical assumption by the modernization school of the 1960s. Leonard Binder, Rupert Emerson, Eric Nordlinger and Dankwart Rustow, among others, argued that democratization was most likely to succeed in those cases where the first phase, the precondition for subsequent phases, was the establishment of a sense of national political identity which could be 'accepted as unchangeable for the future' (Rustow, 1967: 125). The American modernization theorists of the 1960s suggested, in various formulations, that the modernization process implied progress towards national integration, either as the 'melting pot' consequence of increased interactions, or via a state-directed 'nation-building' programme. The nation thus developed as a political community conscious of itself as a 'people' with their own linguistic, religious, cultural, political and historical commonalities and distinctiveness (Alter, 1989: 19). The equal citizenship rights inherent in this idea of political community provided the basis for democratic procedures, and its cultural commonalities provided the basis for democratic discourse. This argument has survived the partial eclipse of modernization theories both as the implicit basis for the 'civil society' intrinsic to recent discussions of democratization (Held, 1989: 286), and also in the frequent protestations by authoritarian rulers in 'new states' that much as they admire and aspire to democracy, it must be delayed, since their societies, unfortunately, are not yet sufficiently modernized to possess the precondition of nationhood.

3 The Consociational Prescription

At first glance, the consociational argument seems to assert that, after all, ethnic pluralism and democracy might be compatible. It does this by redefining democracy as government by a power-sharing coalition of ethnic elites, rather than as a system of competitive majority rule which would merely lead to dictatorship by the largest ethnic segment. However, both on the grounds of its track record (which must include Yugoslavia and the Lebanon) and on theoretical grounds, the consociational argument in many respects reinforces assumptions as to ethnic pluralism's inhospitability towards democracy. Even Lijphart, the main proponent of consociational democracy, accepts that it is elitist, that it is prone to immobilism and the destabilizing politics of outbidding and, most worryingly, that it is a form of government which may encourage secession (Lijphart, 1977). It seems to promise a just basis for government, but it is in part its very promise of an institutionalized fair political balance which makes it so inherently fragile. By institutionalizing ethnic claims it ensures that politics focuses on disagreement as to competing criteria for 'fair' political allocations. Since there can be no objectively neutral criterion, consociationalism engenders either the authoritarian assertion of one criterion, or the rejection, by a weaker segment, of the 'unfair' rules of the game. If even the limited consociational form of democracy is so unstable, then the prospects for democracy in societies lacking political and cultural nationhood seems bleak indeed.

4 The Nation as the Garrison Under Siege

The above arguments thus combine to indicate that effective democratization cannot be attained in the absence of the nation. Accordingly they have been repeatedly quoted by rulers seeking justification for their policies of exclusion and suppression. They are, however, frequently supplemented by a fourth argument in which the absence of an ethnic basis for national unity, and therefore for democracy, combine with the presence of an external threat, so as to generate the perception of a society in crisis, which can survive only on the basis of unquestioning allegiance to the incumbent authoritarian regime and leader.

The authoritarian leader of the ethnically plural society is faced with an apparent dilemma. He needs to deny the existence of 'the nation' in order to justify his suppression of democracy; but on the other hand he can command allegiance only if he can claim to be the father figure or the saviour of the whole community – 'the nation'. The problem is resolved if he can define the nation in reactive, rather than interactive, terms. If he dramatizes the existence of an external enemy against which the garrison under siege must, under its incumbent commander, unite, then the articulation of internal ethnic divisions can be immediately condemned as subversive of national defence, and branded with appropriate epithets – tribalism, ethnic chauvinism, sectarianism or communalism. This is why 'the efficacy of [nationalism] as a basis for non-democratic rule . . . depends in large part on the existence of a credible enemy to the national aspirations of the people' (Huntington, 1991: 46). Each country does of course face its own particular constellation of enemies and threats, but for all developing countries, the twin enemies of neocolonialism and communism could almost always be cited during the cold war era, to provide the necessary justifications for authoritarian rule. Internal disunity, and specifically the spectre of ethnic chaos, become, in such circumstances, the 'fifth column'; so that authoritarianism becomes directed internally, as the suppression of ethnic politics, rather than externally, as aggression against the 'enemy'.

These various models of the 'non-nation', characterized by ethnic cleavages, lack of national integration, the impossibility of institutionalizing a fair consociational balance, and the depiction of a society in crisis, have combined to generate the conventional wisdom that democracy without nationhood is impossible. When this argument is applied to Asia – in particular to the newly industrializing countries of Taiwan, South Korea, Thailand, Malaysia, Singapore and Indonesia – its message is clear. While the socio-economic theories of political change suggest that such industrialization promotes democratization, the ambiguities in their national identities pose a problem. As has been frequently noted, the impact of colonialism on Asia was to create states rather than nations; countries which either because of ethnic bifurcation or ethnic pluralism, had to be held together more by the strength of the state apparatus than by any strong national consciousness (Tinker, 1981). If democratization were to be attempted from such a base, then it would presumably be incomplete and fragile, and would revert to some form of authoritarianism. Moreover, if national identity is indeed a precondition for democratization, then democratization could not itself be successfully employed as a means of nation-building.

But the facts no longer seem to fit the theory. Democratization *has* occurred in South Korea and Taiwan. It has begun in Thailand, and there are various signs of incipient democratization in Malaysia, Singapore and Indonesia; and in all these latter cases it no longer seems to be the ambiguities of national identity which are impeding the process, indeed they may be promoting it.

The phenomenon of the East and Southeast Asian NICs, indeed, demands a reassessment of many of our preconceptions. Taiwan, South Korea, Thailand, Malaysia, Singapore and Indonesia appear increasingly to be out of step with the rest of the world. Instead of economic stagnation, they are experiencing rapid and sustained economic growth; instead of joining Francis Fukuyama's wagon train towards liberal democracy, they assert their own 'strong state' variant – Asian democracy; and instead of indulging in introverted discussions of cultural decline, they are aggressively asserting the superiority of their own 'Asian values'.

A similar disjunction is developing as regards the politics of ethnicity. The recent ethnic conflicts in Europe and Africa have reinforced the view that ethnicity constitutes an intrinsic threat to political stability and democracy. But the Asian NICs are remarkable in that they have experienced prolonged inter-ethnic harmony. Since these states, which have clearly not resolved the tensions between their ethnic and national identities, have sustained political stability and are experiencing a form of democratization, there is perhaps a need to rethink the conventional understanding that nationhood must precede democratization. The purpose here is to point attention to the current renegotiations of ethnic and national identities in East and Southeast Asia, and to suggest that the ambiguities of national identity might be facilitating democratization. This leads to a further suggestion, that the democratic politics of ethnic renegotiation may indeed look significantly different from the democratic politics of liberal pluralism.

THE NATURE OF ASIAN DEMOCRATIZATION

If we are to move towards a distinction between liberal democracy and the democracy of ethnic accommodation, we must begin by examining the process of democratization, and its relationship to national identity. The democratization process is frequently depicted as a causal change in the power relationship between state and civil society. The assumption, derived from western experience, is that this relationship can be described in 'see-saw' terms, such that a strengthening of civil society implies a corresponding 'weakening' of the state. The argument is that the industrialization process engenders a strengthening and pluralization of civil society 'pressures', which weaken the previously strong authoritarian state – causing it to become less autonomous and more responsive; so that the pluralization of civil society, and the associated liberalization of the culture, come to be reflected in the emergence of pluralistic liberal democracy.

If this model of democratization were to be applied to the East and Southeast Asian NICs, it produces a puzzle, in that Asian democratization seems to be accompanied neither by the weakening of the state nor by liberalism. It seems likely that the ability of the KMT, DLP, UMNO, PAP and Golkar to remain in power is not explainable simply by the assertion that we have not yet reached the impending democratic high tide; but paradoxically denotes the possibility that Asian democratization might refer to the strengthening of the fragile authoritarian state, rather than to any weakening of the strong authoritarian state.

It is not being denied here that civil society may expand as industrialization progresses; but it is suggested that the civil society may in some respects support authoritarianism and in others support democratization, may in some respects depend on the strong state and in others may desire autonomy from a weaker state. The rise of civil society does not inevitably weaken the state. In this chapter therefore, the core of the democratization process will not be located in a shift in the state–civil-society balance, but rather in changes internal to the state. Specifically, the term refers here to two competing tendencies, which interact in different weightages to produce variations in the manifestations of democratization in each Asian NIC. These are, firstly, the erosion of elite cohesion; and secondly, the shift to a state strategy of resolving the problems of 'the isolation of power' by creating new intermediary linkages with society.

The authoritarian regimes of the Asian NICs in the 1970s were characterized by the autocratic certitude of the strong nationalist leader, the cohesion of his elite, and their consensus as to the imperative goals of political stability, national economic development and anti-communism. The 1980s raised the issue of the impending departure of the strong leader, the potential completion of the stable development goal, and the loss of relevance (apart from in South Korea) of the anti-communism goal. The outcome is the erosion of the cohesion and certitude of the state-elites, and thence the decline of the moral authority of the autocratic regimes. It has been reflected most obviously in the increased elite factionalism within the governing regimes and parties, and in the elite defections to new competing parties.

Given the personalization of power in Asian cultures, this growth of elite factionalism is reflected in the personal clientelist basis for much of the electoral and political participation. Moreover, it signifies that the politics of democratization is not so much a move to replace the rule of men by the rule of law; but more a search for a new generation of virtuous men, who can restore the absolutist certitudes which constitute the goal of Asian politics by employing managerial, rather than coercive or charismatic, means.

The politics of elite factionalism generated by the succession problem thus coexist, in each of the Asian NICs, with the deliberate efforts by the dominant factions in the regime to strengthen their position by managerial strategies of accommodation and cooptation. The inherent weakness of the authoritarian regimes lay in their tendency, periodically, to expose the coerciveness and arbitrariness of state power. The Asian conception of power is not just as a personal attribute, but also as the ability to create the illusion of harmony and consensus. This goal can be promoted by the deployment of the language and many of the procedures of democracy. Concessions and consultations, and the legitimation derived from constitutionalism, can each promote the strength of state power. It is true that there are some features of democracy – most notably the open voting – which threaten to expose and indeed to exacerbate the divisions which it is the purpose of power to hide. But even here, the language of democracy allows the majority to proclaim itself as the legitimate 'middle ground', or as the incipient general will.

In general then, democratization is not understood here as referring to the inevitable shift in the state-civil society balance brought about by the industrialization and modernization processes; and it does not imply any necessary movement towards political and cultural liberalism. It refers instead to the growth of debate and factionalism within the state elites, and to the concern to prevent any consequent weakening of the state by employing strategies to create new intermediations with society. Clearly there is a tension between these two facets of democratization, in that the more evident the factionalization of the elites, the less coherent and comprehensive is the inclusionary cooptation strategy likely to be. Moreover, the adoption of the democratizing strategy, proclaimed as a new and distinctive 'Asian Democracy' claiming superiority over its Western variant, serves to counteract the elite uncertainties and doubts which gave rise to it.

Thus the extent and the features of democratization vary from country to country. Nevertheless, we can outline the most frequent manifestations. Firstly, the political influence of the military is eroded, in line with the shift from autocratic and coercive rule, towards conciliation. This appears to be happening most clearly in Thailand, South Korea and Indonesia. Secondly, the unity of the dominant party is eroded, and its electoral majority declines as a result of the mobilization activities of disaffected elites. This has occurred in varying degrees. Support for Taiwan's KMT fell from 79 per cent in 1975 to 47.3 per cent in November 1993; support for Malaysia's Barisan went from 60 per cent in 1982 to 53 per cent in 1990, Singapore's PAP went from 76 per cent in 1980 to 61 per cent in 1991, and even Indonesia's Golkar went from 73 per cent in 1987 to 68 per cent in 1992.

Thirdly, there occurs the opening up by the state of fora for public political discussion on a widening range of issues. One of these issues being that of national identity. The issue of the relationship between national identity and democratization is particularly salient in the Asian context because of the oft-noted claim that Asian democratization is distinctively communitarian in character. If Asian democracy gives priority to communal allegiance over individual autonomy, then the question of which community the citizen owes allegiance to, would seem to be of prime political importance. After all, in a liberal-democracy it is not really 'the people' who govern, but rather the competing individuals and the contending pluralistic interest groups. A communitarian democracy however, practices 'the politics of the common good' (Kymlicka, 1990: 206) and so must seek to define itself in terms of the specifics of the 'way of life' of a particular community, so that the democratic legitimacy of the state must rest, presumably, on the way in which it manages the debate as to the identity of that community. In this context then, the authoritarian regime is one which seeks to impose unilaterally a definition of the national community; while the democratic regime in one which opens up societal debate on this issue.

The governing regimes of East and Southeast Asia varied significantly prior to the mid-1980s, both over time and in comparison with each other; but recognition of such variations is not impaired by their designation as authoritarian. As has been frequently noted, the states differed greatly in their degree of 'hardness', 'softness' (Chalmers Johnson, 1987), 'strength' and 'weakness' (Buzan, 1983) depending, in part, on whether the regimes were elected or unelected, military or civilian, coercive or bureaucratic. The concept of authoritarianism is a broad one, but not thereby a particularly loose one. The defining characteristic of the authoritarian state is its unresponsiveness to societal pressures. Thus the term connotes a regime which has high autonomy in that its policy making process is autocratic; and also one whose legitimacy claim rests on some assertion of 'expertise' (traditional, regulatory, or technocratic), rather than on any claim to be representative. It would be rather surprising then, if such an authoritarian regime were to derive its depiction of the national identity, in a responsive way, from the actual contemporaneous values and perceptions of its citizens. Rather than soliciting the views of its citizens, we would expect such a regime unilaterally to assert a national ideology which it considered to be conducive to its own dominance. But the assertion of such a national identity by the state-elites does not indicate the emergence of national consciousness among the society; indeed it might be designed precisely to pre-empt any such development.

THE AMBIGUITIES OF NATIONAL IDENTITY

The states of East and Southeast Asia were each formed in circumstances which posed dilemmas of one kind or another as to their national identity, but these dilemmas remained unresolved (frozen or cemented) under the authoritarian regimes of the 1970s. Firstly, the state-elites' assertions that the national identity was unproblematic and cohesive served to inhibit the kind of societal dialogues which might have allowed the ambiguities as to national identity to be resolved. Secondly, the state's unilateral assertions of national identity themselves each contained an inherent ambiguity. They purported to define the national community in terms of common allegiance to clearly demarcated cultural attributes; but since these cultural attributes were not in fact uniquely shared by the populace, national cohesion was generated only reactively – by assertions of the imperative of national unity against a proclaimed threat or enemy. Both these aspects of the 'pre-democratization' national identity need to be explored.

The ambiguities of national identity in East and Southeast Asia arose not so much from the issue of territorial state boundaries as from the character of the community inhabiting those boundaries; should it be identified in terms of equal citizenship rights, or in terms of the culture of a core ethnic community?

In the first formulation – the political nation – the state claims that its people constitute a nation because they have willingly come together to form a community of equal citizens irrespective of their racial, religious or linguistic backgrounds. Such a formulation of a political nation might seem to be particularly appropriate for societies which contain several ethnically conscious cultural communities. It would seem to imply, most clearly, a depiction of the nation as an overarching ethnically-neutral community in which ethnicity is regarded as politically irrelevant to the national politics of the meritocratic, democratic or universalistic procedures which are employed to define citizenship rights.

The alternative formulation of the nation is as the cultural nation; the community which constitutes a distinct people with its own language, way of life, history and homeland. The claim to cultural nationhood allows the state to demand the allegiance of its people in ways which echo the imperative of ethnic loyalty. The more that the state can point to, or itself generate, the commonalities of language, religion or (fictive) ancestry which define the cultural nation, the more claim it has to the allegiance of its members. Similarly, the more clearly an individual possesses these cultural attributes defining the national community, the more fully does that individual deserve the citizenship rights accruing to membership of the nation. Thus the depiction of the society as a cultural nation implies, in a multi-ethnic society, the prioritizing of one ethnic segment over the others. In its extreme form this emerges in the 'ethnocratic' state which defines national identity specifically in terms of the cultural values and attributes of one dominant ethnic segment, facing the other ethnic groups with the options only of assimilation or marginalization.

Each of the East and Southeast Asian societies (excluding Singapore) can derive, from their pre-colonial history, an image of a set of dominant cultural attributes and values which may be employed to form the core for the definition of contemporary nationhood. The culturally plural society can thus be portrayed as one which is potentially culturally homogeneous in that it already has a cultural core around which nationhood can develop.

The tensions between political and cultural bases for national identity were inherent in the circumstances of state formation in East and Southeast Asia, and remained unresolved under authoritarian regimes determined to inhibit debate and disagreement on such fundamental issues. The East Asian states of Taiwan and South Korea are sometimes likened to Japan, in being remarkably ethnically homogeneous, and therefore lacking any significant national identity problems; whereas the ambiguities of national identity in the multi-racial countries of Southeast Asia, are often much more readily admitted (and indeed tend to be exaggerated by assumptions of primordial racial antipathies). But to accept that South Korea has an unproblematical pan-Korean identity, and that Taiwan has an unproblematical pan-Chinese identity, involves both an uncritical acceptance of the authoritarian regimes' formulations, and a neglect of the impact of the unification issue in generating dilemmas of national identity.

In pre-1947 Taiwan, 'there was probably not much sense . . . of any specifically Taiwanese identity. If people thought about it at all, most would probably have identified themselves as Chinese' (Moody, 1992: 39). But this weak sense of pan-Chineseness was ruptured by the 1947 confrontations between the native Taiwanese and the Mainlander KMT troops. Thereafter, the central ambiguity of Taiwanese national identity has been that of how to relate a pan-Chinese sense of unity with the Mandarin-speaking mainland, a sense of cultural Hokkien-speaking identity *vis-à-vis* the Mainlander 'other', and a Taiwanese political identity which could accommodate both the Mainlander 20 per cent and the 'indigenous' Taiwanese 80 per cent. Should its national identity be focused on the KMT's 'founding myth' of pan-Chineseness, or on the realities of *de facto* independence and cultural pluralism and bifurcation?

In the South Korean case, the ethnic homogeneity of the populace and their commitment to the ideal of unification, have sometimes detracted attention from the fact that this is the classic case, in Asia, of unresolved nationhood. The 'nation before democracy' argument does not say merely that the aspiration for nationhood should precede democratization; it postulates rather that there can be no democracy until the resolution and attainment of the nation.

South Korea was created both as a divided nation and as a client-state of the USA, so that its national identity was problematical at the outset. The continuation of the North-South division has generated real doubts as to the nature of South Korean identity, in that South Koreans may be united as to the desirability of unification with a non-communist North; but so long as the North remains communist, they are faced with an unresolved dilemma of how to reconcile the depiction of North Koreans as both the alien communist enemy, and also as their co-ethnic brothers. The question as to whether unification with a bankrupt communist north would destroy the prosperity and culture of the South, or would promote the fulfillment of the South's destiny as the true inheritor of pan-Korean identity – is not merely a foreign policy problem, or a question of timing and tactics; but one which goes to the heart of the 'who are we' question. The dilemma has been sustained, not resolved, by political regimes whose legitimacy was overtly based on the 'Unification' goal, but who practised a politics based on 'two-Koreas', 'go-it-alone' policies.

The Southeast Asian dilemmas were somewhat different in that they arose primarily from ethnic pluralism. In the Malaysian case, the attempt to forge a political nation of equal citizens – in the 1945 Malayan Union scheme, had given way to the Malayan/Malaysian Federation which was based on an incoherent compromise which defined Malaya neither culturally as an unambiguous Malay homeland, nor politically as a Malayan nation. As Araffin Omar has recently noted,

> The failure to evolve a nationality that was acceptable to all was evident in the creation of the Persekutuan Tanah Melayu (Federation of Malaya) which gave citizenship rights to the non-Malays but denied them a nationality. For Malays and non-Malays alike, the federation perpetuated a sense of ethnic consciousness as it did not lead to a common identity for all. (Araffin, 1993: 121–2)

For Singapore, the problem was that the multiracialism of its population and its geopolitical position as a predominantly Chinese island in a predominantly Malay region both implied the need for a new national identity based on ethnically neutral, meritocratic principles of political nationalism. But the absence of any precolonial history deprived it of any unifying historical symbols around which this could be built, other than Western ones relating to its English language, its colonial heritage, or its capitalist endeavour. The weakness of the resultant national identity arose both from this lack of unifying myths and symbols, and also from the failure to tackle the crucial question as to how the depoliticization of ethnic identities could be combined (in the absence of a cultural assimilation policy), with the attainment of a politicized national consciousness.

For Indonesia, the sense of national cohesion which was generated by confrontation with the Dutch, was vitiated at the outset by squabbles for governmental power among elite groups with competing notions of national identity. In 1945 Sukarno and Hatta had sought to build a bridge between the 'santri' Muslims who envisaged themselves as leaders of an Islamic Indonesia, and the 'abangans' who envisaged a more pluralistic and secular basis for the nation. The Pancasila formulation sought to define a nationalist 'umbrella' under which all who accepted belief in one deity could come together. But it was never fully successful in resolving the ambiguities and tensions of Indonesian national identity. Between 1945 and 1953, there was indeed some articulation of the competing views; but from 1953 onwards – when Sukarno made his Umuntai speech which depicted the unity of a Pancasila Indonesia as under threat from those espousing 'a state based on Islam' – any concern to debate and resolve the ambiguities in the Pancasila 'unity in diversity' formula gave way to the concern to restrict such debate by moving towards increasingly authoritarian controls. Beneath the assertions that Indonesia was united by the Pancasila formulation, lay the unresolved ambiguities and tensions as to the political role of Islam in an Indonesia which is not an Islamic state, but which is 90 per cent Muslim in its composition.

In the case of Thailand, the shift by the state from the pre-1939 'Siam' designation to the name 'Thailand' had signified a problematical attempt to move from an absolutist monarchy with only intermittent control over its peripheral regions, to a nation-state which would assimilate the Chinese, the Malays, the hilltribes and the Lao, into a Central Thai national identity. But this merely highlighted the incongruence between the nation as defined by its territorial borders, and the nation as defined in ethnic-cultural terms. This incongruence was potentially resolvable if cultural assimilation could be achieved, but since the state lacked the capacity to effect such assimilation, the incongruence was intensified.

In each country therefore, the circumstances of state formation implied inherent ambiguities of national identity. But the incumbent authoritarian state-elites had, by and large, no intention of responding to such societal concerns, both because of their general authoritarian stance of promoting depoliticization and departicipation, and also because of their particular concern with legitimating themselves as the managers of a distinct and consensual national community, whose problematical and ambiguous identity could therefore not be admitted or debated.

Their solution was to identify an external 'enemy', most notably the communist threat; but they all also raised the spectre of an internal vulnerability which, they argued, made unity behind their regimes an imperative. They argued that anyone who questioned their definitions of national identity by raising alternative formulations of the relationship between the *ethnie* and the nation, constituted a subversive threat to the state. They then used this as a blanket excuse whereby to justify authoritarian rule and suppress calls for democratization. In the 1970s, the various governments did not have to make up the 'threats' to the unity and stability of the society. But it was not the objective existence of such threats which itself spontaneously generated a sense of national identity. Rather, it was the skillful deployment and exaggeration of these threats by incumbent regimes, in order to impose a state-defined national unity, which served to pre-empt and inhibit the emergence of national consciousness. They thus made use of the 'nation before democracy' argument to try to prevent democratization; but this strategy was only ever partially and temporarily effective.

This garrison nationalism was deployed in diverse ways. In Thailand, the image of the communist menace was used as the main basis for pre-empting popular debate on the nature of Thailand's national identity during the 1970s. In the process, the involvement of Thai insurgents was conveniently ignored, so that anti-communism could provide the basis for mobilizing a reactive national political unity behind the bureaucratic regimes. As Chai-anan has noted:

The Thais must unite themselves . . . in order to ensure their own survival against the Chinese and the un-Thai activities of the communists . . . . communists . . . were either Vietnamese, Chinese, or Northeastern Lao, but never 'Thai'. Communism as an ideology has been regarded as a totally un-Thai enterprise, a negation of the livelihood, history and civilization of the Thai race. (Chai-anan, 1991: 72–3)[2]

In the case of Singapore, the PAP regime sought, with particular intensity during the early 1970s, to compensate for the lack of any clear national identity through the assertion of an 'ideology of survivalism', which demanded national unity and political acquiescence as the only way to overcome Singapore's vulnerability as a small, fragile resourceless island besieged by the dangers of international communism, regional uncertainty, primordial ethnicity, and the cycles of international capitalism. It was the assertion of these threats which demanded the reaction of 'survivalism'; and it was the assertion of 'survivalism' which provided the ideological basis for the surrogate national unity of the Singapore garrison.

The Barisan regime in Malaysia, for its part, sought to paper over the ambiguities and tensions of Malaysian national identity by employing the 'spectre of May 13th', the 1969 ethnic riots, as the ever-present threat which demanded national unity. By directing attention to this threat, the post-1970 authoritarian regimes could pursue the otherwise divisive pro-Bumiputra policies upon which their position depended.

In Indonesia, communism was the focus of siege nationalism in the mid-1960s, and after the 1965 coup Golkar was formed to mobilize support for the new regime on an anti-communist basis. But from the early 1970s onwards, Golkar increasingly became a means for mobilizing support by depicting political Islam as the threat to national unity. By the late 1970s there was a distinct intensification by Suharto's New Order government in its employment of the Pancasila national ideology as a means to marginalise Islamic activists (Suryadinata, 1989: 106). Devout Muslims were accused of trying to change Indonesia into an Islamic state community, and the 1984 imposition of Pancasila as the only state ideology was widely interpreted as a confrontationalist gesture; signifying that the PPP and Islamic identity were now being defined as not fully compatible with Indonesian national identity; and therefore as a threat against which all loyal Indonesians could unite, under the Pancasila and Golkar umbrella.

It was however the garrison nationalisms of the South Korean and Taiwanese governments which were the most dramatic. This was not of itself due to the immediate and direct nature of the perceived threats – the prospect of invasion from, respectively, North Korea and mainland China. Rather it was due to the crises of low legitimacy and support facing the authoritarian regimes of Park Chung Hee's 'Yushin system' and of Chun Doo Hwan in South Korea; and the KMT regimes of Chiang Kai Shek and Chiang Ching Kuo in Taiwan.

In the Taiwan case, the actual risk of invasion was significant only in the 1950s and 60s. With Chiang Ching Kuo's accession to the Presidency in 1978, the PRC's shift towards a policy of peaceful unification with Taiwan in late 1978, and the breaking of relations with the USA in 1979 (Hung-ma Tien, 1992: 240), the invasion threat lessened. But the KMT, factionalized by the impending succession problem, continued to employ the communist threat to justify the repression of opposition and criticism on the grounds that: 'It is necessary to maintain the fictitious notion that we could experience invasion from the mainlanders because it serves as propaganda that the people can rally behind' (ROC official, 1988).

In the South Korean case, President Park, faced with growing unrest and opposition, proclaimed a 'national emergency' in December 1971, asserting that P'yongyang's preparations for invasion, and communist infiltration in the south, necessitated suppression of 'all social unrest' on grounds of 'national security' (Koon Woo Nam, 1989: 54). Opponents of the regimes who demanded democratic rights, and all those who demanded real efforts at unification, were branded as pro-communist agitators, subversive of national unity (Won Mo Dong, 1988: 173).

Park subsequently initiated unification talks with the North so as to try to generate the legitimacy which adhered to the 'unification' myth; but this initiative was accompanied by actions which guaranteed the failure of the talks, and which identified the North as the culprit (Kay-Kyo Sohm, 1989: 53, 54). Thus, in a confrontational atmosphere, the talks 'were themselves used by Park as a rationale for cracking down on dissidents and tightening up political control, claiming that such measures were needed to conduct the dialogue from a position of strength and internal cohesion' (Koon Woo Nam, 1989: 61).

Given the questionable status of the claims to democratic legitimacy of both the South Korean and the Taiwanese regimes, they were committed by the nature of their origins to try to legitimate themselves by reference to the goal of pan-ethnic unification. However, since in each case this goal was impossible to attain, legitimacy could only be pursued by dramatizing the *obstacles* to unification. If they could generate a siege mentality by dramatizing the threat of invasion, then this would legitimate the regimes as the only available defence. The assertion of the imperative of internal unity as a defence against the aggressor provided a justification for the suppression of public political debate about the real issues of national political identity.

The authoritarian state strategy towards national unity, of each of these regimes, was thus a problematical one, in that it relied on the assertion of inherently ambiguous formulations of national identity, and depended upon the maintenance of a siege mentality. So long as authoritarianism persisted, so did the ambiguity and vacuousness of the national identity formulas. But these very incoherences of national identity contributed, in turn, to the weakening of the legitimacy and autonomy of the authoritarian regimes.

There were three main reasons for the declining utility of the garrison nationalism strategy of denying debate on the national identity issue and suppressing calls for democratization. Firstly, the very success of these regimes in maintaining political stability and ethnic harmony, bred a complacency which progressively undermined belief in the spectre of ethnic unrest. Secondly, the repeated deployment of the threat, and its crude overuse to suppress democratic debate, exposed it as a manipulative strategy and undermined its credibility. Thirdly, the more the authoritarian regimes denied and distanced themselves from the doubts and anxieties as to their political and cultural identity, and papered over the cracks in their asserted definitions of the nation, the more they added to their isolation of power, and fuelled the growing intra-elite doubts as to the direction of their nation-building goals.

Thus the strategy of denying the ambiguities of national identity by the assertion of a garrison national identity was one which could not be sustained. As its utility declined, the authoritarian regimes began to shift strategies; instead of denying and excluding debate on the national identity issue, they began to try to accommodate and manage it.

DEMOCRATIZATION AND NATIONAL IDENTITY

The most crucial aspect of democratization is the opening up of political debate, beyond the confines of the state elites, which follows from the growth of regime factionalism and the employment of inclusionary cooptation and accommodationist strategies. It is thus not the institution of competitive elections which defines democracy, but the extent and range of political debate which underlies this competition. The extent and rapidity of democratization has been dramatic in Taiwan and South Korea, but is much weaker in Southeast Asia. In part this is because the military basis of the Taiwanese and South Korean regimes made them much more vulnerable to charges of being undemocratic than did the overtly constitutional and elected regimes of, most clearly, Malaysia and Singapore. Partly also, the continuation of authoritarian politics in Southeast Asia merely reflects the fact that they have not yet had to face up to the final departure of the autocratic rulers who provide the patrimonial and paternalistic focus for their authoritarian regimes. But even in Southeast Asia, the erosion of authoritarian cohesion and certitude has impelled incumbent regimes to seek new managerial strategies to conciliate or coopt those societal interests which appear not directly to threaten their own power and legitimacy. This was recently exemplified in the Suharto government's capitulation to Islamic demands for the abandonment of the state lottery. It should be noted however, on the other hand, that the loss of elite certitude and self-confidence also implied that the state-elites have often been insecure and in some cases perhaps paranoid, as regards any interests which cannot be fitted within prevailing ideological boundaries. In this respect, the democratization process is always likely to be characterized by outbursts of authoritarian repression. But even such outbursts might serve to promote ethnic accommodation. Thus Mahathir's recent 'undemocratic' maneuverings to replace the newly elected opposition PBS government in Sabah has probably ended the exclusion of the Kadazan community by coopting them.

But even were 'democratization' to be merely a new state ideology, it necessarily opens up political debate, since the critics of the regime can also appeal to the ideals and ideas of democracy to facilitate their demands for access to state power. Societal groups do not discuss those issues about which there is agreement among themselves and with the state-elites; it is disagreement, not agreement, which generates discussion. If it is factional elite rivalries which constitute the fundamental 'engine' of democratization; it is the ambiguities as to national identity which comprise the main 'fuel'; the political issue which translates intra-elite dissensus into societal discourse.

The ambiguities of national identity fuel the democratization process in the Asian NICs in four respects. Firstly, the national identity issue become the major focus for the democratizing political contention because of the absence of other ideological disagreements. In the European experience, democratization had involved confrontations between a dominant class (classically the landowning aristocracy) and the emergent bourgeoisie and proletariat classes. Each class had distinct and divergent interests, cultures and political goals, and they articulated these in the distinctive ideologies of conservatism, liberalism and socialism; so that the politics of democratization took the form of a political debate between competing ideologies. By contrast, one of the distinctive features of Asian democratization is that it involves contestation between emergent societal interest groups which are predominantly middle class, and regimes whose developmental policies serve primarily middle class interests and whose elites are themselves identified with or predominantly recruited from the middle classes. The contending groups disagree, in some cases bitterly, about the distribution of political power, whether it should be monopolized by the state bureaucracy segment of the middle class, or dispersed. They disagree, in other words, about the desirability of democracy. But there is remarkably little ideological disagreement as to the normative goals of power – the main consensual goal being that of export-oriented industrial development. In the absence of such ideological disagreement, the politics of democratization is focused upon competing formulations of national identity; since the alternative answers to the 'who are we?' question have direct implications for the relative power and status of the different groups in society.

The expansion of the middle classes means that professionals and entrepreneurs who are not part of the state sector, begin to seek access to the resources of the state hitherto monopolized by the state bureaucratic bourgeoisies. Those sections of this excluded middle class who do not possess, or do not fully possess, the attributes of cultural nationalism, and who thereby are in some sense of lower status than those who possess the prescribed cultural attributes, can demand a reformulation of the cultural basis for national identity, or can appeal to the image of the political nation which gives equal citizenship status and rights to all. The political implication of this is that such culturally marginalised segments of the new middle classes might become the main articulators of calls for democratization through their desire for a change in the characterization of the nation towards a 'political community' formulation, or towards a shift in the 'cultural community' definition. The paradigmatic case here is clearly that of Taiwan, where claims by Taiwanese middle class groups for a share of the state power monopolized by the Mainlander state-elites, were articulated and legitimated in terms of the Taiwanization of the country's politics and culture.

The second way in which the national identity issue propels the democratization process, arises out of the eroding credibility of both the ethnic and the communist threats postulated by garrison nationalism. In Singapore and Malaysia for example, the facts of political stability and economic development undermined the regimes' depiction of the society in terms of incipient collapse, crisis, danger and fragility. In Thailand and Taiwan particularly, the decline of communism undermined any attempt to sustain an image of it as an inherently expansionist and subversive threat.

The erosion of garrison nationalism necessarily directs attention to both the fragility and the ambiguities of national identity, in that it raises the question – 'What else holds us together apart from a common enemy?' As authoritarian state-elites become aware of the declining credibility of their garrison nationalism, they may try to inhibit the opening up of debate either by trying to revive the garrison nationalism – finding new enemies and threats (as with Mahathir's attacks on the West over the Keating affair in later 1993, and the Pergau dam affair in 1994); or they may try to compensate by putting more effort into defining a non-reactive national identity, as with the Singapore regime's attempt to define Singaporean-ness in terms of an 'Asian values' ideology in 1988–9. But the very act of trying to articulate a new focus for national identity, one that differs from the focus which has been asserted previously by the regime – makes its uncritical acceptance by the populace less likely. The outcome is likely to be the opening up of debate on the national identity issue.

The third link between the national identity issue and the democrat-ization process, is that both aspects of politics are in part responses to the process of socio-economic development. In particular, when such develop-ment implies the emergence of new economic disparities between class, urban-rural, and regional communities within the country, or generates new cultural disparities (between 'traditional' and 'westernized' sections of the populace), it begins potentially to undermine the already fragile sense of national unity, and thus further stimulates attempts to define that unity, either around a core culture, or in political accommodationist terms.

Finally, the national identity issue is politically significant in that it is inter-twined with the problem of leadership succession. Authoritarian rulers frequently legitimate themselves as the 'fathers' or 'saviours' of the nation, in that they claim credit for 'saving' the nation either from colonialism, as with Lee Kuan Yew, or from a trauma deriving from the previous regime, as with Suharto. In terms of political symbolism, the identity of the nation is to some extent manifested and guaranteed in the identity of the leader. Since the present-day successors cannot make any such claim to be the fathers or the saviours of the nation, the debates as to their qualifications for the post necessarily attain a wider significance – as debates on how the nation is now to be depicted and symbolized.

SOUTH KOREA AND TAIWAN

In South Korea and Taiwan, the attempts by the authoritarian regimes to suppress dissent on the national identity issue became progressively ineffective, leading them to move towards accommodation and cooptation strategies. In these countries then, both societal democratic dissent, and state democratic responses, have been directed in large part to the national identity issue.

In the case of South Korea, it has been the unification problem which has provided the focal issue for the politics of democratization. The erosion of legitimacy of the Park and Chun regimes arose in part from their failure to offer a coherent formulation of the nation, other than that of the repeatedly reasserted 'surrogate' garrison nationalism. Their opponents, however, legitimated their demands for democratic reform by articulating a vision of Korean identity which combined political and cultural characterizations, and which was embodied in the *sammin* (three-peoples) ideology combining three principles: *minjung* (the people), *minjok* (the nation), and *minju* (democracy) (Lee, 1990: 7–8). This synthesis of political and cultural nationalism was articulated most vociferously by student groups, and it arose from the development of a new sense of incipient national self-confidence which was specifically South Korean in that it grew out of South Korea's economic development, and it focused on the demand for South Korea to be recognized as an independent political community, based on democratic equal citizenship (Hong Nack Kim, 1988: p. 223).

Prior to the referendum for the new democratic constitution in 1987, and the subsequent accession of Roh Tae Woo, this formulation seemed to indicate a basis for a consensual national identity, since it offered a way of combining the aspiration for South Korean nationalism with the aspiration for pan-Korean unification. It was the very strength and self-confidence of South Korean nationalism which generated the argument that the South could re-absorb the communist North back into its fold, on the South's terms.

But since 1987 this incipient convergence of South Korean political nationalism with pan-Korean cultural nationalism has eroded, and is being replaced by a disagreement between two formulations. One position gives priority to pan-Korean cultural nationalism, and has been articulated in a radical form by dissident students. In a more moderate form it underpinned President Roh's concern, from 1989 onwards, to get immediate rapprochement with the North, culminating in the December 1991 reconciliation pact.

The alternative position gives priority to South Korean political nationalism, and stresses that any common Confucianist heritage of North and South has been seriously weakened by 45 years' experience of contrasting lifestyles and cultures. Unification would cripple the economy and democracy of the South and could only be achieved in the short term by 'selling out' to Kim Il Sung. From this perspective, the Korean Unification goal should be retained for now only as a symbolic myth, since its implementation would only threaten the burgeoning South Korean national identity. It is interesting that Kim Young Sam got elected in early 1993 by using a 'red-scare' tactic against his Democratic party opponent, 'declaring that a vote for Kim Dae Jung was a vote for North Korea's President Kim Il Sung' (Shim Jae Hoon, 1993: 21). The new President is opposed to student demands for progress on unification on the grounds that South Korean development could not survive a German-type reunification, and that 'North Korea is an unpredictable community. You can't trust them' (Kim Young Sam, *Far East Economic Review*, 24 June 1993: 20). Thus the disagreement on the Unification issue reflects an underlying unease as to South Korea's national identity, in which the tensions between South Korean political national identity, and Pan-Korean cultural national identity, are nor resolved, but are becoming more clearly articulated.

In the Taiwanese case, the authoritarian KMT regime had denied 'that there can be any such thing as a Taiwanese as distinct from any other kind of Chinese' (Moody, 1992: 56), and it sought to wipe out any indigenous Taiwanese identity by teaching Mandarin and discouraging the use of Hokkien and Hakka. But this effort at assimilation did not promote assimilation; indeed it seems to have had the reactive effect of promoting a Taiwanese identity directed against the mainlander regime. This took various forms; the use of Hokkien, the revival of Formosan folk religious practices, support for the Christian Presbyterian church which used Hokkien; and increasingly, the advocacy (initially coded) of independence. By the 1980s, it emerged in support for overtly political movements; first the 'Dangwai' (non-KMT) groups, and then in 1986, the formation of the Democratic Progressive Party (DPP).

Democratization thus involved the challenging of the national founding myth of unification, which began to be ignored in practice (both by the regime itself and by opposition groups). Taiwan was increasingly treated as a de facto independent state, and by the late 1980s assertions of an independent Taiwan national identity became explicit. 'Various political movements have in varying degrees challenged the definition of the state in terms of China and Chinese nationalist identity, and have argued for an independent Taiwanese Taiwan'. Increasingly, the regime itself has pragmatically adjusted, and instead of branding such ideas as subversive, it has modified but not abandoned its own founding myth (Huntington, 1992a: xii).

Thus the ambiguities of Taiwan's national identity have been clarified, but not resolved. On the one hand, the KMT, which is over 70 per cent indigenous Taiwanese in its membership and support-base, appears to be shifting from a pan-Chinese assimilationist definition of national identity, towards a more pluralist political definition, in which the term 'Taiwanese' refers equally to all inhabitants, and not just to the non-mainlanders. On the other hand, there are signs that a pan-Chinese assimilation identity is giving way to a 'Taiwanization' cultural identity. Bruce Jacobs recently noted

> the surge of 'Taiwanese consciousness'. Until a few years ago the ruling Kuomintang (KMT) emphasized Taiwan's Chineseness and did not permit the accentuation of Taiwanese culture. Now the publication of thousands of books concerned with Taiwan's politics, history and culture has supplanted the dearth. Similarly, restaurants featuring Taiwanese cuisine flourish while even residents who fled the mainland in 1949 have begun to learn Hokkien – the main Taiwanese dialect. (Jacobs, 1993)

Thus in Taiwan, as in the other countries discussed, it was the unresolved national identity issues which provided much of the impetus and focus for the development of democratic debate. The ensuing political discussion seems to involve the articulation and reformulation of the national identity ambiguities, but not necessarily their resolution.

THE IMPLICATIONS FOR SOUTHEAST ASIA

The assertions by Southeast Asian governments that their authoritarian tendencies have been necessitated by the ethnic pluralism and weak national identity of their societies, has been repeatedly echoed by academics. But such arguments glide too easily from the reasonable assertion that incidents of overt ethnic rebellion or rioting in the 1950s and 1960s provided justifications for anti-democratic government responses; into the far less convincing assertion that resurgences of such ethnic hostility would occur if there were to be more democratization. Indeed it is arguable that ethnic tensions in Southeast Asia have frequently been generated precisely by the authoritarian strategies of the various states (Brown, 1994). There are indeed signs that the authoritarian governments in Southeast Asia have begun to recognize that suppression of ethnic and national identity issues may no longer by the most effective way of dealing with them. While the shift from elite certitude to elite dissensus is not, in Southeast Asia, focused only on the issues of how to deal with ethnic pluralism and national identity, these problems nevertheless play a contributory, rather than an inhibitory role in the ongoing shift from the politics of authoritarian exclusion to the politics of managerial accommodation.

SINGAPORE

The extent of democratization is limited in Singapore, and siege strategies for evoking a garrison form of national unity are still employed intermittently; but the weakness and ambiguities of Singaporean national identity have recently been explored and articulated in public debate, in response to the PAP government's initiative in trying to arrive at a viable cultural definition of the nation based on the 'Asian Values' formula.

This state initiative was an outcome of the assumption by Singapore's leaders, that economic development would lead, by the end of the 1980s, to the growth of a new self-confident middle class who would not easily stomach an autocratic form of government. In order to pre-empt this possibility, the government began moving towards a more inclusionary corporatist form of politics which offered new channels for public debate and discussion, but only within the institutional and ideological boundaries defined by the state-elites. The most visible manifestations of this were the creation of the state-sponsored ethnic organizations, Mendaki, Sinda and the CDAC, for the management of, respectively, Malay, Indian and Chinese interests; and the introduction of the Religious Harmony Act, to define the boundary between politics and religion. Any such inclusionary corporatism presupposed the existence of a consensual corporatist nation. The government was thus impelled to define more clearly the Singaporean national identity so as to establish clear ideological boundaries for the new corporatist politics.

But instead of achieving a new clarity and consensus as to the national identity, the 'Asian Values' initiative, has had the effect of translating the previous ambiguities into a new dissensus. The 'Asian Values' definition of the nation was itself based on an attempt to attenuate and sanitize the cultural values of each component ethnic community in Singapore so as to make them compatible with each other and with the ideological preferences of the governing elite. The previous depoliticization of ethnicity thus gave way to a new politicization in which the approved ethnic interests and values were to be articulated through licensed institutions and within the approved 'Asian values' ideological framework. Instead of being depicted ambiguously as an ethnically-neutral meritocracy, Singapore was now to be defined explicitly in Asian ethnic terms. But such a definition was immediately divisive since it appeared to prioritize Confucianist and

Chinese values over Malay and Indian values; and it dichotomized the 'Asian' and 'Western' values which were so inter-mingled in Singaporean society. Its impact, therefore, has been to stimulate the ongoing and unresolved debate between the merits of an ethnically-neutral political identity, and those of an ethnically-based cultural national identity. The airing of debate and dissensus about this issue is thus one of the key measures of the extent of democratization in Singapore, and the government's partial climb down on the 'Asian values' issue is a key signal of the decline in its hegemonic autonomy.

MALAYSIA

In Malaysia, the extent of democratization is again clearly limited, but is evidenced in the decline of the cohesion and autonomy of the state-elite. The increase in factionalism and disunity within the Barisan, within the Malay community, and within UMNO, does not yet, of itself, constitute democratization; but it does make the development of democratic competition and debate more feasible. Until recently, the ambiguities as to Malaysia's national identity had been camouflaged by the Bumiputra ideology, which asserted as an unquestionable truth that the Malay-Muslims be given priority in political status and in the economic allocations of the NEP. But the progressive erosion of united Malay support for UMNO, and of Chinese acquiescence via the MCA; together with the problematical ending of the NEP and the prospects of economic links with a resurgent China, have prompted new debate as to whether to move away from a Bumiputra priority position, or whether to widen the understanding of Bumiputra to include non-Malays (first the non-Muslim indigenese of Sabah and Sarawak, then the Babba Chinese and the Malaccan Portuguese, then the Chinese). The previously unresolved and largely unarticulated ambiguities as to the relationship between Malay identity and Malaysian identity are thus important bases for the emergent political dissensus in Malaysia. These new debates and uncertainties are epitomized in Anwar Ibrahim's concern to distinguish between a 'narrow, parochial, chauvinistic Malay agenda', and his projected image as a 'new Malay' with a 'national Malay agenda which accepts the new political and economic realities . . . [of] the full participation of the Malays, Chinese, Indians and other communities in the country' (*Far East Economic Review*, 30 September 1993: 20). The airing of these ambiguities constitutes, from the perspective of the opposition DAP, the shift of the government towards 'more liberal and open . . . nation-building policies' (Vatikiotis, 1993a: 32).

THAILAND

In Thailand, the demands for democratization which have periodically erupted among Central Thai students and urban middle-class groups since 1973, have been depicted as arising out of their exclusion from the establishment patronage network which constituted the bureaucratic–military state (Jackson, 1989: 36–8). In this politics, the issue of national identity provoked political dissension in two significant respects. Firstly, it was the pressures towards assimilation into a Central Thai national identity which underlay much of the support for autonomy and communism, during the 1970s and 1980s, among Sino-Thai students, Northern hill-tribes, Pattani Malays and Isan Thai-Laos. Consequently, the democratization process has been punctuated by various calls for administrative devolution, cultural pluralism, and political accommodation, which imply the search for a new, non-ethnocratic, Thailand identity. This implies, as Chai-anan has noted, attempts to define national identity in political, rather than ethnic-cultural terms:

> Political parties, elections and the legislative process . . . provide for new institutional frameworks in which ethnicity is not a factor. In this new political context, the names of political parties which are purely Thai (such as Chart Thai, Prachakorn Thai, Ruam Thai) and have no ethnic connotations serve as a legitimating instrument. (Chai-anan, 1991: 75–6)

But this attempt to reformulate Thailand's national identity in political terms, remains in tension with attempts by democratizing forces to employ new versions of cultural national identity. Thus democratization has involved 'a series of identity crises especially among the younger generation' (Chai-anan, 1991: 74) which have been manifested in various confrontations between establishment and middle class factions articulating divergent interpretations of the Buddhist basis for Thai identity; fundamentally, between the establishment view of Buddhism as legitimating absolutist rule, which survived, until May 1992 at least, in the symbolism of the monarchy; and reformist interpretations which have offered justifications for capitalist enterprise and the democratic decentralization of power. The middle classes have not tried to reject Buddhism as the basis for defining national identity, since no alternative legitimatory symbols have been available to them; rather they have sought to refashion Buddhist principles in ways which modify the character of that national identity:

[Their] efforts to demonstrate Buddhism's scientificity and rationality and its compatibility with Western ideas and practices . . . provide educated and middle class Thais with a means of affirming their cultural and political identity and independence while still accepting foreign ideas and technologies. Consequently the religious rationalism of middle class Buddhism . . . may . . . act as a cultural lubricant for the process of socio-economic change . . . so long as Thais seek to . . . define their national identity in Buddhist terms. (Jackson, 1989: 55–6)

Thus the democratization process in Thailand is characterized by the new expression of divergent characterizations of national identity, in which ideas of political nationality compete with ideas of cultural nationality. The democratization of the state is signalled by its inability, any longer, to impose unilaterally a state-defined national identity upon society. One recent prediction is that the outcome of the democratization process in Thailand will be 'a serious national identity crisis' (Chai-anan, 1991: 82).

INDONESIA

The emergence of major economic problems in the mid-1980s, the prospect of leadership succession, and the lessening of Suharto's control over the military, and also over parliament and the press, all combined to bring about some lessening of authoritarian controls during the late 1980s, and an increase in the responsiveness of the state to societal interests (MacIntyre, 1991: 31–40, 59; Suryadinata, 1989: 153). Thus, as Andrew MacIntyre has noted,

In Indonesia . . . political change is now underway. . . . The tight grip the government has held over political life generally, and the policy-making process in particular, is now showing signs of loosening in some areas. But Indonesia does not appear to be following the paths of . . . other countries. The signs of change which have emerged so far suggest that while there is movement in the direction of a diffusion of power and greater political input by societal groups, Indonesia is unlikely to move far in the direction of liberal democracy for some time. (MacIntyre, 1991: 1)

The unresolved issue of Islam's place in Indonesia's national identity, and thence the uneasy relationship between Islamic groups and Golkar, has impelled political change in a democratizing direction. Having failed to resolve the issue by confrontationist strategies, Suharto has shifted towards a strategy of 'wooing' the Islamic community so as to gain its support (Suryadinata, 1989: 153). This shift of strategy was first evident in the 1984 elections, when Golkar began to adopt Islamic symbols, overtly to show respect to Islamic sensibilities, and to recruit Islamic leaders as activists. This strategy of cooptation was followed in 1990 by Suharto's formation of the Association of Indonesian Muslim Intellectuals (Schwartz, 1993).

It is noticeable that the impact of this Islamization of Indonesian government has not been to generate any consensus as to the political role of Islam in the national identity, but indeed to reopen the disagreements as to that role. This is because Suharto's purpose has been to expand support for his regime by trying to coopt and to depoliticize Islam; bringing it within the Golkar and Pancasila umbrellas. This has only increased the salience of the question as to how to combine the image of Indonesia as a political and pluralistic community, with its Islamic cultural character. A possible resolution of this ambiguity has been suggested by the revival of the Nahdatul Ulama, which is Indonesia's largest Muslim organization and which accepts Islam as being fully compatible with Pancasila, and espouses 'a philosophy of Islam as a pluralistic force which poses no danger to democracy and democratic values' (Schwartz, 1993). But this clashes directly with the depoliticized version of Islam which is being promoted within Golkar; and the unresolved clash between the two was recently symbolized in the attempt by the government to disrupt Nahdatul Ulama's mass rally in March 1992. The tentative opening up of debate as to Islam's place in Indonesian national identity does not offer the promise of consensus, but rather of engagement between proponents of an Islamic state, proponents of pluralistic Islam, and proponents of depoliticized Islam.

CONCLUSIONS

When political scientists asserted that there was a close link between the processes of democratization and the development of a sense of nationhood, they were no doubt correct; but they were perhaps mistaken in erecting some contingencies of European political history into a universifiable theoretical formula. The argument here has been that, in East and Southeast Asia, democratization is proceeding in part because and not despite of, the ambiguities of national identity which inhered in the circumstances of state formation. These ambiguities had been ignored or denied, until the late 1970s, by authoritarian state-elites who sought to inhibit political debate on such contentious issues by their assertion of a reactive garrison national unity. It was the erosion of the cohesion, certitude and autonomy of these authoritarian state regimes and of their garrison nation ideologies, which facilitated the articulation of the national identity ambiguities, and their clarification, through political discourse, into divergent political and cultural characterizations of the nation.

While it is of course possible that the democratization process might generate consensus on this central issue of national identity, it seems more likely that increasingly open debate will simply generate a clarification of the disagreements as to national identity. Democracy, after all, refers not to an end-state of harmonious consensus, but rather to a commitment endlessly to explore disagreements by political means. There are indeed variations as to the centrality of the national identity issue to the causation, content and consequences of democratization, but the discussion has indicated that the formation of the nation might not precede democratization; rather, democratization might be the articulation of the ambiguities of national identity.

The political salience of the national identity issue does have important implications for the character of the emergent democratic politics. Firstly, it ensures that political interests will be clothed in the language of competing communitarian claims; and therefore that the character of democratization differs markedly from a western liberal democratic politics in which demands are clothed primarily in the language of individual rights and interests. It is not that Asians are less selfish or more patriotically or ethnically loyal, merely that their self-interests will only be accepted as valid political claims if they are legitimated in communitarian language.

But there is another, more important, implication. Autocratic regimes have repeatedly justified their authoritarianism, in East Asia as elsewhere, by the argument that ethnic communal loyalties are inherently irrational and absolutist; and therefore incompatible with democracy. The democratization process involves, therefore, the erosion of this view of cultural allegiances. It implies a recognition, by state-elites and by those in civil society, that the disjunction between the claims of political and cultural nationalism can indeed be managed in various ways, and can be so managed either democratically or undemocratically. But it follows from this that the emergent political debate which characterizes democratization, does not involve simply a pluralistic bargaining process. Debates as to the extent of Malay priority in Malaysia, the role of Islam in Indonesia, the relative merits of Hokkien and Mandarin in Taiwan, cannot be conducted as if they were only the bargaining chips of competing interest groups, and resolvable simply by the mobilization of numerical majorities. Competing cultural claims are indeed amenable to debate and discussion, and even reconciliation, but this is so only if it is recognized by all concerned that they involve not assertions of 'absolutist, primordial, inalienable, natural' rights; but rather, that they relate to negotiable historical, social and cultural claims which are resolvable through involvement in what Alasdair MacIntyre calls, 'the conversation between traditions' which relies on and demands that members of each community imaginatively empathize with each other, recognizing and accepting the internal logic of each others values and claims (MacIntyre, 1988: 395).

The argument that democratization necessitates a prior settling of the national identity question had its origin in the liberal view that the democratic state is one which must not impose upon society any particular or partial definition of justice and virtue, but rather seeks to act neutrally and impartially, defending or promoting the rights and arbitrating the interests of differing individuals and groups in society. Such neutral government is possible only when there is broad agreement on the nature of the rights to be defended or promoted, and on the cultural or ideological goals to which the interests are directed.

But the form of democratization being developed in East and Southeast Asia is clearly not a liberal one which focuses on the neutrality of the state. It approximates more to the kind of polity which Sammy Smooha has recently described as 'ethnic democracy', and which combines features of political and cultural nationalism (Smooha, 1990). In such a polity, all individuals enjoy equal citizenship rights irrespective of ethnic origin, but the state is not ethnically or ethically neutral, since it prioritizes the culture of the dominant or core ethnic segment. At the same time however, the state is committed to 'multiculturalism' in that it offers various forms of autonomy or protection to ethnic minorities so as to coopt and accommodate them, rather then subjecting them to exclusion and control. Instead of institutionalizing, and removing from the arena of political debate, any specific formula for the balancing of ethnic representation or allocation, such a state actively facilitates and promotes such debate on ethnic issues. Ethnic debates are not however 'free for alls', since the state must manage the articulation of ethnic claims so as to distinguish those which are political from those which are absolutist.

The implication then is for a shift from autocratic and coercive authoritarianism, towards a form of managerial government in which the procedures of democracy are employed not for the promotion of liberalism; but rather for the managed incorporation and cooptation of competing ethnic claims. There is indeed, therefore, a precondition for democratization in Asia. Not the resolution of the national identity issue; but rather the acceptance, by state-elites as well as by civil society, that national identity claims are a debatable issue. This, however is always problematic in an Asia that fails to recognize the value of debate.

7 Towards a Model of Illiberal Democracy

Jones, Jayasuriya, Bell and Jones

If you diminish the paternal authority, or even if you retrench the ceremonies that express your respect for it, you weaken the reverence due to the magistrates . . . Retrench but one of these habits and you overturn the state. (Montesquieu on China in *The Spirit of the Laws*)

We find it necessary, from time to time, like a good father would, to help members of the family to progress. The West say, 'Why are you interfering?' but we have a different problem and we have to solve it our way. (Goh Chok Tong, Singapore's Prime Minister interviewed by *Le Monde* 19/10/1994)

Enlightenment rationalism has, to a very large degree, shaped our contemporary understanding of democracy and democratization. The key performers in this drama are autonomous social actors who push the state towards democratic forms. The significance of the role played by these social actors varies according to the scriptwriters' modernization or Marxian preference.

A common theme of this work is that the application of this understanding to Pacific Asia is deeply flawed. Indeed, it is not entirely surprising to find that when modernization occurs within particular and contingent historical circumstances, and under the influence of a radically different ethic, it facilitates social, political and economic arrangements vastly different from those intimated by Anglo-American liberalism. What is more disturbing, is how difficult it is both for western trained economists and political scientists to accept this possibility.

The conclusion of this study is that political change in Pacific Asia is likely to lead to a form of illiberal democracy. What then does the model of illiberal government that has developed in Pacific Asia since 1945 involve? In our view there are three distinctive features of East Asian illiberal democracy: first, a non-neutral understanding of the state; second, the evolution of a rationalistic and legalistic technocracy that manages the developing state as a corporate enterprise; finally, the development of a managed rather than a critical public space and civil society.

THE NON-NEUTRAL STATE

Classically, western liberal theory is founded on the assumption that rulers must respect an individual's equal right rationally to choose, enact and revise (if need be) his or her own conception of the good life in a world of incommensurable values. By contrast, East Asian political actors conventionally maintain that governments may justifiably intervene in most if not all aspects of social life in order to promote an officially predetermined conception of the good.

Conventionally, in contemporary Pacific Asia, this good is presented in technocratic, developmentalist terms. The state constitutes an enterprise to be rationally managed towards bureaucratically determined goals. Thus Malaysia has its Vision 2020, while Singapore's PAP establish Singapore's 'moral markers' twenty years in advance. Politics, in such an understanding, is clearly subordinate to the pursuit of these conceptions of the good.

Moreover, alongside such developmental considerations, the good often comes to be identified with yet to be fully realized religious and/or national ideals towards which the larger community needs to be collectively mobilized. In order to steer the people towards this collective unity, the post-colonial technocratic elite sets the rationally determined and consequently unarguably certain standards. In this context, furthermore, the developmental polis draws selectively upon traditional Asian understandings of balance and harmony, filial piety, *gotong royong* (cooperation) and non-contentious consensus building to establish order, growth and unity.

This paradoxically conservative weave of tradition and national development increasingly explains the understanding of procedural democracy in contemporary Pacific Asia. Regular elections not only offer an important source of feedback on elite initiatives, they also offer a test of the rationality of the ruled. Those irrational enough to support opposition candidates in Singapore lose their kindergartens, while in Malaysia, the ruling UMNO coalition offers Sabahans the promise of infrastructural development if they abandon their attachment to the locally prominent PBS. In illiberal democracy the election constitutes a test of the ruled rather than the rulers. The ruled pass the test when they confirm the rule of the dominant party. In a liberal understanding, democracy succeeds when elections change governments, in the illiberal version democracy succeeds when elections legitimate the rule of an incumbent elite.

This understanding is further facilitated by the absence in Pacific Asia of any clear distinction between political office and the person of the officeholder. Without such a distinction, moreover, it is difficult to establish the notion of a loyal opposition. The absence of those checks and balances that emerged historically and contingently in the Anglo-American world favour an illiberal style of rule.

LAW AS ADMINISTRATIVE TECHNIQUE

> Be immeasurably great, be unfathomably deep; make certain that names and results tally, examine laws and customs, punish those who act wilfully, and the state will be without traitors. (Han Fei Zi)

In order to instrumentalize the developing understanding of the national goal, the technocratic elites of Pacific Asia increasingly have recourse to administrative law in order to establish the latest technocratically designed objective. Thus, law is an extension of administrative technique and supplements the vision or the national plan. This understanding, in Taiwan, South Korea and Singapore, has its roots in East Asian legalism adumbrated by attenuated understandings of a Confucian provenance, which considers administrative law as part of the ruler's technical equipment.

Such a view contrasts with an Anglo-American understanding of law as a constitutional machinery. Centrally, as we have suggested, such 'legalistic Confucianism' is politically authoritarian. It accommodates neither a popular right to partipation, nor any indefeasible individual right. The people consequently constitute a managerial problem. Ideally, rule is firm and efficient. There is limited room here for politics as an essentially pluralistic activity or for the notion that government reflects a popular will.

Law, therefore, constitutes a precisely defined code of conduct equally applied to all subjects and specifying the specific duties of certain actors whether civil servants or heads of families or children towards parents. The reinvented East Asian conception of law, although it may use the vestigial institutions and codes of former colonial rulers, has little in common with Anglo-American jurisprudential thought. East Asian legalism applied either to chewing gum or opposition leaders, cannot readily accommodate legal right. It provides only a strict delineation of duties. Consequently, Asian understandings of *fa* or *adat* have difficulty in accepting an idea of contract as an agreement mutually enforceable through an independent judiciary. Indeed legalism ultimately seeks to reduce law to bureaucratic technique.

The purpose of Pacific Asian rule is apolitical. In place of a constitutional understanding that articulates a common and evolving association in terms of law, we find legalistically prescribed performances with little space for a critical or creative interrogation of what such performances might involve. Moreover, it is the technocratic elite that possesses the necessary skill to adjust mutable laws and constitutions to the new demands of modernization. Thus, Korea currently enjoys its sixth constitution since 1950, Taiwan plays with the notion of an elected President and Singapore adds an elected Presidency to its erstwhile Westminster style parliament. Such changes should not be viewed as a shift from the rule by good men to the rule of law. Instead Asian constitutions represent the mutable by-product that eventuate from the anxious search for new men of prowess modified according to the current requirements of an apolitical technocracy.

THE MANAGED PUBLIC SPACE AND THE DEPENDENT CIVIL SOCIETY

The evolution of this techno-paternalism has further implications for the character of civil society in an Asian modernity. Political development conventionally assumes a benign relationship between the emergence of civil society and pressure for democratic change. As civil society grows it allows emerging social groups to challenge authoritarian rule. From this perspective, civil society constitutes an autonomous space of association unregulated by the state. This autonomy exists in dynamic tension with the demands of the state and is crucial to the politics of liberal democracy.

A brief acquaintance with the conditions of emergence of the Pacific Asian states must ultimately question the universality of the liberal demo-cratic state-civil society dyad. From a Pacific Asian perspective liberal democratic civil society is a product of particular, historically contingent configurations of states and markets.

Indeed, a notable feature of illiberal democracy consists in the existence of formal democratic procedures without politics. Rule develops without the critical public or civil realm vital to the existence of liberal democracy. Instead, the ruling technocracies of Pacific Asia seek to manage emerging social, ethnic and religious groups and channel their activities along state determined lines. Consequently, the democratization process in Pacific Asia largely reflects a shift from coercive to managerial regulation of these groups. Yet the development of this managerial style rarely implies the emergence of autonomous critical actors or permits even a loyal opposition.

Intriguingly, such intrusive management does not seem to exacerbate tensions between the omnicompetent elite and the emerging civil society. Social and political associations, media and non-governmental organizations that evolve under technocratic guidance remain effectively in its thrall. Exposure to state education and a culture of dependency inures in the mem-bers of these associations narrow specialism, and a lack of interest in wider issues. Specialization and deference facilitate an essentially illiberal civil society that supports the management that techno-paternalism affords.

The technocracies of Pacific Asia have spawned civil societies that are notable for the extent of their state dependence. Civil society is state regulated and affords little opportunity for the development of a critical public realm. The state in fact functions as the gatekeeper licensing civil discourse and managing its terms of debate. Rather than the communicatory discourse of the Anglo-American public bar, the ersatz imitation of the karaoke lounge is the appropriate discursive image for contemporary Pacific Asian society.

THE TAO OF MANAGEMENT

Political change in Pacific Asia then constitutes neither an authoritarian response to pressure from civil society nor reflects a burgeoning demand for the polymorphous pleasures of a free media and a tolerant pluralism. Instead, such change represents the anxious and often proactive attempt by a virtuous mandarinate to maintain harmony, balance and economic growth in a world that always threatens to dissolve into deracinating uncertainty. Moreover, not only do the state managers require a leadership principle, their clients also seek the certainty that techno-paternalism affords. This anxious pursuit of hierarchically coded relationship is daily manifest in the ostensibly communitarian politics practised in Pacific Asia.

An Asian understanding of power as the capacity to harmonize, balance and transmit an ethical understanding has further facilitated this managerial project. Traditionally, the power of the ruler rested in his ability to absorb difference and maintain consensus. In this context, the military autocratic style popular in a variety of Asian states in the early 1980s disturbingly intimated the actual or potential threat of violence. Such an intimation of conflict implies imminent dissolution in Pacific Asian political thought. The potential recourse to a military solution signifies not only a lack of sophistication but, more disturbingly, an absence of consensus and moral authority. Consequently, in the course of the 1980s East and Southeast Asian states devised a series of managerial strategies, not only to maintain the authority of the state, but also to assuage the anxieties of emerging middle-class urban groups and so render them both more visible and more pliable in order to restore the desired equilibrium. A consensual arrangement that gives the civil societies of East Asia their peculiarly conformist character.

Thus just as the ethic that has governed the East Asian miracle and formed both its ruling elite and its new middle-class social groups is antithetical to the liberalism that shaped the historically contingent civil societies of western Europe and North America, it also favours political arrangements that are both stable and inimical to Western civic understandings of equality, freedom and pluralism.

Notes

2 Democracy in Confucian Societies: The Challenge of Justification

1. This is a revised version of a paper presented at the 1993 annual meeting of the American Political Science Association and to members of the National University of Singapore's Department of Political Science, subsequently published in the French language periodical *Lekton* (Fall 1993, vol. III, no. 2). Thanks are due to those audiences, and I am especially grateful to my co-authors and to Selina Chen and David Fott for their most helpful written commentary, as well as to Lekton editor Daniel Weinstock for permission to reprint sections of the article.

2. Contemporary communitarians, however, have challenged the view that our interest in personal autonomy ought to (always) take priority over our interest in community, particularly in view of the erosion of community and widespread social malaise in Western societies – see Etzioni (1993) and Bell (1993).

3. This seemingly obvious point must be made because cynical Western visitors to East Asian countries often assume that since 'Confucianism' is (at times) an ideology manipulated by state elites to justify their rule, it is nothing more (interesting) than that.

4. Some scholars also include Vietnam in the 'Confucian camp' – see, e.g., Tu, 1989: 1; Moody, 1988: especially chapters 6 and 9; Pye, 1985: especially chapter 8.

5. Japan is the exception in East Asia, however, as loyalty to other groups sometimes takes precedence both in theory and practice over family relationships – see Moody, 1988: 8; Wargo, 1990: 500; and Tai, 1989: 16.

6. Thus, e.g., the 'Confucian Ethics' curriculum prepared for Singaporean schools in the late 1980s (consultants included Confucian scholars Yu Ying Shih, Tu Wei-ming and Theodore De Bary) gave prominence to heroines such as Nie Rong (a courageous Warring States era woman who chose to commit suicide rather than forsake blood ties to her younger brother) and left out explicitly patriarchal elements from their interpretation of Confucian ethics.

7. The legalist Han Fei Zi, for example, argued that the 'family obligations over all others' principle is incompatible with successful warfare:

   > There was a man of Lu who accompanied his sovereign to war. Three times he went into battle, and three times he ran away. When Confucius asked him the reason, he replied, 'I have an aged father and, if I should die, there would be no one to take care of him'. Confucius, considering the man filial, recommended him and had him promoted to a post in the government. Thus we see that a man who is a filial son to his father may be a traitorous subject to his lord . . . Confucius rewarded a man, and as a result the people of Lu thought nothing of surrendering or running away in battle. (Han, 1967: 106)

Han Fei apparently fabricated this story about Confucius for his own purposes, but none the less one can surmise that Confucius and Han Fei would offer opposing pieces of advice to the young man in Sartre's famous example torn between staying to care for his ill mother or leaving to fight with the Free French Forces (although Han Fei would probably favour a third alternative – to fight with the Nazis).

8. Divorce was difficult to obtain even during Mao's era in the PRC when efforts were made to transfer (at least some) loyalty from the family to the Party and to Mao (see, e.g., (Honig, 1991: 350–9).

9. PRC authorities have discouraged for economic reasons such traditional practices as lavish funerals (better that the money go to build schools) and the siting of graves in arable fields, but these practices have been reviving in response to the post-Mao liberalization (Whyte, in Dernberger, *et al.*, 1991: 718).

10. For example, Japanese households have kept 'alive many traditions such as the observation of rituals before tablets within the home to honor individual ancestors' (Rozman, 1991: 194), and in Korea the ritual of ancestor worship 'is carried on as an important part of family life'. (Robinson, 1991: 221)

11. My claim, it should be noted, is not that any particular manifestation of Confucian familism is an essential part of social landscape in East Asia (e.g., that the Japanese had a low savings rate in the late nineteenth century does not falsify my argument; those interested in doing so would have to demonstrate that at time *x* East Asians do not typically fulfill more obligations for the sake of family members in comparison with Westerners, and that this situation cannot plausibly be attributed to an ultimately ineffective Chinese Communist Party-style plan to eradicate family loyalties).

12. It is interesting to note that feminist 'care theorists' in Western countries are similarly unmoved by appeals to the value of autonomy. As Will Kymlicka explains:

> Justice not only presupposes that we are autonomous adults, it seems the presuppose that we are adults *who are not care-givers for dependants*. Once people are responsible for attending to the (unpredictable) demands of dependants, they are no longer capable of guaranteeing their own predictability. Perhaps the whole picture of autonomy as the free pursuit of projects formed in the light of abstract standards presupposes that care for dependent others can be delegated to someone else, or to the state. It is interesting to note how little care theorists talk about the sort of autonomy that male theorists discuss at length – the setting of personal goals, the commitment to personal projects. According to Baier, the care perspective 'makes autonomy not even an ideal. . . . A certain sort of freedom is an ideal, namely freedom of thought and expression, but to "live one's own life in one's own way" is not likely to be among the aims of persons'. (Kymlicka, 1990: 285; quoting Bair, 1987: 46)

But care theorists and Confucians differ in the sense that whereas the former focus primarily on the implications of responsibilities for dependent children, the latter focus primarily on the care owed to elderly parents.

13. Peter Moody, Jr, however, argues that the exam system tested technical

proficiency rather than moral worth, hence that 'at its heart it was a legalist rather than a Confucian institution' (Moody, 1988: 26). But Moody's interpretation cannot account for the following facts: the exams were dominated by the Confucian Classics until 1905 and were thought to confer moral knowledge as well as administrative ability, and officials defined themselves in Confucian rather than legalist terms (as Moody himself notes on p. 26).

14. But that is not to say Confucian scholar bureaucrats always had the capability to serve the public – in fact, they were 'all too often alone in facing the power concentrated in the ruler [and were] rarely successful statesmen achieving noble goals' (De Bary, 1989a: 19).

15. As Gilbert Rozman explains,

> Bureaucrats are more secure [in East Asian societies than in Western capitalist societies], their positions based on high educational qualifications and professional competence. Public opinion is less fickle; it is more trusting of behind-the-scenes political maneuvring and paternalistic decision-making by a small group of officials. . . . East Asian societies usually have the advantage of being able to carry out reform through their bureaucracies. This is reform through bureaucratic consensus, in contrast with . . . the Western method of public opinion appeals. (Rozman, 1991: 37, 38)

In terms of particular East Asian countries, the bureaucracy continues to attract top talent, command respect, and exert a disproportionate share of political power in Korea, Singapore and Taiwan. Even in Japan, the most democratic country in Confucian East Asia, the former US ambassador to Japan Mike Mansfield notes that 'the nearly autonomous Japanese ministries . . . run the country on a day to day basis and often frustrate . . . mandates from the increasingly discredited leadership' ('Consumers will benefit from Japan's political blow-up', in the *Straits Times*, 25 June 1993: 34; see Van Wolferen, 1989: for a book-length defence of this thesis), and it is unclear to what extent the new reformist coalition government has the will and power to strengthen the political leadership's position *vis-à-vis* the bureaucracy. In China, bureaucrats have power but little prestige, massive corruption and past blunders having undermined the legtimacy of CCP cadres, but one can expect the re-emergence of traditional esteem for bureaucrats if the government pursues with attempts to professionalize the civil service (see Song, 1992).

16. Working on this assumption, J. S. Mill in chapter 7 of *Representative Government* argued against equal universal suffrage on the grounds that granting extra votes to educated persons minimizes the danger of class legislation.

17. Singapore has periodic elections for Parliament, but the elections are not free, fair, and competitive – individual ballots are numbered (the government can check at least in principle who voted for what party), promising opposition candidates face serious forms of retaliation, and the press is tightly-controlled and generally pro-government.

18. Will Kymlicka criticizes Charles Larmore's defence of liberalism founded on the plurality of different people's ends (see Larmore, 1987: 70–7) on the grounds that the freedom of individuals to dissent and convert (a freedom liberals care about) isn't needed to ensure tolerance between groups:

Let us assume that the members of different groups are bound to their
present ends. Representatives of each group meet and attempt to come
to an 'overlapping consensus' (Rawls), or a 'modus vivendi' (Larmore).
Each group would agree to let the members of other groups engage in
their practices. But why would either group demand that individuals be
free to convert from one group to another, or that individuals have state
protection of their rights to dissent and to non-discrimination within
their current group? (Kymlicka, 1989: 60)

A real-life example comes to mind (see also Kymlicka, 1992) – in Singapore, religious groups are free to preach to their own flock but not to Muslims,
and one might add that plurality and mutual respect do not even require
democracy, so long as a relatively benign paternalistic government allows
ethnic and religious groups to pursue their own cultural activities in peace.

19. Implicitly admitting the failure of 'nation building' exercises such as the
promotion of official core values, the splitting up of ethnic groups in various
public housing estates, and lengthy national service, the Singaporean government has recently implemented 'ethnic-based welfare schemes' operating under the assumption that 'blood ties' run deeper than national feelings,
whereby Malays contribute to a fund for underprivileged Malays, Chinese
contribute to a fund for underprivileged Chinese, and Indians contribute to
a fund for underprivileged Indians. Some have criticized this scheme on the
grounds that it may rekindle latent ethnic tensions and disproportionately
favour the relatively well-off Chinese group (Chee, 1994: 22–4).

20. It should be noted that whereas Buchanan invokes this point to make the
case that liberal rights such as the freedom of association are a strong bulwark against attempts to destroy or dominate various communities within
nation states, I do so to make the case that the democratic method interpreted as fair competitive elections is a strong bulwark against attempts
to destroy communities.

21. The 'state-first' policy in practice meant not only betraying family members but also neglecting basic family obligations – see, e.g., Jung Chang's
(1991) vivid account of her father's insensitive behaviour towards his pregnant wife in the heady days after the revolution.

22. Some regime insiders argue that the government also employs military conscription to instill a sense of patriotism, at least in the sense of instilling a
military 'fighting spirit', but anecdotal evidence from my own students fresh
from two and a half years of national service suggests that this strategy is
ineffective if not counterproductive – most say the experience was miser-
able, and others said they would fight but on account of their family (living
in Singapore), not 'for the sake of the nation'.

23. Singaporeans have a word for this phenomenon – Kiasuism, literally meaning 'fear of losing', but referring to all kinds of petty, selfish, and overly
self-protective behaviour. The local branches of MacDonald's, presumably
as part of the chain's interesting world-wide policy to adapt their food to
local habits and culinary practices (MacDonald's in Quebec serve poutine,
MacDonald's in American cities with large Jewish populations serve bagels,
and so on), have recently begun to sell 'kiasuburgers', a spicy chicken
sandwich launched with a humorous advertising campaign that pokes fun at
kiasu behaviour. Some Singaporeans have criticized MacDonald's in the

172   *Notes*

       letters page of the local newspaper, arguing that the campaign may have the unintended effect of glorifying such undesirable behaviour and projecting a bad image of Singapore abroad.

24. Cherian George, an unusually frank Singaporean journalist, makes a similar point – one can hardly blame people for ignoring their political obligations, he says, 'When they hear so many cautionary tales: of Singaporeans whose careers came to a premature end after they voiced dissent; of critics who found themselves under investigations; of individuals who were detained without trial or even though they seemed not to pose any real threat; of tapped phones and opened letters. . . . The moral of these stories: In Singapore, better to mind your own business, make money, and leave politics to the politicians'. (*Sunday Times* (Singapore), 11 July 1993: 7)

25. This is an exaggeration from a Confucian standpoint, however, for the family above all provides mark and dignity for common people. But one need not endorse this part of Hegel's argument to support his point that intermediary non-governmental associations are especially conducive to a broader sense of public spiritedness.

26. It is important to note that de Tocqueville argued there must be a place for individual independence within such associations, for associations that are tyrannical within themselves produce passive and servile behaviour instead of training members in the use of their energies for the sake of common enterprizes (de Tocqueville, 1840: 198). In other words, patriotism requires intermediary associations with established norms and practices of individual independence, a form of association which may not be readily transferable to East Asian contexts that downplay the significance of personal autonomy.

27. Thus, e.g., the Germans and the Japanese seemed patriotic in World War II, but on the other hand it is difficult to gauge the extent of genuine patriotism in authoritarian contexts (how much obedience stems from fear?). More importantly, even if we assume that Germans and Japanese were deeply patriotic, the particular social and historical factors that made them so are complex and not readily exportable, unlike the easily adoptable practice of free, fair, and competitive elections for choosing rulers.

5 The Political Economy of Democratization

1. For an outline of the notion of 'research programme' see Lakatos (1970); what is especially useful in this notion is that research programmes are identified in terms of the research problems generated.

2. These pacts are bargains between political actors, which limit the exercise of power and secure the vital interests – usually economic – of these actors.

3. For an attempt to place the evolution of citizenship in historical context, see Keane (1988).

4. For an elaboration of these concepts, see Keane (1988) and Cohen (1982).

5. For example, Moore (1966) analyses the impact of coercive rural labour relations in the transition to democracy. See also the work of Rueschemeyer *et al.* (1992).

6. For a review of the work Barrington Moore see Skocpol (1973) and, more generally, Skocpol and Somers (1980). Scokpol's general argument about Moore focuses on the absence of 'state variables' in regime transition.

7. For corresponding emphasis on the role of the working class in democratic transition see Therborn (1977); Rueschemeyer *et al.* (1992) and Luebbert (1987).

8. Though of course Fukuyama does suggest that East Asia may prove to be the exception.

9. This was, of course, Moore's (often forgotten) central point that the English route to liberal democracy was the exception rather than the norm.

10. For a similar theme see Aglietta (1978), Lipietz (1988).

11. Although given the fact that late industrialising is the norm for a great many nations, the term 'German exceptionalism' may be somewhat misleading.

12. See Mooers (1991) for an excellent historiography of German exceptionalism.

13. For general reviews of the NIEs see Haggard (1990), Deyo (1987) and Wade (1990).

14. Modernization theory, in the Huntingtonian (1968) variant, posits a fundamental conflict between participation and development. The political mobilization that democracy engenders, it is argued, disrupts the capacity of the state to develop the economy.

15. From this view, corporatism is more akin to exchange in an oligopolistic market with two or more large parties. As such, the analysis can be extended to include a range of areas not usually covered under the rubric of corporatism.

16. Although of course the extent of dependence of these measures may vary from state to state.

17. However, it needs to be pointed out that because Taiwan had a large number of small to medium sized enterprizes, the incentives to organize structures for collective action were not high.

18. For an analysis of the Bretton Woods system see Gilpin (1987).

19. It should be noted that as the economy became more and more complex, inter-capitalist rivalry increased in salience. For example, domestic private financial capital, as opposed to manufacturing capital, was increasingly against domestic protection.

20. In particular, the FKI has complained about the unofficial taxes it is required to pay the ruling party.

21. For example, the recent elections to Golkar are symptomatic of these tensions.

22. Authors such as Rosenbluth (1989) have drawn attention to a similar producer bias in Japanese politics.

23. Indeed representation of interests may in fact suffer under this kind of clientelism.

24. In fact, the dominant party systems probably best approximate Kircheimer's (1964) 'catch all party'.

6 Democratization and the Renegotiation of Ethnicity

1. This chapter is a rethinking and a reworking of the paper on 'The Nation, the *Ethnie* and the *Demos*: Political Change in the East and Southeast Asian NICs', presented at the Workshop on Ethnicity and the State, Department of Political and Social Change, Research School of Pacific and Asian

Studies, Australian National University, January 1994. It is envisaged that the collected workshop papers be published, edited by Dr Ron May.

2. As Chai-anan notes, the designation of communists as non-Thais was strongest during the 1940s and 1950s. The myth was eroded during the 1970s in the face of the Thai student revolt of 1973. It is important to note that it was the position of Northeastern Thailand as the main communist stronghold, which promoted the redesignation of Thai-speaking Buddhist peoples of the Isan region as 'Lao', rather than as 'Thai'.

Bibliography

Agillieta, M. (1978) *A Theory of Capitalist Regulation: the US Experience*. London: New Left Books.

Almond, G. and Verba, S. (1963) *The Civic Culture*. Princeton, N.J.: Princeton University Press.

Alter, Peter (1989) *Nationalism*. London: Edward Arnold.

Anderson B. (1990) *Language and Power: Exploring Political Cultures in Indonesia*. Ithaca, N.Y.: Cornell University Press.

Anderson, B. (1992) 'The New World Order', in *24 Hours*, special supplement entitled 'Whatever Happened to the New World Order?', February, Sydney: Australian Broadcasting Service.

Anderson, B. and Mcvey, R. (1971) 'A Preliminary Analysis of the October 1st 1965 Coup in Indonesia', *Modern Indonesia Project*. Ithaca, N.Y.: Cornell University Press.

Araffin, Omar (1993) *Bangsa Melayu: Malay Concepts of Democracy and Community, 1945–1950*. Kuala Lumpur: Oxford University Press.

Arato, A. (1990) 'Revolution, Civil Society and Democracy', *Working Papers on Transitions from State Socialism*, no. 905, Ithaca, N.Y.: Cornell University Press.

Arblaster, Anthony (1987) *Democracy*. Milton Keynes: Open University Press.

Arneson, Richard (1993) 'Democratic Rights at National and Workplace Levels', in David Copp, Jean Hampton and John Roemer, eds, *The Idea of Democracy*. Cambridge, UK: Cambridge University Press.

Asia Watch Report (1989) 'Silencing all Critics: Human Rights Violations in Singapore'.

Baier, Annette (1987) 'Hume, the Woman's Moral Theorist?', in E. K. Hay and D. Meyers, eds, *Women and Moral Theory*. Savage, Md.: Rowan & Littlefield.

Barber, Benjamin (1984) *Strong Democracy: Participatory Politics for a New Age*. Berkeley, Calif.: University of California Press.

Barry, Brian (1991) *Democracy and Power: Essays in Political Theory I*. Oxford: Clarendon Press.

Barthes, R. (1987) *Empire of Signs*. New York: Hill & Wang.

Bartley, R., Chan Heng Chee, Huntington, S. and Ogata, S. (1993) *Democracy and Capitalism: Asian and American Perspectives*. Singapore: Institute for Southeast Asian Studies.

Bell, Daniel A. (1993) *Communitarianism and Its Critics*. Oxford: Clarendon Press.

Bellows, Thomas (1994) 'Politics Elections, and Political Change in Taiwan', *Asian Journal of Political Science*, 2(1).

Bernal, M. (1991) *Black Athena*. London: Vantage.

Bollen, K. A. and Jackman, R. (1985) 'Economic and Noneconomic Determinants of Political Democracy in the 1960s', in R. G. Braungart, ed., *Research in Political Sociology*. Greenwich, Conn.: Jai Press.

Bradford, C. J., Jr (1990) 'Policy Intervention and Markets: Development Strategy Typologies and Policy Options', in G. Gereffi and D. L. Wyman, eds, *Manufacturing Miracles. Paths of Industrialization in Latin America and East Asia*. Princeton, N.J.: Princeton University Press.

Bresnan, J. (1993) *Managing Indonesia: The Modern Political Economy*. New York: Columbia University Press.

Brown, David (1994) *The State and Ethnic Politics in Southeast Asia*. Routledge, London/New York: Routledge.

Buchanan, Allen (1989) 'Assessing the Communitarian Critique of Liberalism', *Ethics*, 99 (July): 4–23.

Buchwalter, Andrew (1992) 'Hegel's Concept of Virtue', *Political Theory*, 21 (November).

Burmeister, L. (1991) 'State, Industrialization and Agricultural Policy in Korea', *Development and Change*, 21(1): 197–223.

Buzan, B. (1983) *People States and Fear: The National Security Problem in International Relations*, Brighton: Harvester Wheatsheaf.

Caney, Simon (1992) 'Liberalism and Communitarianism: A Misconceived Debate', *Political Studies*, lx (June): 5–19.

Carroll, W. K. (1990) 'Restructuring Capital. Reorganizing Consent: Gramsci, Political Economy and Canada', *Canadian of Sociology and Anthropology*, 27(3): 390–416.

Chai-anan Samudavanija (1991) 'State-Identity Creation, State-Building and Civil Society 1939–1989', in Craig J. Reynolds, ed., *National Identity and its Defenders: Thailand, 1939–1989*, Monash Papers on Southeast Asia, no. 25.

Chalmers, I. (1991) 'Indonesia 1990: Democratization and Social Forces', *Southeast Asian Affairs 1991*. Singapore: Institute for Southeast Asian Studies.

Chan Wing Tsit (1973) *A Source Book in Chinese Philosophy*. Princeton, N.J.: Princeton University Press.

Chee Soon Juan (1994) *Dare to Change: An Alternative Vision for Singapore*. Singapore: Singapore Democratic Party.

Cheng Chung Ying (1991) *New Dimensions of Confucian and neo-Confucian Philosophy*. New York: State University New York Press.

Cheng Tung Jan (1989) 'Democratizing the Quasi-Leninist Regime in Taiwan', *World Politics*, 41(4).

Cheng Tung Jan (1990a) 'Is the Dog Barking? The Middle Class and Democratic movements in the East Asian NIC's', *International Study Notes*, spring: 11–22.

Cheng Tung Jan (1990b) 'Political Regimes and Development Strategies: South Korea and Taiwan', in G. Gereffi and D. L. Wyman, eds, *Manufacturing Miracles. Paths of Industrialization in Latin America and East Asia*. Princeton, N.J.: Princeton University Press.

Cheng Tung Jan and Haggard, Stephen, eds (1992) *Political Change in Taiwan*, Boulder, Col.: Lynne Rienner.

Chew, M. (1994) 'Human Rights in Singapore: Perceptions and Problems', Occasional Paper Series no. 11, National University of Singapore, Political Science Department.

Chowdhury, A. and Islam, I. (1993) *The Newly Industrialized Economies of East Asia*. London: Routledge.

Chu, Yun-han (1992) *Crafting Democracy in Taiwan*. Taipei: Institute for National Policy Research.

Clark, C. (1989) *Taiwan's Development: Implications for Contesting Political Paradigms*, Connecticut: Greenwood.

Clark, D., ed. (1993) *Korea Briefing: Festival of Korea*. Boulder, Colo.: Westview.

Clifford, M. (1988) 'Filing for Divorce', *Far Eastern Economic Review*, 21 April.

Cohen, J. L. (1982) *Class and Civil Society: the Limits of Marxian Critical Theory*. Amherst: University of Massachusetts Press.

Cohen, Joshua and Rogers, Joel (1983) *On Democracy: Toward a Transformation of American Society*. Harmondsworth: Penguin.

Confucius (1938) *The Analects of Confucius*, trans. Arthur Waley. London: Allen & Unwin.

Confucius (1979) *The Analects of Confucius*, trans. D. C. Lau. London: Penguin.

Copper, J. (1993) *Taiwan, Nation State or Province?* Boulder, Col.: Westview Press.

Cotton, J. (1991) 'On the identity of Confucianism: Theory and Practice', *Political Theory Newsletter, no. 3:* 13–26.

Cotton, J. (1992a) 'Understanding the State in South Korea; Bureaucratic Authoritarian or State Autonomy Theory', *Comparative Political Studies*, 24(4) (June): 319–37.

Cotton, J. (1992b) 'Civil Societies in the Political Transition in North Korea: the Limitation of the East European Model', *Korea and World Affairs*, VI(2): 319–37.

Cotton, J., ed. (1993) *Korea Under Roh Tae Woo*. Sydney: Allen & Unwin.

Crouch, Harold and Morley, James (1992) 'The Dynamics of Political Change', in James Morley, ed., *Driven by Growth: Political Change in the Asia–Pacific Region*. Armonk, N.Y.: M. E. Sharpe.

Cumings, B. (1987) 'The Origins and Development of the Northeast Asian Political Economy: Industrial Sectors, Product Cycles, and Political Consequences', in F. C. Deyo, ed., *The Political Economy of the New Asian Industrialism*. Ithaca, N.Y.: Cornell University Press.

Cumings, B. (1989) 'The Abortive Abertura: South Korea in the Light of Latin American Experience', *New Left Review*, 173: 5–32.

Cutright, P. (1963) 'National Political Development: Measurement and Analysis', *American Sociological Review*, 28(2): 253–64.

Dahl, Robert (1956) *A Preface to Democratic Theory*. Chicago: University of Chicago Press.

Dahl, R. (1971) *Polyarchy: Participation and Opposition*. New Haven, Conn.: Yale University Press.

Dawson, Raymond (1981) *Confucius*. Oxford: Oxford University Press.

Dahl, Robert (1985) *A Preface to Economic Theory*. Cambridge, UK: Polity Press.

Dahl, Robert (1989) *Democracy and Its Critics*, New Haven, Conn.: Yale University Press.

Dahl, Robert (1992) 'The Problem of Civic Competence', *Journal of Democracy*, 3(4): 20–35.

De Bary W. T. (1981) *Neo-Confucian Orthodoxy and the Learning of Mind-and-Heart*. New York: Columbia University Press.

De Bary, W. T. (1983) *Liberal Tradition in China*. Hong Kong: Chinese University Press.

De Bary, W. T. (1986) *Confucianism as an Aspect of East Asian and World Civilizations*. Institute of East Asian Philosophies (Singapore) Public Lecture Series, no. 3.

De Bary, W. T. (1988) *A Forum on 'The Role of Culture in Industrial Asia – The Relationship Between Confucian Ethics and Modernization'*. Institute of East Asian Philosphies (Singapore) Public Lecture series, no. 7.

178   *Bibliography*

De Bary, W. T. (1989a) *Confucius as a Noble Man?*. Institute of East Asian Philosophies (Singapore) Public Lecture series, no. 12.

De Bary, W. T. (1989b) *The Trouble with Confucianism*. Institute of East Asian Philosophies (Singapore) Public Lecture Series, no. 13.

Dernberger, Robert, De Woskin, Kenneth, Goldstein, Steven, Murphy, Rhoads and Whyte, Martin, eds (1991) *The Chinese: Adapting the Past, Facing the Future*. Ann Arbor, Mich.: Center for Chinese Studies Publications.

De Tocqueville, Alexis (1840) *Democracy in America, vols I and II*. New York: Vintage.

Deyo, F. C. (1987) 'State and Labour: Modes of Political Exclusion in East Asian Development', in F. C. Deyo, ed., *The Political Economy of the New Asian Industrialism*. Ithaca, N.Y.: Cornell University Press.

Deyo, F. C. (1992) 'Coalitions, Institutions, and Linkage Sequencing – Toward a Strategic Capacity Model of East Asian Development', in F. C. Deyo, ed., *The Political Economy of the New Asian Industrialism*. Ithaca, N.Y.: Cornell University Press.

Diamond, Larry (1992) 'Economic Development and Democracy Reconsidered', *America, Behavioral Scientist*, 35(4, 5): 450–91.

Diamond, L., Linz, J. and Lipset, S. M. (1989) *Democracy in Developing Countries: Asia*, vol. 3. Boulder, Colo.: Lynne Rienner.

Doner, R. (1991) *Driving a Bargain: Automobile Industrialization and Japanese Firms in Southeast Asia*. Berkeley: University of California Press.

Dunn, J. (1991) *Western Political Theory in the Face of the Future*. Cambridge, UK: Canto.

Dunn, John, ed. (1992) *Democracy: The Unfinished Journey, 508BC to AD1993*. Oxford: Oxford University Press.

Dutton, M. (1992) *Policing and Punishment in China*, Cambridge, UK: Cambridge University Press.

Duyvendak, J. L. (1928) *The Book of Lord Shang*. London: Probstain.

Dworkin, Ronald (1989) 'Liberal Community', *California Law Review*, 77: 479–504.

Ebrey, Patricia (1991) 'The Chinese Family and the Spread of Confucian Valves', in G. Rozman, ed., *The East Asian Region*. Princeton, N.J.: Princeton University Press.

Eckert, C. J. (1990–1) 'The South Korean Bourgeoisie: a Class in Search of Hegemony', *Journal of Korean Studies*, 115–47.

Economist, The (1994) 'Fings Ain't Wot They Used to Be', 28 May 1994.

Ekiert, G. (1991) 'Democratization Processes in East Central Europe: A Theoretical Reconsideration', *British Journal of Political Science*, 21 (July): 285–313.

Elman, B. (1987) 'Confucianism and Modernization, a Re-evaluation', in J. P. L. Jiang, ed., *Confucianism and Modernization: A Symposium*, Taipei: Freedom Council.

Elvin, M. (1986) 'The Double Disavowal, The Attitudes of Radical Thinkers to the Chinese Tradition', in Shan Yu Ming (ed.) *China and Europe in the Twentieth Century*, Chengchu, Taiwan: Chengchu University Press.

Esping Anderson, G. (1985) *Politics Against Markets: the Social Democratic Road to Power*. Princeton, N.J.: Princeton University Press.

Etzioni, Amitai (1993) *The Spirit of Community: Rights, Responsibilities, and the Communitarian Agenda*. New York: Crown.

Fairbank, John and Reischauer, Edwin (1989) *China: Tradition and Transformation*. Boston, Mass.: Houghton Mifflin.

Fajnzylber, F. (1990) 'The United States and Japan as Models of Industrialization', in G. Gereffi and D. L. Wyman, eds, *Manufacturing Miracles. Paths of Industrialization in Latin America and East Asia*. Princeton, N.J.: Princeton University Press.

Fallows, James (1994) *Looking at the Sun: The Rise of the New East Asian Economic and Political System*. New York: Pantheon.

Fingarette, H. (1972) *Confucius: The Secular and the Sacred*. New York: Harper.

Fishkin, James (1991) *Democracy and Deliberation*. New Haven, Conn.: Yale University Press.

Fu Hu and Yun-Han Chu (1992) 'Electoral Competition and Political Democratization', in Tung Jan Cheng and Stephen Haggard, eds, *Political Changes in Taiwan*. Boulder, Col.: Lynne Rienner.

Fukuyama, F. (1992) *The End of History and the Last Man*. London: Hamish Hamilton.

Galston, William (1991) *Liberal Purposes: Goods, Virtues, and Diversity in the Liberal State*. Cambridge: Cambridge University Press.

Geertz, C. (1960) *The Religion of Java*. Glencoe, Col.: Free Press.

George, Cherian. 'Here to Stay', *Sunday Times* (Singapore), 11 July 1993.

Gereffi, G. and Wyman, D. L., eds (1990) *Manufacturing Miracles. Paths of Industrialization in Latin America and East Asia*. Princeton, N.J.: Princeton University Press.

Gershenkron, A. (1943) *Bread and Democracy in Germany*. Berkeley: University of California Press.

Gilpin, R. (1987) *The Political Economy of International Relations*. Princeton, N.J.: Princeton University Press.

Gould, Carol (1988) *Rethinking Democracy*. Cambridge: Cambridge University Press.

Government of Singapore (1991) *The Next Lap*. Singapore: Times Press.

Gullick, J. M. (1991) *Malay Society in the Late Nineteenth Century*. Oxford: Oxford University Press.

Gutmann, Amy (1987) *Democratic Education*. Princeton, N.J.: Princeton University Press.

Habermas, J. (1987) *The Theory of Communicating Action*. Cambridge, Mass.: Beacon Press.

Habermas, J. (1989) *The Structural Transformation of the Public Sphere: An Inquiry into the Category of Bourgeois Society*. Oxford: Polity Press.

Haggard, S. (1990) *Pathways from the Periphery: the Politics of Growth of the Newly Industrializing Countries*. Ithaca, N.Y.: Cornell University Press.

Hall, D. G. (1991) *A History of South-East Asia*. London: Macmillan.

Hamilton, Nora and Biggart, G. (1991) 'The Organization of Business in Taiwan: Reply to Numazaki', *American Journal of Sociology*, 96(4): 999.

Hamilton, Nora and Kim, Eun Mee (1993) 'Liberalization in South Korea and Mexico', *Third World Quarterly*, 14(1): 109–36.

Han Fei Zi (1964) *Basic Writings*. New York: Columbia University Press.

Han Fei Zi (1967) *Basic Writings of Mo Zi, Hsün Zi, and Han Fei Zi*, trans. Burton Watson. New York: Columbia University Press.

Hansen, M. H. (1991) *The Athenian Democracy in the Age of Demosthenes*. Oxford: Clarendon Press.

Harland, Bryce (1993) 'Whither East Asia', *Pacific Review*, 6(1): 12–21.

Hayek, Friedrich (1979) *Law, Liberty, and Legislation, vol. 3*. London: Routledge & Kegan Paul.

Heine-Geldern, R. (1956) 'Conceptions of State and Kingship in Southeast Asia', *Southeast Asia Programme Data Papers*, no. 18. Ithaca, N.Y.: Cornell University Press.

Held, David (1989) *Models of Democracy*. Cambridge, UK: Polity Press.

Held, David (1992) 'Democracy: From City-States to a Cosmopolitan Order?', in David Held, ed., *Political Studies*, vol. XL.

Held, D. (1993) *Prospects for Democracy*. Cambridge, UK: Polity Press.

Henderson, G. (1968) *Korea the Politics of the Vortex*. Cambridge, Mass.: Harvard University Press.

Hewison, R., Robison, R. and Rodan, G. (1993) *Southeast Asia in the 1990's*. Sydney: Allen & Unwin.

Ho, Wei-ming (1989) 'Value Premises underlying the transformation of Singapore', in K. Sandhu and P. Wheatley, eds, *Management of Success. The Moulding of Modern Singapore*, Singapore: Institute for Southeast Asian Studies.

Hong Nack Kim (1988) 'The 1987 Political Crisis and Implications for US-Korean Relations', in Ilpyong J. Kim and Young Whan Khil, eds, *Political Change in South Korea*. New York: Korean PWPA.

Honig, Emily (1991) 'Courtship Love and Marriage: The Life and Times of Yu Luojin', in Robert Dernberger, Kenneth De Woskin, Steven Goldstein, Rhoads Murphy and Martin Whyte, eds, *The Chinese: Adapting the Past, Facing the Future*. Ann Arbor, Mich.: Center for Chinese Studies Publications.

Hsu, L. (1932) *The Political Philosophy of Confucianism*, New York: Dutton.

Hung-ma Tien (1992) 'Transformation of an Authoritarian State: Taiwan's Development Experience', in Tung Jan Cheng and Stephen Haggard, eds, *Political Change in Taiwan*. Boulder/London: Lynne Rienner.

Huntington, S. (1968) *Political Order in Changing Societies*. New Haven, Conn.: Yale University Press.

Huntington, S. (1991) *The Third Wave: Democratization in the Late Twentieth Century*. Norman: University of Oklahoma Press.

Huntington, Samuel P. (1992a) 'Forward', in Tung Jan Cheng and Stephen Haggard, eds, *Political Change in Taiwan*. Boulder, Colo.: Lynne Rienner.

Huntington, Samuel P. (1992b) 'Will More Countries Become Democratic?', *Political Science Quarterly*, 99(2).

Huntington, Samuel (1993) 'American Democracy in Relation to Asia', *Democracy and Capitalism: Asian and American Perspectives*. Singapore: Institute of Southeast Asian Studies.

International Herald Tribune (1994) 'A Graying Holland Votes, Fearing Welfare's Future', 3 May.

Ivanhoe, Philip (1991) Review of David Hall and Roger Ames's 'Thinking Through Confucius', *Philosophy East and West*, 44(3): 559–64.

Jackson, Peter A. (1989) *Buddhism, Legitimation and Conflict: The Political Functions of Urban Thai Buddhism*. Singapore: Institute for Southeast Asian Studies.

Jacobs, B. (1985) *The Korean Road to Urbanization and Development*. Urbana: University of Illinois Press.

Jacobs, Bruce (1993) 'Rip Van Winkle Returns to Taiwan', *Far Eastern Economic Review*, 13 May, p. 36.

Jiang, J. P. L., ed. (1987) *Confucianism and Modernization: A Symposium*. Taipei: Freedom Council Press.

Johnson, Chalmers (1987) 'Political Institutions and Economic Performance: The Government Business Relation in Japan, South Korea and Taiwan', in F. C. Deyo, ed., *The Political Economy of the New Asian Industrialism*, Ithaca, N.Y.: Cornell University Press.

Jones, D. and Sakong, I. (1980) *Government, Business and Entrepreneurship in Economic Development: the Korean Case*. Cambridge, Mass.: Harvard University Press.

Jung Chang (1991) *Wild Swans: Three Daughters of China*. New York: Simon & Schuster.

Kahan, A. (1992) *Aristocratic Liberalism: the Social and Political Thought of Jacob Burckhardt, J. S. Mill and Alexis de Toqueville*. Oxford: Oxford University Press.

Kahn, J. and Loh, F. (1992) *Fragmented Vision: Culture and Politics in Contemporary Malaysia*. Sydney: Allen & Unwin.

Kateb, George (1992) *The Inner Ocean: Individualism and Democratic Culture*. Ithaca, N.Y.: Cornell University Press.

Kay-kyo Sohm (1989) *Authoritarianism and Opposition in South Korea*. London/New York: Routledge.

Keane, J. (1988) *Democracy and Civil Society*. London: Verso.

Kennedy, Paul (1993) *Preparing for the 21st Century*. New York: Random House.

Kim, D. and Joo, Y. (1982) *The Food Situation and Policies in the Republic of Korea*. Paris: Organization for Economic Cooperation and Development.

Kim Ilpyong and Young When Khil (1990) *Political Change in Korea*. New York: Paragon House.

Kircheimer, O. (1964) 'The Waning of Opposition', in R. Macridis and B. E. Brown, eds, *Comparative Politics*. Homewood, Ill.: Dorsey Press.

Koon Woo Nam (1989) *South Korean Politics: The Search for Political Consensus and Stability*. London/New York: University Press of America.

Kuo Tai Chun and Myers, R. (1988) 'The Great Transition: Political Change and the Prospects for Democracy in the Republic of China on Taiwan', *Asian Affairs*, 15(3) (Fall): 115–35.

Kurth, J. (1979) 'The Political Consequences of the Product Cycle: Industrial History and Political Outcomes', *International Organization*, 33(1), 1–34.

Kymlicka, Will (1989) *Liberalism, Community, and Culture*, Oxford: Clarendon Press.

Kymlicka, Will (1990) *Contemporary Political Philosophy: An Introduction*. Oxford: Clarendon Press.

Kymlicka, Will (1992) 'Two Models of Pluralism and Tolerance', *Analyse & Kritik*, 5, 33–56.

Kymlicka, Will (1993) 'Appendix I: Some Questions about Justice and Community', in D. Bell, *Communitarianism and Its Critics*. Oxford: Clarendon Press.

Lakatos, I. (1970) 'Falsification and the Methodology of Scientific Research', in I. Lakatos and A. Musgrave, eds, *Criticism and the Growth of Knowledge*. Cambridge and New York: Cambridge University Press.

Landes, D. (1965) 'Japan and Europe: Contrasts in Industrialization', in W. Lockwood ed., *The State and Economic Enterprize in Japan*. Princeton, N.J.: Princeton University Press.

Laothmatas, Anek (1992) *Business Associations and the New Political Economy of Thailand.* Singapore: Institute of Southeast Asian Studies (ISEAS)/Oxford: Westview Press.

Lapidus, I. (1991) *A History of Islamic Societies.* Cambridge: Cambridge University Press.

Larmore, Charles (1989) *Patterns of Moral Complexity.* Cambridge: Cambridge University Press.

Lee, C. H. (1992) 'The Government, Financial System, and Large Private Enterprises in the Economic Development of South Korea', *World Development*, 20(2): 187–97.

Lee, Man Woo (1990) *The Odyssey of Korean Development. Korean Politics 1981–90*, New York: Praeger.

Legge, J. (1893) *The Great Learning*, vol. 1 of *The Chinese Classics*, 7 vols, Oxford and London: Spottiswoode.

Leng, Shao-chuan and Lin, Cheng-yi (1993) 'Political Change in Taiwan: Transition to Democracy?', *The China Quarterly*, 136: 805–39.

Levenson, J. R. (1965) *Confucian China and its Modern Fate*, 3 vols. London: Routledge & Kegan Paul.

Leys, Simon, *New York Review of Books*, 11 October 1990.

Li, Victor (1991) 'Two Models of Law', in Robert Dernberger, Kenneth De Woskin, Steven Goldstein, Rhoads Murphy and Martin Whyte, eds, *The Chinese: Adapting the Past, Facing the Future.* Ann Arbor, Mich.: Center for Chinese Studies Publications.

Liddle, R. (1992) 'Indonesia's Democratic Past and Future', *Comparative Politics*, 24(4): 443–62.

Lijphart, Arend (1977) *Democracy in Plural Societies: A Comparative Exploration.* New Haven, Conn.: Yale University Press.

Link, Perry (1992) *Evening Chats in Beijing: Probing China's Predicament.* New York: Norton.

Lipietz, A. (1988) 'Reflections on a Tale: the Marxist Foundations of the Concept of Regulation and Accumulation', *Studies in Political Economy*, 26, 7–36.

Lipset, S. M. (1960) *Political Man: The Social Basis of Politics.* Baltimore, Md.: Johns Hopkins University Press.

Lipset, S. and Rokkan, S. (1967) *Party Systems and Voter Alignments.* New York: Free Press.

Lo, Shiu-Hing (1992) 'Taiwan Business People, Intellectuals, and Democratization', *Pacific Review*, 5(4): 382–9.

Lodge, G. (1991) *Two Public Lectures.* Singapore: Singapore University Press.

Luebbert, G. M. (1987) 'Social Foundations of Political Order in Interwar Europe', *World Politics*, 39(1): 449–78.

McCormick, Barrett (1994) 'Democracy or Dictatorship?: A Response to Gordon White', *The Australian Journal of Chinese Affairs*, no. 31, January.

Macedo, Stephen (1990) *Liberal Virtues.* Oxford: Clarendon Press.

MacIntyre, Alasdair (1988) *Whose Justice? Which Rationality?* London: Duckworth.

MacIntyre, Andrew (1991) *Business and Politics in Indonesia.* Sidney: Asian Studies Association of Australia/Allen & Unwin.

Macpherson, C. B. (1973) *Democratic Theory: Essays in Retrieval.* Oxford: Oxford University Press.

Macpherson, C. B. (1977) *The Life and Times of Liberal Democracy.* Oxford: Oxford University Press.

Mahathir, Mohamad (1989) *The Malay Dilemma*. Singapore: Times.

Mahbubani, K. (1994) 'The United States: Go East Young Man', *The Washington Quarterly*, 17(2): 5–23.

Mahmood, N., Ahmad, Z. (1990) *Political Contestation: Case Studies from Asia*. Singapore: Heinemann.

Maisrikrod, S. (1992) *Thailand's Two General Elections in 1992*, ISEAS Research Notes and Discussion Papers no. 75, Singapore: Institute for Southeast Asian Studies.

Mansfield, Mike (1993) 'Consumers will Benefit from Japan's Political Blow-up', *Straits Times* (Singapore), 25 June.

March, J. G. and Olsen, J. (1984) 'The New Institutionalism: Factors in Political Life', *American Political Science Review*, 78(3): 734–49.

Marshall, T. H. (1950) *Citizenship and Social Class*. Cambridge: Cambridge University Press.

Mencius (1970) *Mencius*, trans. D. C. Lau, London: Penguin.

Metraux, D. (1991) *Taiwan's Political and Economic Growth in the Late Twentieth Century*. Lampeter: Edwin Mellin.

Metzger, Thomas (1977) *Escape from Predicament: Neo-Confucianism and China's Evolving Political Culture*. New York: Columbia University Press.

Mill, J. S. (1970) *Utilitarianism, On Liberty and Essay on Bentham*, ed. M. Warnock. London: Fontana.

Mill, John Stuart (1975) 'The Subjection of Women', *Three Essays*. Oxford: Oxford University Press.

Miller, David (1992) 'Deliberative Democracy and Social Choice', in David Held, ed., *Prospects for Democracy: North, South, East, West*. Cambridge, UK: Polity Press.

Minchin, James (1990) *No Man Is an Island: A Portrait of Singapore's Lee Kuan Yew*. Sydney: Allen & Unwin.

Minogue, K. R. (1987) 'Loquocentricity and democracy: the communicative theory of modern civil unity', in B. Parekh, ed., *Political Discourse Explorations in Indian and Western Political Thought*. New Delhi: Sage.

Moody, Peter (1988) *Political Opposition in Post-Confucian Society*. New York: Praeger.

Moody, Peter R. (1992) *Political Change in Taiwan: A Study of Ruling Party Adaptability*. New York: Praeger.

Mooers, C. (1991) *The Meaning of Bourgeoisie Europe: Absolutism, Revolution and the Rise of Capitalism in England, France and Germany*. London: Verso.

Moon, Chung-in (1991) 'The Politics of Structural Adjustment in South Korea: Analytical Issues and Comparative Implications', *Korean Journal*, 31(3): 54–68.

Moore, Barrington (1966) *The Social Origin of Dictatorship and Democracy*. Boston, Mass.: Beacon Press.

Morley, J., ed. (1992) *Driven by Growth: Political Change in the Asia–Pacific Region*. New York: M. E. Sharpe.

Mostov, Julie (1992) *Power, Process, and Popular Sovereignty*. Philadelphia: Temple University Press.

Munck, G. (1993) 'Between Theory and History and beyond Traditional Studies: A New Comparative Perspective on Latin America', *Comparative Politics*, 24(4): 475–95.

Munro, Donald (1977) *The Concept of Man in Contemporary China*. Ann Arbor: University of Michigan Press.

184 *Bibliography*

Muzaffar (1987) *Islamic Resurgence in Malaysia*. Selangor: Penerbit Fajar Bakti.
Namazaki, I. (1991) 'State and Business in Post War Taiwan: Comment on Hamilton and Biggart', *American Journal of Sociology*, 96(4): 993.
Needham, J. (1978) *The Shorter Science and Civilization in China*, 2 vols, Cambridge, UK: Cambridge University Press.
Nivison, D., ed. (1959) *Confucianism in Action*. Stanford, Calif: Stanford University Press.
Nordlinger, E. (1981) *On the Autonomy of the Democratic State*. Cambridge, Mass.: Harvard University Press.
Nussbaum, Martha (1992) 'Justice for Women!', *The New York Review of Books*, 8 October 1992.
O'Donnell, G. (1979) 'Tensions in the Bureaucratic Authoritarian State and the Question of Democracy', in D. Collier, ed., *The New Authoritarianism: Studies in South American Politics*, Princeton, N.J.: Princeton University Press.
O'Donnell, G., Schmitter, P. and Whitehead, L. (1986) *Transitions from Authoritarian Rule: Prospects for Democracy*. Baltimore, Md.: John Hopkins University Press.
Oi, J. C. (1992) 'Fiscal Reform and the Economic Foundations of Local State Corporatism in China', *World Politics*, 45(1): 99–126.
Okin, Susan Moller (1989) *Justice, Gender, and the Family*, New York: Basic.
Orme, J. (1988) 'Dismounting the Tiger: Lessons from Four Liberalizations', *Asian Survey*, 193(2): 245–65.
Palliser, J. (1991) *Politics and Policy in Traditional Korea*. Cambridge: Harvard University Press.
Parekh, Bhikhu (1993) 'The Cultural Particularity of Liberal Democracy', in David Held, ed., *Prospects for Democracy: North, South, East, West*. Cambridge, UK: Polity Press.
Pateman, Carole (1970) *Participation and Democratic Theory*. Cambridge: Cambridge University Press.
Patterson, Orlando (1991) *Freedom*. New York: Basic.
Pempel, T. J. and Tsuenekawa, K. (1979) 'Corporatism without Labour: the Japanese Anomaly', in P. Schmitter and G. Lembruch, eds, *Trends Towards Corporatist Intermediation*. Beverly Hills, Calif.: Sage.
Phillip, Roderick (1988) *Putting Asunder: A History of Divorce in Western Society*. Cambridge: Cambridge University Press.
Pilger, J. (1994) 'Great Mates with Suharto', *New Statesman*, 11 April 1994.
Pocock, J. G. A. (1977) *The Machiavellian Moment: Florentine Political Thought and the Atlantic Republican Tradition*. Princeton, NJ: Princeton University Press.
Prseworski, A. (1985) *Capitalism and Social Democracy*. Cambridge: Cambridge University Press.
Pye, L. (1985) *Asian Power and Politics: the Cultural Dimensions of Authority*. Cambridge, Mass.: Harvard University Press.
Pye, L. (1988) *The Mandarin and the Cadre: China's Political Cultures*. Ann Arbor, Michigan: Center for Chinese Studies.
Pye, L. (1993) 'An Introductory Profile: Deng Xiaoping and China's Political Culture', *China Quarterly*, 135.
Quah, Jon, ed. (1990) *In Search of Singapore's National Values*. Singapore: Times Academic Press.
Rawls, John (1980) 'Kantian Constructivism in Moral Theory', *Journal of Philosophy*, 77 (Sept.): 35–71.

Rawls, John (1987) 'The Idea of an Overlapping Consensus', *Oxford Journal of Legal Studies*, 7.1, 1–25.

Rawls, John (1988) 'The Priority of Right and Ideas of the Good', *Philosophy and Public Affairs*, 17 (Fall): 78–114.

Reed, A. (1993) *Southeast Asia in the Age of Commerce 1450–1680*. Vol. 2. *Expansion and Crisis*. Newhaven, Conn.: Yale University Press.

Robinson, T., ed. (1991) *Democracy and Development in East Asia Taiwan South Korea and The Philipines*. Washington: AEI Press.

Robinson, Michael (1991) 'Perceptions of Confucianism in Twentieth-Century Korea', in Gilbert Rozman, ed., *The East Asian Region: Confucian Heritage and Its Modern Adaptation*. Princeton, N.J.: Princeton University Press.

Robison, R. (1989) 'Authoritarian States, Capitalist Owning Classes and the Politics of Newly industrializing Countries: the Case of Indonesia', *World Politics*, 41(1): 52–74.

Robison, R. (1993) 'Indonesia: Tensions in State and Regime'. In K. Hewison, R. Robison, and G. Rodan (eds), *Southeast Asia in the 1990s. Authoritarianism, Democracy and Capitalism*. Sydney: Allen and Unwin.

Rodan, G., ed. (1993) *Singapore Changes Guard*. New York: St Martin's Press.

Rorty, Richard (1989) *Contingency, Irony, and Solidarity*. Cambridge: Cambridge University Press.

Rosenbluth, F. M. (1989) *Financial Politics in Contemporary Japan*. Ithaca: Cornell University Press.

Rousseau, J. J. (1968) *The Social Contract*. Harmondsworth: Penguin.

Roy, Denny (1994) 'Singapore China, and the "Soft Authoritarian" Challenge', *Asian Survey*, XXXIV(3) (March): 231–42.

Rozman, Gilbert, ed. (1991) *The East Asian Region: Confucian Heritage and Its Modern Adaptation*. Princeton, N.J.: Princeton University Press.

Rueschemeyer, D., Stephen, E. H. and Stephens, J. D. (1992) *Capitalist Development and Democracy*. Cambridge, Mass.: Polity Press.

Ruggie, J. (1982) 'International Regimes, Transactions and Change: Embedded Liberalism in the Postwar Economic Order', *International Organization*, 36(2): 379–415.

Rupesinghe, K., ed. (1992) *Internal Conflict and Governance*. London/New York: Macmillan/St Martin's.

Rustow, Dankwart, A. (1967) *A World of Nations*. Washington, D.C.: Brookings Institute.

Schmitter, P. (1979) 'Still the Century of Corporatism?' In P. Schmitter and G. Lembruch, eds, *Trends Towards Corporatist Intermediation*. Beverly Hills, Calif.: Sage.

Schue, Vivienne (1992) 'China: Transition Postponed?', *Problems of Communism*, XLI(1, 2): 157–68.

Schumpeter, Joseph (1943) *Capitalism, Socialism, and Democracy*. London: Allen & Unwin.

Schwartz, Adam (1993) 'Islam and Democracy', *Far Eastern Economic Review*, 19 March 1993, p. 32.

Schwartz, Benjamin (1960) 'Some Polarities in Confucian Thought', in D. Nevinson, ed., *Confucianism in Action*. Stanford, Calif.: Stanford University Press.

Schwartz, Benjamin (1985) *The World of Thought in Ancient China*. Cambridge, Mass.: Harvard University Press.

Shea, Jia-dong and Yen Tzung-tu (1992) 'Comparative Experience and Financial Reform in Taiwan and Korea: Implications for the Mainland of China', in R. Garnaut and L. Guoguang, eds, *Economic Reform and Industrialization: China and the Pacific Region*. Sydney: Allen & Unwin.

Shim Jae Hoon (1993) 'Civilian Mandate', *Far Eastern Economic Review*, 7 January, p. 21.

Skocpol, T. (1973) 'A Critical Review of Barrington Moore's Social Origins of Dictatorship and Democracy', *Politics and Society*, 12(2): 1–34.

Skocpol, T. and Somers, M. (1980) 'The Uses of Comparative History in Macrosocial Inquiry', *Comparative Studies in Society and History*, 22(2): 174–97.

Smith, A. D. (1991) *National Identity*. London: Penguin.

Smooha, Sammy (1990) 'Minority Status in an Ethnic Democracy: The Status of the Arab Minority in Israel', *Ethnic and Racial Studies*, 13(3): 12–26.

Song Bing (1992) 'The Reform of Mainland China's Cadre System – Establishing a Civil Service', *Issues and Studies: A Journal of Chinese and International Affairs*, 28(10): 23–43.

Sorensen, George (1992) 'Kant and Processes of Democratization: Consequences for Neorealist Thought', *Journal of Peace Research*, 29(4): 13–26.

Sorensen, George (1993) *Democracy and Democratization: Processes and Prospects in a Changing World*, Boulder: Westview Press.

Spence, J. (1990) *The Search for Modern China*. Norton: New York.

Springborg, P. (1992) *Western Republicanism and the European Prince*. Cambridge, UK: Polity.

Steinberg, D., ed. (1989) *In Search of Southeast Asia: A Modern History*. Sydney: Allen & Unwin.

Stepan, A. (1985) 'State Power and the Strength of Civil Society in the Southern Cone of Latin America', in P. B. Evans, D. Rueschemeyer and T. Scokpol, eds, *Bringing the State Back In*. Cambridge and New York: Cambridge University Press.

Stiglitz, J. E. (1989) 'Markets, Market Failures and Development', *American Economic Review*, 79(1): 197–203.

Suffian Tun Mohammed, Suffian Tun Mohd, Lee, H. P. and Trindads, F. A. (1979) *The Constitution of Malaysia and Its Development*. Oxford: Oxford University Press.

Suh Kuk Sang, ed. (1983) *The Identity of the Korean People: A History of Legitimacy on the Korean Peninsula*. Seoul: National Unification Board.

Suryadinata, Leo (1989) *Military Ascendency and Political Culture: A Study of Indonesia's Golkar*. Athens: Ohio University.

Tai, Hung-chao, ed. (1989) *Confucianism and Economic Development: An Oriental Alternative?* Washington, D.C.: Washington Institute Press.

Tamir, Yael (1993) *Liberal Nationalism*. Princeton, N.J.: Princeton University Press.

Taubert, A. (1991) 'Liberalism Under Pressure in Indonesia', *Southeast Asian Affairs*, new issue: 121–41, Singapore: Institute of Southeast Asian Studies.

Therborn, G. (1977) 'The Rule of Capital and the Rise of Democracy', *New Left Review*, 103: 124–53.

Therborn, G. (1992) 'The Right to Vote and the Four World Routes To/Through Modernity', in Rolf Torstendahl, ed., *State Theory and State History*. London: Sage.

Tinker, Hugh (1981) 'The Nation-State in Asia', in Leonard Tivey, ed., *The Nation-State: The Formation of Modern Politics*. Oxford: Martin Robertson.

Touraine, A. (1989) *Palavra e Sangue Politica o Sociedade A America Latina*. São Paulo: Editora da Universidade Estudual de Campinas.

Tsang, S. (1993) *In the Shadow of China: Political Developments in Taiwan Since 1949*. London: Hurst.

Tu Wei-ming (1984) *Confucian Ethics Today: the Singapore Challenge*. Singapore: Federal Publications.

Tu Wei-ming (1987) 'Confucian Humanism in a Modern Perspective', in J. P. L. Jiang, ed., *Confucianism and Modernization: A Symposium*, Taipei: Freedom Council Press.

Tu Wei-ming (1989) *Confucianism in an Historical Perspective*, Institute of East Asian Philosophies (Singapore) Occasional Paper and Monograph Series no. 15.

Tu Wei-ming, ed. (1991) *The Triadic Chord: Confucian Ethics, Industrial East Asia and Max Weber*, Singapore: Institute of East Asian Philosophies.

Van Wolferen, Karel (1989) *The Enigma of Japanese Power*. London: Macmillan.

Vatikiotis, M. (1993a) 'In Search of a New Role', *Far Eastern Economic Review*, 9 December.

Vatikiotis, M. (1993b) *Indonesian Politics under Suharto*. London: Routledge.

Vogel, E. (1991) *The Four Little Dragons*. Cambridge, Mass.: Harvard University Press.

Vogel, E. and Lodge, G. (1987) *Ideology and National Competitiveness: a Comparison of Nine Different Countries*. Boston, Mass.: Harvard Business School Press.

Wade, R. (1990) 'Industrial Policy in East Asia: Does it Lead or Follow the Market?', in G. Gereffi and D. L. Wyman, eds, *Manufacturing Miracles. Paths of Industrialization in Latin America and East Asia*. Princeton, N.J.: Princeton University Press.

Walzer, Michael (1983) *Spheres of Justice*. Oxford: Basil Blackwell.

Wang Yang Ming (1963) *Instructions for Practical Living*. New York: Columbia University Press.

Wargo, Robert (1990) 'Japanese Ethics: Beyond Good and Evil', *Philosophy East and West*, October.

Weber, Max (1951) *The Religion of China*. Glencoe, Cal.: Free Press.

Weinstock, Daniel (1993) 'Introduction: Le Défi du Pluralisme', in *Lekton*, III, 2(1): 7–28.

White, Gordon (1994) 'Democratization and Economic Reform in China', *Australian Journal of Chinese Affairs*, no. 31 (January): 73–95.

Winclar, E. A. (1992) 'Taiwan Transition?', in Tun-Jen Cheng and Stephen Haggard, eds, *Political Change in Taiwan*. Boulder/London: Lynne Rienner.

Wollstonecraft, Mary (1975) *A Vindication of The Rights of Women*. Harmondsworth: Penguin.

Wolters, O. (1982) *History, Culture and Religion in Southeast Asian Perspectives*, Singapore: Institute for Southeast Asian Studies.

Wonmo Dong (1988) 'Student Activism and the Presidential Politics of 1987 in South Korea', in Ilpyong J. Kim and Young Whan Kihl, eds, *Political Change in South Korea*, New York: Korean PWPA.

World Bank (1993) *The East Asian Miracle: Economic Growth and Public Policy*. Oxford: Oxford University Press.

Wright, M. C. (1957) *The Last Stand of Chinese Conservatism: the Tung Chih Restoration 1862–74.* Stanford, Calif.: University Press.

Yang, Martin (1945) *A Chinese Village: Taitou, Shantung Province.* New York: Columbia University Press.

Yu Ming Shaw, ed. (1986) *China and Europe in the Twentieth Century*, Chengchu, Taiwan: Chengchu University Press.

Yu-shan, Wu (1989) 'Marketization of Policies: the Taiwan Experience', *Asian Survey*, XXIX(4): 388–400.

Zolo, Danilo (1992) *Democracy and Complexity: A Realist Approach*, trans. David McKie. University Park, Penn.: Pennsylvania State University Press.

Index

189